NEGOTIATING IDENTITY IN SCANDINAVIA

NEGOTIATING IDENTITY IN SCANDINAVIA

Women, Migration and the Diaspora

Edited by
Haci Akman

berghahn
NEW YORK · OXFORD
www.berghahnbooks.com

First published in 2014 by

Berghahn Books

www.berghahnbooks.com

© 2014, 2021 Haci Akman
First paperback edition published in 2021

Library of Congress Cataloging-in-Publication Data

Negotiating identity in Scandinavia : women, migration and the diaspora /
edited by Haci Akman.
    pages cm
    Includes bibliographical references and index.
    ISBN 978-1-78238-306-2 (hardback : alk. paper) — ISBN 978-1-78238-307-9
(ebook)
    1. Women immigrants—Scandinavia—Social conditions. 2. Women
immigrants—Scandinavia—Political activity. 3. Women—Scandinavia—
Identity. 4. Scandinavia—Emigration and immigration. I. Akman, Haci,
editor of compilation.

JV8198.N44 2014
325.48--dc23

2013029906

British Library Cataloguing in Publication Data

A catalogue record for this book is available from the British Library

Printed on acid-free paper

ISBN: 978-1-78238-306-2 hardback
ISBN: 978-1-80073-180-6 paperback
ISBN: 978-1-78238-307-9 ebook

ꙮ Contents

☺⟫ Illustrations

⤷⟩⟩ Preface

This volume draws impetus from the realization that women's diaspora is vastly different and more complex than men's and that more research is needed on the topic. The choice to focus primarily on women stems from the recognition that migration impacts men and women differently, and that women and men respond differently to the changes brought about by migration and to experiences of inclusion and exclusion. The intention is not to invalidate men's migratory experiences but rather to give women more visibility, particularly in Scandinavia, where, as in much of the global North, women have historically migrated as dependents of men. Women's particular experience of diaspora became an inspiration and the driving force behind the anthology.

I suppose readers may be curious to know why a male researcher is the sole editor of a book on women's diaspora. I guess there is no good answer, other than the fact that I have spent thirty-five years in diaspora myself. I came to Norway in 1980 as a Kurdish refugee in the aftermath of a coup d'état in Turkey that year. Throughout the years since, the situation of exiled people from all over the world, the creation of diaspora communities and the politics of immigration have been my main concerns within my research as well as my personal life. However, research on women's diaspora is indeed primarily conducted by female researchers; hence most of the contributors to this volume are women.

The chapters in *Negotiating Identity in Scandinavia: Women, Migration and the Diaspora* address, with varying emphases, the processes that produce diasporas and the structures that work to impede their formation. The chapters' themes relate to major issues and situations women in Scandinavia encounter in diaspora or have experienced in their countries of origin, displacement or uprootedness, their struggles to create meaning in new environments and the ways they bargain and negotiate meaning along the way. Diaspora seems to represent a new learning site for immigrant women. Many have learned to read and write, while others have acquired higher education; they are involved in community work and politics, among many other things. New experiences and knowledge also provide opportunities for political involvement – in the host country as well as in the country left behind.

It is no secret that the work on this book has been a road with many stumbling blocks. Nonetheless, the final product of this journey is a unique, highly interesting, rewarding book that provides new knowledge and insight into women's diaspora in Scandinavia.

Bergen, 2014
Haci Akman
Associate Professor
University of Bergen

𝒮⟫ Acknowledgements

Various people contributed meaningfully to this anthology. I especially wish to thank Associate Professor Gaudencia Mutema at the Centre for Women and Gender Research at the University of Bergen, who coordinated the work in its initial phase and wrote a major part of the introduction, to which Minoo Alinia, a contributor to this book, also made valuable contributions.

Great thanks to Associate Professor Marguerite Daniel at the HEMIL Center, University of Bergen, for her help with the language. I would like to express special gratitude to Hanne Dale, project employee at the Museum Centre in Hordaland and translator at Språkfolk AS, Bergen, for her constructive comments and help with editing and language in the final phase of the work. I also wish to thank the authors of this anthology for their interesting and highly relevant contributions to the understanding of women's diaspora in some Scandinavian countries – and for being so patient.

Last but not least I wish to express my great appreciation to former Senior Editor Ann Przyzycki DeVita at Berghahn Books for her tireless assistance and valuable advice along the way.

Introduction

REASSERTING THE CENTRALITY OF WOMEN IN DIASPORAS

Haci Akman

Since the early 1990s, significant developments have affected how gender and migration are conceptualized. A reading of works from that period, such as those by Anthias (1992), Buijs (1993), Indra (1999) and Anthias and Lazardis (2000), among others, suggests that gender continued to occupy a peripheral position in analytical and theoretical discussions, despite its pervasiveness in the processes of conflict, forced migration and subsequent settlement in the diaspora. The 2000s saw a marked increase in the attention paid to the connection between gender and migration, although as Palmary et al. (2010) argue, the nature of the 'and' in 'gender and migration' is rarely interrogated.

This book aims to examine the very nature of these interactions and their effects on studies of gender and diaspora, which together offer suitable territory for a fruitful exploration of frequently overlooked mechanisms. The authors in this anthology draw connections between gender and migration by reflecting on *how* gender becomes a preoccupation in thinking about migration. Some of the links they find lie in the absences, silences and exclusions in understandings of gender in knowledge production about migration.

The book purposes to revisit the concept of diaspora through the experiences of women living in Norway, Sweden and Denmark. Some aspects of these texts are particular to their Scandinavian setting, but the relevance of the themes they raise extends far beyond this geographical region. Consequently, the authors often invoke studies on gender and migration in other regions by way of comparison. The primary focus on women recognizes that migration impacts men and women differently, and that as actors, women and men typically respond differently to the changes generated by migration and to experiences of inclusion and exclusion. As diaspora communities are often considered homogeneous or gender-neutral, we emphasize the importance of a gendered analysis of the migration process, of integration and welfare policies and practices, and of home-host relations as well as ways the migrants themselves are gendered and characterized by various subject positions that affect their everyday experiences and their access to political, economic and cultural forms of citizenship.

This emphasis on women's experiences relative to men's is not intended to invalidate men's migratory experiences but rather to give women more visibility, particularly in Scandinavia, where women have historically migrated as dependents of men, as is the case throughout the global North. It is also fitting to focus on women because family reunification laws in Scandinavia are still premised on the notion of a male sponsor/breadwinner. Women's different positionalities can provide insights into the structures and forces that operate to reproduce economic disparities and institutional injustices for some migrants but not for others.

The general scope of the book extends to the experiences of migrants (including refugees, asylum seekers, exiles and labour migrants) in three Scandinavian countries who view themselves as members of national, ethnic, linguistic, cultural and political communities living outside their habitual 'home'. With varying emphases, the articles address the processes that produce diasporas as well as structures that work to impede their formation. Another theme is the role that 'home' and 'host' play in understandings of citizenship, interactions across and within communities, identity formations, the sense of belonging or alienation, and emerging new power relations.

The title of the book, *Negotiating Identity in Scandinavia*, reflects an observation that concurs with Bhatia and Ram's (2001) argument that throughout the process of migration, migrants constantly negotiate between here and there, past and present, homeland and country of settlement, the self and the other. These negotiations may be in response to affirmations or contradictions that individuals or communities might encounter about who they are, where they belong, which religious and cultural values they hold and how they 'fit into' the host society. This book contends that migrants reaffirm identities that may have been distorted by adopting different strategies with ambivalent outcomes, including acts of resistance. As its articles illustrate, trying to make sense of what to take from one's culture and what to leave behind, and what to take from the dominant culture and other subcultures and what to leave out, can be a particularly challenging everyday task.[1]

Most research within the field of migration studies is based on the experiences of male immigrants. However, many investigations have documented differences between women's and men's experiences of migration to highlight and theorize women's experiences (Wright 1995; Alicea 1997; Hondagneu-Sotelo and Avila 1997; Jones-Correa 1998;

Sassen-Koob 1984; Sassen 1996; Pessar 1995; Basch, Glick Schiller and Szanton Blanc 1995; Alinia 2004; Eliassi 2010).

These studies focus mainly on family situations and responsibilities; women's role in the creation, development and maintenance of transnational communities and transnational family and kinship networks; and the ways migration to a highly industrialized society affects gender (Alicea 1997; Hondagneu-Sotelo and Avila 1997; Basch, Glick Schiller and Szanton Blanc 1995; Pessar 1995; Darvishpour 2002). Others explore women's sense of belonging in the community and their political participation (Jones-Correa 1998; Alinia 2004), or attend to the impact of the restructured global economy and global relations between capital and labour in terms of women's migration (Sassen-Koob 1984; Basch, Glick Schiller and Szanton Blanc 1995). Sassen-Koob describes the global processes of economic restructuring as 'one element in the current phase of Third World women's domestic and international migration' (1984: 1161–62).

The 'feminization of the job supply'– that is, the household's becoming a global market for women's labour – and the increase in female migration are therefore strongly interrelated (Lutz 2011). Women who create, develop and sustain the transnational kinship networks and communities and 'transnational motherhood' (Hondagneu-Sotelo and Avila 1997: 548) migrate both with or without their families in search of a job. They are often forced to leave behind their families and children, to be looked after by other female relatives or the children's fathers (Alicea 1997; Hondagneu-Sotelo and Avila 1997).

The above-mentioned studies provide a broad perspective on postcolonial migration in general and women's migration in particular. Several studies show that irrespective of differences in the structures of the host societies and their migrant policies, respondents share many experiences in being women and immigrants from the Third World (Jones-Correa 1998: 336; Alicea 1997). On the one hand, they are objects of racism and xenophobia and are excluded from the national community; on the other, as women they are better positioned within the family and in society in general. Thus women, who are supposed to be bearers of tradition, often become the first to challenge it.

Previous studies have highlighted gender differences in social mobility, sense of belonging and political participation (Jones-Correa 1998: 327, 335). They show the impact of wage earning on women's social and family life – for instance, conflicts within families become more visible as women's economic independence and resources offer them more confidence and they assert their rights to greater autonomy and equality within the household (Darvishpour 2002; Eyrumlu 1998; Alinia 2004). According to these studies, the family as an institution goes through significant change that in turn affects the relationship between couples and also between parents and children.

However, as Alicea rightly points out, women's sense of belonging-ness and their relationship to their countries of settlement and countries of origin cannot be seen within the framework of a 'home/host dichot-omy' (1997: 600). This dichotomization, according to her and other re-searchers (Bhabha 1999; Sassen 1999), results from categorizing 'host' and 'home' in terms of binary opposites such as modernity and tradi-tion, progressiveness and backwardness, and so on. In reality, however, the relationship often proves both contradictory and ambivalent. The achievement of economic independence and improved social status en-courages women to grow closer to their countries of settlement, but at the same time they feel that unfavourable racial and class conditions discriminate against them (Mohanty 2003). Alicea (1997) argues that placing transnational networks at the centre of the debate might in it-self be a way to prevent such dichotomizations and simplifications.

Many women have believed that their migration would equal an es-cape from gender oppression. They highlight inequities at home and their desire to break away from repression. Paradoxically, traditional gender expectations, coupled with women's sense of moral obligation and their desire to resist racial oppression and disadvantaged class con-ditions, keep them tied to subsistence work that extends across national boundaries (Alicea 1997; Lutz 2011). These women construct homes and homeland communities as familiar places that give a feeling of comfort, yet they are aware of the gender oppression that makes up 'home' (Ali-cia 1997: 621–22; Alinia 2004).

On the Structure of This Book

The book is divided into two parts. The first addresses issues of bar-gaining and negotiating identities in view of the displacement and uprootedness caused by migration, providing examples of the various forms of meaning-making that migrants to Scandinavia engage in. The second deals with home politics, host policies and resistance. Each part highlights central aspects of the migrant experience, although the cat-egories are by no means separated by strict boundaries.

Bargaining and Negotiating Identities

The first part revolves around how refugee or exile status affects peo-ple's lives and experiences.

It describes problems faced by refugees and exiles, from more prosaic everyday issues to struggles with identity, the sense of belonging and tensions between homeland and their new environment. It explores art as way of mending the fracture caused by exile, creating meaning and even empowerment. Its chapters also investigate Muslim women's self-positioning in relation to dominant discourses in Swedish and Danish society, detailing how they navigate the mechanisms, beliefs and prejudices of their host society and the diaspora community in order to represent their religious identity and gender, and how they carve out new identities for themselves at the intersection between these groups.

Haci Akman's 'Art as Political Expression in Diaspora' explores exile's alienating, confusing impact on those who are forced into involuntary migration. Having left all that is familiar, they must make their way in an unknown, bewildering environment where they strive to find 'new understanding, new goals and new meaning'. Akman focuses on the role of female artists in the diaspora, some of whom have been imprisoned and tortured because their art is perceived as challenging the political system. He considers the internal and external forces that influence an exile's need to create a sense of belonging, to find a new 'home'. It is existentially vital to the exile to feel accepted and affirmed, not only by the new society but also by fellow members of her ethnic group in the diaspora. However, as Akman observes, many female exiles feel 'locked out' of their new community both personally and institutionally. Relationships that previously defined identity no longer exist. New roles and responsibilities lead to contradictions in how the self is experienced in the homeland and in the diaspora. Akman illustrates the pain and suffering of exile with reference to the paintings and experiences of the artist Kwestan Jamal Ali, who was born in Kurdistan but now lives and works in Norway. Through her strongly political art she explores motifs inspired by her own experiences and memories of oppression, flight and exile.

Pia Karlsson Minganti, in 'Islamic Identity as Third Space: Muslim Women Activists Negotiating Subjectivity in Sweden', analyses the complexity in the negotiations of Muslim women as they position themselves relative to the dominant discourses of a 'Swedish' and a 'Muslim' sphere. She uses the concept of an ambiguous, creative, critical *third space* that provides a 'location' for negotiations within and between groups perceived as dominant and homogeneous. After describing the women's experiences of and responses to the dominant discourses, Karlsson Minganti explores how, neither rejecting nor overemphasizing the bipolar categories, they negotiate a third position defined as 'Islamic', inspired by their engagement in Muslim youth associations.

Influenced by the Islamic revival, the women in the study see the Koran as granting many rights to women, for instance, permitting them to be educated and to educate others. The women counteract stereotypes of passive, oppressed Muslim women in that they have agency and see themselves as both bearers of Islam and active citizens in Swedish society. However, Karlsson Minganti points out, their actions may also maintain power structures, particularly related to gender issues; thus the third space accommodates collective norms even as it contests them. As a hybrid space that allows for transgression and empowerment while simultaneously reproducing domination, it runs the risk of being disciplined and incorporated by essentializing discourses.

Rikke Andreassen's 'Political Muslim Women in the News Media' furthers the focus on Muslim women in Scandinavia. Examining the Danish news media's debates on veiled Muslim women, she concentrates on the case of Asmaa Abdol-Hamid. Rather than focusing explicitly on diaspora, Andreassen's text provides a valuable contextualization of the general political-public discourse that frames diasporic discourses, practices and identities. These debates offer insight into the media's construction of ethnicity/race, gender, sexuality and nationality. When Abdol-Hamid became a presenter at a Danish public-service TV station in 2006, an outcry by a feminist organization claimed her attitudes threatened women's rights in Denmark. This sparked a debate through press releases, national newspapers and TV about the interpretation of headscarves as oppression of women. Andreassen argues that this is also a debate about how to define feminism, and about the relations between different feminisms. The headscarf issue challenges the hegemonic view within Danish second-wave feminism that the headscarf prevents the emancipation of women, particularly with regards to education and employment. In 2007, Abdol-Hamid became a candidate in the parliamentary elections. Andreassen argues that Abdol-Hamid and other female Muslim candidates were treated differently, especially when it came to their attitudes towards sexual minorities and gender equality. Andreassen shows how accusing Abdol-Hamid of being homophobic and hence against sexual liberation functions as a national mechanism of exclusion: sexual tolerance is racialized and associated with the white, ethnically Danish community, whereas homophobia and intolerance are reserved for the Muslim community. By analysing Yildiz Akdogan's 2011 election campaign, Andreassen also shows how female Muslim candidates faced criticism from not only Danish politicians and news media but also certain Muslim groups. Andreassen's text reveals how these debates highlight the intersection between race, ethnicity, religion, sexuality and the construction of nationality. She maintains that the media, instead of challenging power relations when it comes to Muslim women, has helped maintain and uphold existing power relations in Denmark.

Malene Fenger-Grøndahl follows up on several themes in Andreassen's chapter, discussing Western feminism and its relation to Muslim immigration to Denmark. Her essay considers the case of Maria, who arrived in Denmark from Chile in 1973, seeking political asylum. At the time she was not only granted asylum but also welcomed by Danish left-wing activists with an interest in Latin America. She was encouraged to divorce her husband and set herself free through the Western concept of feminism. Forty years later, the 'headscarf issue' and Muslim women are on the political agenda, and female Muslim newcomers to Denmark as well as children of Muslim immigrants are expected to fit into a new political agenda that sees Islam as a threat to democracy and gender equality. While wearing the veil and behaving 'well' opens up educational possibilities for Muslim girls, taking on the identity of a well-behaved Muslim girl also poses limitations when it comes to choice of career and political influence. Fenger-Grøndahl examines the prejudice, challenges and identities available to, and in some cases imposed upon, immigrant women and men in Denmark from the 1970s onwards, arguing that a new framework incorporating multiple identities might be under way, partly due to the efforts of immigrant women.

Fenger-Grøndahl's contribution contains interesting narratives that in many ways illustrate this anthology's central concerns. It favours a journalistic approach to the theme over narrative analysis, a choice that might have had implications for the conclusions drawn in the text. Nevertheless, her chapter remains a highly relevant, substantial contribution to the body of knowledge on and insight into previous and present experiences of immigrant women in Denmark.

The following chapter moves on to discuss Kurdish diasporic experiences, identities and movements, based on interviews with Kurdish men and women living in Gothenburg, Sweden. In 'Gendered Experiences of Homeland, Identity and Belonging among the Kurdish Diaspora', Minoo Alinia focuses on gender's impact on their relation to Swedish society and the Kurdish diaspora and highlights the complexity of processes of identity and belonging. While both men and women experience political freedom in Sweden, women exercise social and legal rights that frequently go well beyond what they were used to in their country of origin and consequently have a more open, positive attitude to Swedish society. Similarly, migrant men and women may lose both social standing and social networks, but the rights women gain go some way towards compensating for their losses. Moreover, a woman's role as a mother and caretaker provides some continuity and leads to contact with society, whereas there is little to compensate for the losses experienced by men. Both genders experience racism and exclusion in the form of suspicion and discrimination. Alinia discusses perceptions of gendered racism among her respondents, who find that Swedes categorically see Kurdish men as violent and oppressive, and Kurdish women as subordinate and oppressed. Thus, women and men alike feel rejected by Swedish society and find a home and a sense of belonging in Kurdish communities. However, women take a more ambivalent, critical stance towards the Kurdish community and try to challenge its boundaries and create their own spaces.

Home Politics, Host Policies and Resistance

The chapters that form this book's second part exemplify different forms of gendered resistance in relation to homeland politics and public integration policies. The authors further probe the concept of diaspora and its relation to migrants' engagement in political struggles in their home societies, and offer concrete examples of mechanisms within policy management and strategic plans for immigration and citizenship.

Kariane Westrheim's chapter, 'Kurdish Women of the Diaspora and Political Participation', opens this section with an account of the collective imaginations of nation inside and outside Kurdistan. She traces the development of the concept of diaspora and the historical turbulence in Kurdistan, caused by external and internal conflicts, war and deportations, that resulted in Kurds' dispersion from their original homeland to diaspora communities worldwide. Her article provides a brief overview of some characteristics of Kurdish diaspora in Europe, using Norway as one example. Here, Westrheim underlines the dearth of research and academic literature on gendered Kurdish diaspora in Norway. The chapter's main concern is the politicization of Kurdish diaspora and the ways in which diaspora can promote political awareness and political literacy among Kurdish women. Whereas women from traditional Kurdish families previously had limited possibilities to engage in activities outside the home, she argues, the Kurdistan Worker's Party (PKK), which entered the stage in the 1980s, has also actively recruited Kurds with diverse professional and educational backgrounds from diaspora. In North Kurdistan, Kurdish women have been at the forefront of the political and armed struggle, and Kurdish women in diaspora often function as a bridge between structures and organizations in two countries. Westrheim's essay discusses the intersections of learning processes, political participation and gender issues, and the joint efforts of Kurdish women in the diaspora and in the homeland to change the role of women within Kurdish society. These interactions and exchanges, she surmises, are relevant and applicable not only in Scandinavia, but wherever Kurdish communities have settled.

Bolette Moldenhawer's chapter 'Territorial Stigmatization, Inequality of Schooling and Identity Formation among Young Immigrants' continues to focus on education by engaging with host countries' policies of compulsory education, exploring the way social background, ethnicity, gender and residential segregation help produce and reproduce disadvantages for young immigrants. Based on major findings from the EDUMIGROM research project, her text uses select Danish and French cases to show the impact of gender on how immigrant students' schooling and social relations relate to the symbolic and social order of local residential areas and become superimposed onto the stigmata of ethnicity. Inspired by Loïc Wacquant (2007, 2008a, 2008b) this symbolic work around schooling is conceptualized in relation to mechanisms of territorial stigmatization in an age of advanced marginality. Moreover, by addressing the concept of diaspora (Gilroy 2009), Moldenhawer takes identity formation among immigrants into account, discussing its changing patterns and its effects on female students in a context of territorial segregation and stigmatization. Having illustrated important factors in immigrant students' school achievements, the chapter presents an empirical analysis of how gender intersects with social backgrounds and ethnic discrimination in the selected Danish and French cases to create new forms of inclusion and exclusion within compulsory education. Moldenhawer's examination of the mechanisms and policies that create educational differentiation in two countries committed to egalitarianism in the school system also relates various ways immigrant students cope with these issues.

The final chapter of this anthology, Tina Kallehave's 'The Absence of Strategy and the Absence of *Bildung*: When Integration Policy Cannot Succeed', discusses host policies and resistance in a Danish context. Kallehave studies Danish authorities' efforts to integrate Somali immigrants so as to make them self-supporting and able to understand basic Danish norms and values. Kallehave considers the concept and aims of integration as well as unintended effects of sociocultural processes in interaction with Somali immigrants. Integration programmes have evolved into social programmes for those Somalis classified as socially vulnerable. Kallehave uses the theoretical framework of 'interpellation and *Bildung*' to examine the features and challenges of integration. She argues that interpellation has the potential to ease some of the complexities of integration by factoring in resistance to the organizing strategies designed to result in *Bildung*. Kallehave explores complexity and resistance by pinpointing differences between the authorities' and Somalis' varying understandings of responsibilities to family and the gendered implications thereof. She suggests that Danish approaches to integration are not strategic because they fail to take sufficient account of Somali acts of resistance and to differentiate between the objectives of the programmes and the programmes themselves as a means of achieving *Bildung*.

This anthology gathers a diverse set of research questions related to gender, migration and diaspora in Scandinavian countries, and addresses undergraduate and postgraduate students as well as scholars within different scientific disciplines. In doing so, it aims to further nuance the literature within the field and reaffirm the role of women within studies on diaspora.

Notes

1. This does not, however, imply a view of cultures as static entities – rather, they may be seen as dynamic processes that go through continual change.

References

Alicea, M. 1997. '"A Chambered Nautilus": The Contradictory Nature of Puerto Rican Women's Role in the Social Construction of a Transnational Community', *Gender and Society* 11(5): 597–626.

Alinia, M. 2004. *Spaces of Diasporas: Kurdish Identities, Experiences of Otherness and Politics of Belonging*. Göteborg Studies in Sociology 22. Gothenburg: University of Gothenburg.

Anthias, F. 2000. *Ethnicity, class, gender, and migration: Greek-Cypriots in Britain*. Aldershot, England and Brookfield, Vt: Avebury.

Anthias, F. 2000. 'Metaphors of Home: Gendering New Migrations to Southern Europe', in F. Anthias and G. Lazaridis (eds), *Gender and Migration in Southern Europe: Women on the Move*. Oxford: Berg, pp. 15–48.

Basch, L., N. Glick Schiller and C. Szanton Blanc. 1995. 'From Immigrant to Transmigrant: Theorizing Transnational Migration', *Anthropological Quarterly* 68(1): 48–63.

Bhabha, H.K. 1999. 'Liberalism's Sacred Cow', in M. Howard and M.C. Nussbaum (eds), *Is Multiculturalism Bad for Women? Susan Moller Okin with Respondents*. Princeton, NJ: Princeton University Press.

Bhatia, S. and A. Ram. 2001. 'Locating the Dialogical Self in the Age of Transnational Migrations, Border Crossings and Diasporas', *Culture and Psychology* 7: 296–309.

Buijs, G. (ed.). 1993. *Migrant Women: Crossing Boundaries and Identities*. Oxford: Berg.

Darvishpour, M. 2002. *Immigrant Women Challenge the Role of Men: How the Changing Power Relationship within Iranian Families in Sweden Intensifies Family Conflicts after Immigration*. Stockholm: Stockholm University.

Eliassi, B. 2010. *A Stranger in My Homeland: The Politics of Belonging Among Young People With Kurdish Background in Sweden*, Ph.D. dissertation. Härnösand: Mid Sweden University.

Eyrumlu, R. 1998. Iranska familjer i Sverige. Ett nordeuropeiskt samhälle. Göteborg: Bokförlaget Invand-Lit.

Gilroy, P. 2009. 'The Dialectics of Diaspora Identification', in L. Back and J. Solomos (eds), *Theories of Race and Racism. A reader*, 2nd ed. London and New York: Routledge, pp. 564–77.

Hondagneu-Sotelo, P. and E. Avila. 1997. '"I'm Here, but I'm There": The Meanings of Latina Transnational Motherhood', *Gender and Society* 11(5): 548–71.

Indra, D. (ed.). 1999. *Engendering Forced Migration: Theory and Practice*. Oxford: Berghahn.

Jones-Correa, M. 1998. 'Different Paths: Gender, Immigration and Political Participation', *International Migration Review* 32(2): 326–49.

Lutz, H. 2011. *The New Maids: Transnational Women and the Care Economy*. London and New York: Zed Books.

Mohanty, C.T. 2003. *Feminism Without Borders: Decolonising Theory, Practicing Solidarity*. Durham, NC: Duke University Press.

Palmary, I., E. Burman, K. Chantler and P. Kiguwa (eds). 2010. *Gender and Migrations: Feminist Intervention*. London: Zed Books.

Pessar, P.R. 1995. 'On the Homefront and in the Workplace: Integrating Immigrant Women into Feminist Discourse', *Anthropological Quarterly* 68(1): 37–47.

Sassen-Koob, S. 1984. 'Notes on the Incorporation of Third World Women into Wage-Labor Through Immigration and Off-Shore Production', in Robin Cohen (ed.), *The Sociology of Migration*. Cheltenham: Edward Elgar.

Sassen, S. 1996. *Losing Control? Sovereignty in an Age of Globalization*. New York: Columbia University Press.

———. 1999. 'Culture Beyond Gender', in M. Howard and M.C. Nussbaum (eds), *Is Multiculturalism Bad for Women? Susan Moller Okin with Respondents*. Princeton, NJ: Princeton University Press.

——— (ed.). 2002. *Global Networks, Linked Cities*. New York: Routledge.

Wacquant, L. 2007. 'Territorial Stigmatization in the Age of Advanced marginality', *Thesis Eleven* 91: 113–18.

———. 2008a. 'Ghettos and Anti-Ghettos: An Anatomy of the New Urban Poverty', *Thesis Eleven* 94: 66–77.

———. 2008b. *Urban Outcasts. A Comparative Sociology of Advanced Marginality*. Cambridge: Polity Press.

Wright, C. 1995. 'Gender Awareness in Migration Theory: Synthesizing Actor and Structure in Southern Africa', *Development and Change* 26: 771–91.

PART I

BARGAINING AND
NEGOTIATING IDENTITIES

☺⟫ 1

ART AS POLITICAL EXPRESSION IN DIASPORA

Haci Akman

Introduction

Exile is a political phenomenon that touches the inner depths of humanity. Exile status affects all vital aspects of refugee life, destroying the foundation of social reality for those affected and attacking their most fundamental sense of security. A romantic glow veils the word exile, reinforcing the myth that a life between two cultures affects intellectual activity creatively (Eastmond 1997 [1989]). Such a view, of course, omits such key dimensions of the status such as grief, homelessness and lack of belonging.

Migration, a part of human history from the earliest times, has increased in scope and significance globally since 1945 and particularly since the 1980s. Current figures from the Global Commission on International Migration estimate that around 200 million people have spent more than a year outside their home countries. According to the Norwegian Directorate of Immigration these people are commonly termed migrants.[1] Migration appears poised to increase even in this millennium and will probably be one of the most important factors in global change. Some migrants move from country to country without finding stability or protection; others settle down in a new country that can provide opportunities for a better life. Because migration affects not only the migrants themselves, but also the provider and recipient communities, few people today have no personal experience of migration. Many migrants' former lives were disrupted by extreme, life-threatening events, making their journey a one-way passage with no real home to return to. They have, in the metaphorical sense, left the well-beaten track to embark on a road without any instructions or signposts. Somewhere there is another marked highway, but until it is found the environment can seem confusing and chaotic. From this perspective, the migrant's exile, or diaspora existence, is about striving to find new understanding, new goals and new meaning (Akman 1994: 11).

Migrants, including those who flee for political reasons, are typical of our time. In postmodern and postcolonial theory, concepts such as fragmentation, alienation, value relativity, identity problems and destruction are used as part of the contemporary diagnosis (Lewis and Mills 2003). These phenomena can also be used to describe the migrant condition. Migrants are in a way detached from previous contexts and live in a constant process of negotiation with a series of dilemmas that raises and establishes what can somewhat imprecisely be called the postmodern framework (Chambers 1994).

The world has become smaller and more accessible, yet at the same time more complex and interrelated. Again, the migrant is an essential feature in this development and represents all foreigners who suddenly find themselves in what we consider to be known. Migrants have to deal with the complex, master the unknown and develop navigation strategies in the new landscape. Migrants are an issue not just for the migrants themselves, but also with respect to their environment. Encountering the foreign forces locals to realize that they are no longer the world's centre and its only standard, as Western discourses of 'others' tend to claim. Globalization entails a decentring that affects all parties. Increasing globalization and ethnic diversity lend new dimensions to forms of cultural expression in the community and challenge urban life (Chambers 1994). As a result of increasing globalization and mobility, Norway too has gained some of the human resources carried along by globalization.

In the first section of this chapter, I try to show the characteristics of exile and diaspora conditions and depict how people in diaspora sometimes struggle to find a 'new name'. In the second section, I focus on intellectuals in diaspora and female diaspora artists in particular. The third part of the essay explores the political sensitivity of art and artistic expression. The last section draws on a meeting I had with the exiled Kurdish painter Kwestan Jamal Ali, who came to Norway after being a refugee in her own country for ten years. Diaspora artists bring a certain ambiguity to Norwegian art, along with variations, nuances and an otherness that generate an enriching multicultural, global expression.

Diaspora and Exile

The term diaspora originally pertained to the Jewish people's exodus and worldwide dispersion after the Babylonian and Roman conquests of Palestine. Today this concept is used to refer to areas where many people from the same country or region have settled and find new life chances (Safran 1991). People in diaspora have migrated and resettled for many reasons, political exile being one of them. The term exile here means people in diaspora who have fled their home country or the place they used to live to seek refuge and protection elsewhere. The terms diaspora and, even more, exile are associated with freedom and artistic expression. However, such an experience hinges on confirmation in the diaspora of one's previous status and identity (Akman 1994). To experience freedom of expression, artists must have the opportunity to raise their artistic 'voices' through art, whether they 'speak' through literature, paintings, music or dramatic art. Otherwise they perceive their diaspora existence as neither liberating nor inspiring, but perhaps to the contrary, as a straitjacket. Many female exiled artists share the fate of other women through the ages who have had to leave their homelands, voluntarily or involuntarily. They have lived under totalitarian regimes and been imprisoned and tortured. In several known cases, women artists have been surreptitiously killed for their oppositional artistic expressions.

The causes of persecution, exile or escape largely remain the same throughout history, but the people, the society and the context change continuously. The female exile's opposition of a political system often provokes various forms of sanctions as a government response. As mentioned, artists whose activities result in their political persecution may feel forced to choose exile as a solution. The diaspora existence can thus seem like a 'penalty' that affects both individuals and groups. According to Akman (1994), exile in diaspora is an expression of a person's loss of fundamental rights in their homeland – of family and friends, work, cultural manifestation and language. In diaspora, the exile faces a new linguistic context in which their own language often seems useless as a tool for communicating or mastering new surroundings. The feeling of alienation generated by uprootedness from familiar contexts is not something one chooses: it develops over time or is imposed by others, and frequently leads to serious undervaluing, as the exile's experiences, thoughts and hopes do not have the same meaning as before or are difficult to transfer to the new context. Life in diaspora therefore feels very contradictory. For many it goes beyond having a job and a place to stay: it is a quest for belonging, a search for a place to belong where one is recognized as the person one is (Eastmond 1997 [1989]).

To create or to build a sense of belonging is a process that engages internal and external forces. The external forces are best characterized by the community in which the new opportunities arise. Often what is sought is a 'home town' that is not just a geographic point on the map but a source of opportunity to those who live there. The inner force might be the individual's ability and willingness to accept and use the opportunities offered by the home town and the broader environment, financially, materially and relationally. In this way, the exile becomes a part of a process that strengthens attachment to a place and to those who live there, contributing to greater visibility (Akman 1989).

Exile is a process that links changes in personal and social identity with changes in social positions, and vice versa. John C. Knudsen (1990) argues that for those who define themselves as political refugees (exiles), it can be of existential importance that this status is not rendered suspect but on the contrary, is affirmed by others. This applies equally to the new society and to their fellow countrymen or members of their own ethnic group, whose ascription of this status to the person cannot be taken for granted: the exile's former status in the homeland can, in diaspora, be either invalidated, sustained or maximized. This holds true above all in their Norwegian surroundings (Knudsen cited in Akman 1994).

Finding a Name

Migrants' attachment to their country or place of origin, family and friends, and people or ethnic group is often perceived to be more real than life in diaspora. For many, however, years in exile have led to gradual change in this former reality. Nothing is completely real anymore – neither what they left behind, nor what they came to. Such knowledge is a heavy burden and at worst leads to a feeling of alienation, as in a poem by the Prague writer Rainer Maria Rilke (1875–1926) that describes his experience of visiting a new and strange city: looking out over the city from his window, he was overwhelmed by a sense of desolation and alienation. The city seemed impossible to enter – it locked him out.

Being locked out, as Rilke described it, is perhaps characteristic of many women exiles' experience in diaspora at both the personal and the institutional level. Some try to reduce the sense of alienation and desolation by becoming more like 'the others'. But whereas adaptation to others is positive and constructive, it can also lead to losing sight of what seems meaningful in one's own past. Exile thus holds many existential experiences that can work to change personal and ethnic identity. In an existentialist perspective, people bump into the identity issue when they experience loss of all their reference points and their 'name', in other words, when they become aware of their anonymity (Sløk 1966: 65). But through the recognition of this condition – through alienation, so to speak – a new identity can emerge. In order to have an identity, one must be able to establish one's identity with one's own name and reference points, and be able to hold on to this amid life's changing circumstances. One's name and visibility show that one stands in relation to other people, to history, to the world of things and different situations, that is, in the reality of relations experienced as one's own. In exile, however, it happens that such relationships break down and a person is no longer recognized by them. Identity reference points are therefore inadequate in the crisis situation that exile represents.

Today, the term exile is rarely used and is often regarded as a dimension of concepts like migration and diaspora, which also entail political elements.

Female Intellectuals in Diaspora

Intellectuals in diaspora are often identified by the position they had in their home country, and possibly within their own ethnic group. 'Status' refers to a person's legal or social profession or position in relation to others. The concept of status pops up in the political arena as, for example, asylum-seeker status, immigrant status, status as a political refugee. Those who are considered intellectuals have often enjoyed a special status in their home country that they seek to continue in diaspora (Knudsen 1990). Often highly educated, they are defined as readers or cultural translators by the new society. To attain such a position, those concerned must have clear reference points to the past, possess wisdom and be known to have good general knowledge about the diaspora community. These individuals are often sought after to explain, interpret and translate knowledge and information to others of their nation or ethnic group in the diaspora community. How reliably this is done depends on the way the 'reader' relates to the diaspora members. It is insufficient to be perceived as intellectual in the sense of being 'learned' or having such a status; in addition, 'readers' are expected to have the ability to communicate well and give advice that others can use to their benefit (Akman 1994).

Female intellectuals in diaspora are people with rich resources who nonetheless obviously differ in terms of social and professional background and experience. Sometimes they have fled their home country after opposing the authorities there. In diaspora they must deal with new aspects of social and gendered life, and reassess beliefs, expectations and opinions about what a woman is and what an intellectual is, as well as the status, roles and responsibilities of women in the community they have come to. Can a woman hold on to her previous values and norms? Will her role and self-concept as a woman change? The gender role is only part of her culture; she also has a role as a Kurd, an Armenian, a Jew, and an Assyrian.

Many women in diaspora find that women's political pursuits are regarded as merely propping up men's political activity. At the same time, women in diaspora are known to discover their own political issues to fight for, expressed through various cultural forms such as dance, song, music, literature or different types of art. The experience of living in at least two cultures but not fully in any of them may be stressful, but it is also enriching. Women in diaspora participate in several cultures, and through this participation new cultural forms are often created in a continuous process that challenges the culture and changes the society.

Female Artists in Diaspora

Political conflict, war and violence mark the history of the twentieth century in many parts of the world. Like other political dissidents, many artists experience exile and uprootedness because of this history. Many migrants regard diaspora as something temporary and are often heard insisting that they will return home once conditions are favourable. The world changes, and regions once haunted by war might be peaceful ten years later. Many exiled artists therefore have the opportunity to work freely between two and sometimes three cultures. The works of transnational female artists, whether created in the diaspora or in their respective countries, are forging a new consciousness that has no borders. Edward Said (1990) claimed that '[t]he exile knows that in a secular and contingent world, homes are always provisional. Borders and barriers, which enclose us within the safety of familiar territory can also become prisons, and are often defended beyond reason and necessity' (Said cited in Chambers 1994: 2).

The postmodern world is characterized by pluralism and diversity. Today's artists confront the historical and political forces that bind cultures, such as globalization, political conflict and war. Their themes draw attention to social inequities, human rights violations, environmental and economic issues, neo-colonial interests and repressive regimes. Such critical exploration of controversial issues is often censored in the artist's country of origin. Female migrant artists are no exception in this regard.

As the world becomes increasingly diverse and complex, art too receives a multilayered and more complex expression. Female artists in diaspora can contribute to a more comprehensive art concept and diversity of cultural expression in public spaces. Increasing global migration gives Norway a flow of 'specialists' in many areas: food, clothing, newspapers, music, literature, film, ornaments, handicrafts and visuals. Different ethnic artists represent a wide diversity of expressions and genres. Some come from countries where artistic activity has been unproblematic, whereas others' artistic message is a political demonstration and may have been the direct cause of their exile. Previously this meant that the artist lost contact with the art scene in the home country, but new technologies have made it easier to follow political and cultural developments there. Combining technically mediated closeness with geographical distance allows such artists to maintain and develop artistic activity in exile while still following artistic developments and networks in the home country.

Norwegian art is enriched by its inclusion of skilled ethnic artists in its art institutions and artist networks, but this inclusion also sends an important signal to ethnic groups in Norway in general. Norwegian recognition matters – not only to the ethnic artist, but also to what this person is and stands for politically. Ethnic groups in diaspora need symbolic reference points and markers of loyalty, and exile artists and their art can represent some of them.

Art as Political Expression

Encyclo Online defines political art as '…work that contains political subject matter, takes a stand on an issue, addresses a public concern, or awakens viewer sensitivity'.[2]

Cheryl Toman (2009) observes that art forms may range from highly intellectualized artistic projects to grassroots movements. An open mind is able to experience this diversity of artistic expressions and see its relevance. 'Art', defined broadly, includes all visual, literary, and performing arts and combinations thereof. She further claims that it is logical for art to serve as a catalyst for change and reform (Toman 2009: 2), which means that art is a highly political matter.

'Art has served political ends and addressed political themes and issues throughout history. Events experienced during the first half of the twentieth century compelled numerous artists to speak out and use their art to make political statements (Kleiner & Mamiya 2004)' Indeed, art has been a means of expression all through history as artists have used their art to convey political statements in various ways. Whether expressing philosophical or political standpoints, their statements have most often dealt with the political environment, political events or systems. As Jean Roy (2008) puts it, a piece of art 'tells a history in one's life or group of lives. Social injustice, alienation, misery, resettlement, and control of power all affected and took part in the art that incorporated the political statements behind [its] meaning.'

In her editorial on 'Women, Activism and the Arts', Toman (2009) states that women and creativity have always been a topic of interest in the field of women's studies. She looks at women in the Arab diaspora and the way they seem to channel their creativity positively so as to develop tools through their art for 'consciousness-raising and a means of actively participating in the history – past, present, and future – of their own communities and countries as well as of the world in general'. She further claims that '[t]he arts are one of the few unifying forces for such activism since they enable all women to potentially find a common medium of communication regardless of social class, ethnic or religious background, or level of formal education' (2009: 2).

Toman also points to the Lebanese photographer Rania Matar and her series of photos, 'The Forgotten People', portraying refugees in the Shatila camp for Palestinians in Lebanon. Deeply inspired by the people's spirit and resilience, Matar captured powerful images that tell a story common to all refugees. Toman argues that the purpose of Matar's activism is to raise awareness of such situations. Through her art, Matar addresses the world's citizens and appeals to their obligation to right injustice (2009: 2). The art of female artist activists or political dissident artists living in diaspora often directs itself beyond the diaspora context, as the intention is to improve the lives of women regardless of social, cultural, economic or educational backgrounds.

In the field of forced migration, Marita Eastmond (2007: 249) emphasizes that narratives are sometimes the only means researchers have of knowing something about life in times and places to which they otherwise have little access. Narratives can reveal how people themselves, as 'experiencing subjects', make sense of violence and turbulent change. Eastmond argues for the need to distinguish between *life as lived*, the flow of events that touch on a person's life; *life as experienced,* how the person perceives and ascribes meaning to what happens, drawing on previous experience and cultural repertoires; and *life as told,* how experience is framed and articulated in a particular context and to a particular audience (Eastmond 2007: 249). Visual art actualizes all these different narratives. A painting can be seen as a story – a narrative – in which the artist's voice can be heard. In political art this voice tries to tell a story or make a statement. This 'visual narrative' interwoven into the painting is founded in the lived life of the artist, the experiences of the artist and the message told in the painting. The exiled Bolivian painter Eduardo Ibáñez,[3] who throughout his career has always identified with the lower strata of society, sometimes starts his work by writing a poem on the canvas he will paint on. In this way the poetic narrative and the visual image become one. The artist's painting includes his own lived life, the experiences he makes by living this life and the artistic expression that can be viewed as a story that needs to be told.

A Kurdish Artist in Diaspora

Some years back I had the opportunity to meet the exiled artist Kwestan Jamal Ali and talk to her about her art and the political message she tries to convey through her paintings. What follows is my account of our conversation on the background of her paintings and photos.

Kwestan Jamal Ali was born in the late 1960s in the northern part of Iraq that today is termed Kurdistan. She came to Norway after the U.S.-led invasion of 2003. During the Gulf War she, her husband and their newborn child crossed the mountains together with thousands of Kurdish refugees escaping political persecution under the brutal Baath regime to resettle in the safe haven the UN provided near the Turkish border. Educated at Sulaimania College of Arts, she has exhibited her works in her homeland as well as Canada, Germany, and Japan and, later, Norway. Later she also took a master's degree in arts in Norway.

'What drives me when I am in diaspora', Kwestan Jamal Ali says, 'is to speak up against oppression with my paintings.' As a Kurdish woman and artist living under Saddam Hussein's regime, Kwestan Jamal Ali experienced the brutality of life, oppression of women and persecution of artists delivering political messages through their artworks. There she was critical of the regime, but she found her real oppositional voice much later, in the diaspora. Kwestan Jamal Ali's former experiences form the main thread in her paintings, which balance between past and the present, hope and despair. One of her works, 'The Story of the Stone', shows feet entangled in an abstract formation reflecting movement on stones, evoking her own story and symbolizing the Kurdish people's flight into the mountains of Kurdistan. On this gruesome journey the artist witnessed people suffering starvation and illness. Hundreds died on the way. She saw husbands and fathers carrying their sick or dead children. As she was a mother herself, her attention turned to the women – desperate mothers trying to feed and care for their children in a hopeless situation (Kwestan Jamal Ali, personal communication, 5 May 2008). Kwestan Jamal Ali explains how deeply inspired she becomes when listening to other women's stories, whether the context is Kurdistan, Norway or elsewhere.

> I get my inspiration from the plight of women the world over. When I see the suffering around me I feel like expressing myself with a voice in support of all these women, and that voice comes in form of painting. That is why I paint.

Kwestan Jamal Ali's art contains many voices: her own as a woman, the voice of every suffering woman and the voice of her people. But her art also expresses the general problem of oppression, genocide and the silencing of voices under oppressive regimes that is endured by people in many parts of the world. Her art is not hers alone, she says; it belongs to her people and to women in particular. The works discussed below incorporate Kwestan Jamal Ali's experiences as a refugee, a woman, an exile, a Kurd and a member of the Kurdish diaspora.

'Walking without Shoes'

Figure 1.1. Kwestan Jamal Ali, *Tvangsinnvandring* (detail), 2002. Used with permission of the artist.

The Gulf War of 1991 prompted an exodus from Kurdistan, Iraq, an escape in which thousands of refugees died in horrible, extreme conditions of disease, starvation or cold. These experiences, her own fear and her observations of her fellow refugees' suffering made a deep and everlasting impression on the artist, but they also inspired her future artistic production as, in the course of the artistic process, her thoughts were drawn back to her flight. For Kwestan Jamal Ali, words were too limited to convey hunger, distress and death.

One of the things that affected her most strongly as a human being and artist was the many refugees who lost their shoes along the way. It was almost inconceivable that people – women, men, children, the old and the sick – could continue without protective footwear in the snow, cold and dirt of high mountain paths leading through gorges and deep ravines. The artist's explanation was that fear drove people onwards over the mountains. Pain, grief and hatred, but also friendship and solidarity, were faithful companions on the long march. She recalled how parents, seeking emotional release, would cry and scream out their pain as their children looked on, terror-stricken.

'The Story of the Stone'

Having decided to escape, Kwestan Jamal Ali knew that the only road to freedom ran through the mountains of Kurdistan. According to a Kurdish proverb, 'The Kurds have no friends but the mountains'. The

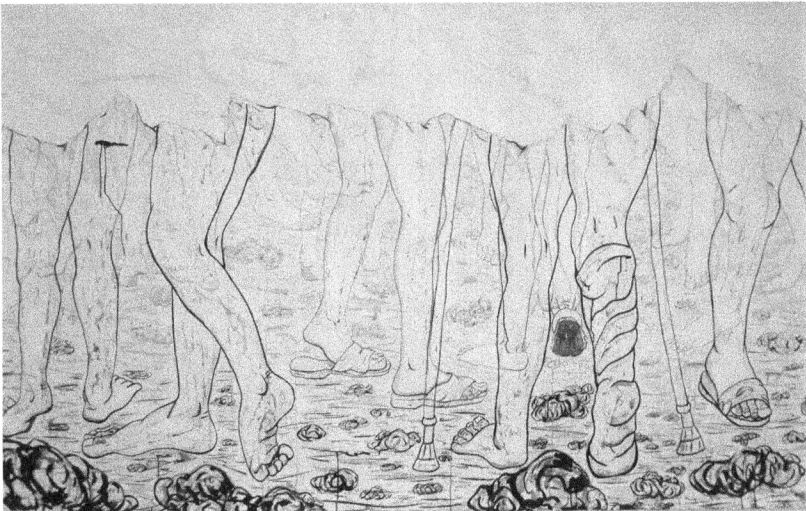

Figure 1.2. Kwestan Jamal Ali, *På flukt*, 2010. Used with permission of the artist.

Figure 1.3. Kwestan Jamal Ali, *Spor i steinene*, 2006. Used with permission of the artist.

mountains of Kurdistan can be inhospitable and dangerous, but they also provide protection. The artist experiences the mountains as the incarnation of care: they embrace their people, and they are kind and loving. Kurdish history is inscribed in mountain caves where people have sought shelter since time immemorial. Their forefathers have written their escape story on the cave walls – and in the hearts of all Kurds. The stories chiselled in the stones seem to have been there forever, and they approach the reader by saying 'I was here long before you'. The message of the stones reminds us that history repeats itself.

In diaspora, memories strengthen over time. The history of the stones and the nature of Kurdistan inspire Kwestan Jamal Ali to create great art. For her, stone is a metaphor, a mental image and a recurring theme in artistic expression. Stone is universal; it is found everywhere. All cultures have a relationship to stone. When people are forced to flee, the stones remain as a silent witness to what has happened.

'Returning Home'

After six years of exile, Kwestan Jamal Ali was finally able to return to her beloved homeland of Kurdistan. During her years in exile, she had dreamed of visiting the caves where she and thousands of others sought refuge. She went with her camera to the mountains and walked along the unending barefoot-trodden road to freedom. The stones and rocks were still there, as if time had stood still. The stones represent history, she claims, including the history of a young painter's escape.

Stone and Political Pain

'The History of the Stone' is an image showing that we can read our history through stone, which becomes a witness to events large and small. The motif points to social and political relations, but upon looking more closely one will find commentaries (in the outlines, the colours and the shapes) carved in stone, or written in Indian ink. The first cultural voice in human history is found in stones and inside mountain caves. Through their history Kurds too have used stone to guard animals and livelihoods, keeping them safe from external danger. Everything can change, but only the stones are protection from enemies and sometimes death.

> As a Kurdish artist, I have experienced a dictatorial system and enemies who have tried to destroy and wipe out my history, culture and language. Each time the stones, caves and rocks became our protectors. Only the stones can tell the story of my people.

Kwestan Jamal Ali emphasizes the distinction between herself, as an artist, and a political scientist or historian whose profession is to write the history of a people or the political system in a given society:

> I have chosen an aesthetic form of communication and express myself with brush and colours on canvas. Art touches people in a different way than the written word. All senses are used. My message is actually simple and universally human, but also political. My paintings tell about the political problems in my homeland and my people's historical suffering, but they are also proud monuments to the peoples' struggle and strength.

Again we see how a painting can function as a visual narrative that the artist needs to tell.

Art as Cultural Struggle

Referring to the black power and women's liberation movements of the 1960s and 1970s (and onwards) in the United States, Lisa Gail Collins (2006: 718) claims that passionate participants and activist artists in both struggles imagined a world where they would thrive, be safe and feel connected, authentic and whole. Activist-participants strove to realize this world by transforming the dominant social order. She refers to the scholar and grassroots organizer Maulana Ron Karenga who once asserted, 'We stress culture because it gives identity, purpose, and direction. It tells you who you are, what you must do, and how you can do it', further claiming that a black cultural revolution was essential to the revolutionary struggle for black power (Karenga 1967, cited in Collins 2006: 724). For Kwestan Jamal Ali, art is central to what Collins terms cultural feminism, that is, ideologies that embrace the creative construction of alternative or oppositional cultures of resistance or resistance through art. Inspired by Lucy Lippard, one of America's most provocative and influential art writers and political activists in the 1970s, Collins emphasizes that art and politics are linked. Both, she believes, have the power to change (Collins 2006: 732). This is also true of resistance artists elsewhere who live under politically suppressive conditions that need to be changed. Kurdish artists have lived under oppressive regimes for decades, but despite positive changes in the situation in Kurdistan (Iraq), oppositional voices still have to be cautious. The struggle for political freedom and freedom of speech, as well as freedom of critical artistic expression, is a process that must be kept alive to continue in different ways.

Conclusion

This chapter has treated a typical phenomenon of our time: people's migration from their countries of origin. When many migrants from the same nation, country or ethic group resettle in a new place, they form a diaspora community. Since the first known diaspora of the Jewish people, diaspora communities have formed all over the world, among them Kurdish diasporas in different European countries, the United States, Canada and Australia. People in diaspora have migrated and resettled for different reasons, political exile among them.

The essay focuses on artwork as political expression and on female exiled artists in particular. Causes of persecution, exile and escape have changed little throughout history, but the peoples, societies and contexts are ever in flux. The female exile has often excited government sanctions by opposing a political system – indeed, many an artist has endured political persecution as a consequence of artistic activity, and exile sometimes appears the best option. The many ways art can serve as a catalyst for change and reform clearly demonstrate its tremendous political potential. An artwork can tell the story of the life of a person, nation or ethnic group. By sending a political message, the artist often takes a stance in favour of a cause, group or people, at the same time opposing an oppressive system or regime. In this way the artwork becomes a narrative – a story giving voice to the artist. In paintings like those by Kwestan Jamal Ali, the 'visual narrative' interwoven in the images is rooted in the artist's lived life and past experiences, and in the message conveyed through the painting.

Female artists in diaspora have a crucial role to play in raising awareness of political issues in their countries of origin with specific attention to gender aspects and the situation of women. Thus they fulfil Lippard's (1995) vision of female art as a force with the power to envision, move and change.

Notes

1. UDI on international migration: http://www.udi.no/Oversiktsider/Interna sjonal-migrasjon
2. ENCYCLO, Online Encyclopedia. Retrieved 17 August 2012 from http://www.encyclo.co.uk/search.php
3. See the home page of Eduardo Ibáñez. Retrieved 26 July 2012 from http://www.eduardo-ibanez.com/?page_id=283

References

Akman, H. 1989. Hjembygd som livsmulighet. *Bergens Tidende* 25(9), p. 27.
———. 1994. *Landflyktighet.* Bergen: Forlaget Migrasjonslitteratur.
Chambers, I. 1994. *Migrancy, Culture, Identity.* London and New York: Routledge.
Collins, L.G. 2006. 'Activists Who Yearn for Art That Transforms: Parallels in the Black Arts and Feminist Art Movements in the United States', *New Feminist Theories of Visual Culture* 31(3): 717–52. Retrieved 20 August 2012 from http://www.jstor.org/stable/10.1086/498991
Eastmond, M. 1997 [1989]. *The Dilemmas of Exile: Chilean Refugees in the U.S.A.* Gothenburg: Acta Gotoburgensis.
———. 2007. 'Stories as Lived Experience: Narratives in Forced Migration Research', *Journal of Refugee Studies* 20(2): 248–64.
Kleiner, F.S. and Mamiya, C.J. (2004). 'Gardner's Art through the Ages: The Western Perspective'. *Online Study Guide.* Retrieved 5 July 2012 from http://wadsworth.com/art_d/templates/student_resources/0495004782_kleiner/studyguide/ch22w/ch22_9.html
Knudsen, J.C. 1990. 'Prisoners of International Politics: Vietnamese Refugees Coping with Transit Life', in *Indochinese Refugees' Experience and Its Asian Response*, special issue of *Southeast Asian Journal of Social Science* 18(1): 153–65.

Lewis, R. and S. Mills. 2003. 'Introduction', in R. Lewis and S. Mills (eds), *Feminist Postcolonial Theory: A Reader*. New York: Routledge, pp. 1–24.

Lippard, L. R. (1995). *The Pink Glass Swan. Selected Feminist Essays on Art*. New York: New Press.

Roy, J. 2008. 'Art as a Political Statement,' *Yahoo! Voices*. Retrieved 29 August 2012 from http://voices.yahoo.com/art-as-political-statement-2013245.html?cat=37

Safran, W. 1991. 'Diasporas in Modern Societies: Myths of Homeland and Return', *Diaspora* 1(1): 83–99.

Sløk, J. 1966. *Eksistensialisme – en innføring*. Oslo: Gyldendal.

Toman, C. 2009. 'Women, Activism and the Arts', *al-raida* 124: 2–6.

꧂ 2

ISLAMIC IDENTITY AS THIRD SPACE
Muslim Women Activists Negotiating Subjectivity in Sweden

Pia Karlsson Minganti

Introduction

The research area 'women in diaspora' concerns fundamentally negative experiences, such as loss, imposed changes, contradictions, degradation and alienation. The flip side of the coin, however, features testimonies of opportunity, creativity and desired change. Too strict a focus on either side of the coin – that is, diaspora simply as pain *or* prospect – risks resulting in stereotypical descriptions. This chapter brings complexity into the picture, exploring young women's negotiations of identity and subjectivity in relation to Islam in Sweden and their particular risk of being framed in the unproductive dichotomy of oppression versus emancipation (Jacobsen 2011a; Bracke and Fadil 2012). My fieldwork among women engaged in Muslim youth associations in Sweden revealed their eagerness to reject simplistic descriptions of themselves as, for instance, clear-cut religious fundamentalists, victims of Muslim fundamentalism or rebels against Western imperialism. The self-stories they tell go beyond dominant frames, but are they heard? Is there any space for these young women to be recognized as subjects, with perspectives as complex and ambivalent as anyone else's? The aim of this chapter is not to present entire life stories but to critically reflect on positioning and belonging in relation to the construction of faith-based identity among women activists in Swedish Muslim youth associations.

People, including the women in this study, routinely use essential identities in order to talk about the self and the other: man, woman, Muslim, Swede. One way of understanding this is to see negotiation of subjectivity as a matter of asserting one's world view by articulating and authorizing stories relevant to oneself. In this manner, identities enable subjectivity in that they assert positions and perspectives (Hall 1990). As constructively formulated by Avtar Brah:

> Subjectivity – the site of processes of making sense of our relation to the world – is the modality in which the precarious and contradictory nature of the subject-in-process is signified or *experienced* as identity. Identities are marked by the multiplicity of subject positions that constitute the subject.... Indeed, identity may be understood *as that very process by which the multiplicity, contradiction, and instability of subjectivity is signified as having coherence, continuity, stability; as having a core – a continually changing core but the sense of a core nonetheless.* (Brah 1996: 123–24, emphasis in original)

Sociologist Manuel Castells claims that in times of rapid, uncontrolled change, people are especially likely to reorganize around 'primary identities' – ethnic, national, territorial and, not least, religious – which make up the most 'formidable force for personal security and collective mobilization' (Castells 1996: 3). These identities are often seen as either biologically or divinely determined. Being an adolescent Muslim in Sweden, however, involves continuous contestation of the meanings and boundaries of significant identities with various actors in the family, peer group, school, workplace, mass media, Internet and other public spheres. The negotiation of subjectivity and identity is a matter of ascertaining a sense and recognition of belonging. Yet, the young women in this study seem to experience a life situation in which they cannot fully identify with one or another national/ethnic identity. This ambivalence may result in their being depicted as deficient subjects. This chapter illuminates how the young women refuse such depictions and instead struggle for full subjectivity and citizenship.

Like most young Swedish Muslims, all the women in the focus of this study have formal citizenship, so the struggle for this right is not at the top of Muslim youth associations' agendas in Sweden. This contrasts with other European countries, such as Germany and Italy, where many young people categorized as second- or third-generation immigrants are denied formal citizenship (Frisina 2006; Yükleyen 2012). Despite being regular citizens, however, the women in this study do not always feel accepted as equals. In contemporary 'Western' imaginaries, Muslims are stereotypically constructed in opposition to the features valued in the modern citizen. Though the notion of the rights-bearing modern citizen is based on a moral subject capable of autonomous reason, this capacity is unevenly ascribed to people in view of aspects such as gender, sexuality, 'race'/ethnicity and class. In the post–9/11 climate, 'the Muslim' has been increasingly associated with lack of rationality and democratic behaviour, attributed to religious and cultural heritage (see Andreassen, this volume; Runfors 2009; Hübinette and Lundström 2011; Moray and Yaqin 2011; Keskinen 2012). Consequently, the young women act to oppose this exclusionary representation and call for recognition as valued and contributing members of society.

As members of Muslim youth associations, they actively participate in proclaiming a new Swedish Muslim subject position, that is, an ordinary citizen of a different faith. I will argue that this position does not benefit from being understood within the frame of hyphenated identity built on the reproduction of essential identities. Rather, my intention is to demonstrate how the women take part in carving out an 'Islamic' position in between, or beyond, dominant discourses of 'Swedish' and 'Muslim' identity. To understand such a process, I point to the utility of cultural theorist Homi K. Bhabha's concept of a *third space* of hybridity, from which new perspectives and positions can emerge (Bhabha 1994: 36–39).

Bhabha introduces the concept of the third space to emphasize ambiguous negotiations within and between perceived homogenous groups, thus describing a creative and critical space that neither rejects nor overemphasizes the available bipolar discourses and positions. Criticism has stressed that the concept of hybridity is itself polarizing and implies the existence of a concept of 'pure culture' (Wolf 2008: 12). However, given a dynamic perspective on hybridity based on a view of culture and identity as consistently heterogeneous and fluid, the concept of the third space has potential: '[A]ll forms of culture are continually in a process of hybridity. But for me the importance of hybridity is not to be able to trace two original moments from which the third emerges, rather hybridity to me is the "third space" which enables other positions to emerge' (Bhabha 1990: 211).

Extensive research on identity formation in terms of hybridity has supplied a frame of reference apt for grasping affirmative implications of life in diaspora (e.g., Vertovec and Rogers 1998; Farahani 2007). Scandinavian researchers have examined young Muslims' hybrid identity construction in conjunction with the creation of a universal Islamic position (Mørck 1998; Schmidt 2004; Jacobsen 2011b) and with consideration of possible variations of identity constructions between organized and non-organized Muslim youth (Jeldtoft and Nielsen 2011; Otterbeck 2011; Jeldtoft 2012). Researchers who have indicated the progressive potential of a third space include Shahnaz Khan (2002) in her study on Muslim female identity in Canada, Katrin Goldstein-Kyaga and María Borgström (2009) in their study on young people of immigrant background in Sweden, Tobias Hübinette on adopted Koreans (2004) and Hanna Wikström (2007) on families of Iranian origin in Sweden.

In her study of Swedish pupils' talk on religion, Kerstin von Brömssen pointed instead to the difficulty of finding expressions of hybrid identities and creation of a third space, thus claiming that the religious dimension seems to reproduce boundary demarcations (von Brömssen 2003: 329). This chapter, on the contrary, illustrates the actual prevalence of hybridity within young women's Islamic circles. Yet I will take up von Brömssen's critical stance in the sense of questioning hybridity as automatically anti-essentializing and empowering (Brah and Coombes 2000; Hutnyk 2005). I will add to the critique of Bhabha's notion of the third space by contextualizing it and demonstrating how it can indeed result in the maintenance of power structures, particularly when viewed from a gender perspective. Inspired by a text by Sara Ababneh, I will discuss the young women's Islamic position as a hybrid third space that 'both reproduces domination but also provides an opportunity to fight it' (Ababneh 2006: 23).

However, I will also question the emphasis on 'resistance to power' that is so common in analyses of Muslim women's actions. Bhabha's third space is understood as a moment of ambivalence in which dominating discourses cannot reproduce their authority and the opportunity for resistance arises (Bhabha 1990, 1994). But, with her seminal work on Muslim women's pious self-formation, Saba Mahmood (2005) helps us rethink the notion of agency in a way that goes beyond a 'traditional' secular-liberal perspective that reduces agency to a matter of individual autonomy and desire for change. She also helps us question the binary rhetoric that depicts women's rights and free choice as core values of Western nations and Muslims as threatening them. In the past decade this rhetoric has given rise to new practices of oppression in relation to immigration, citizenship and what Sirma Bilge and Paul Scheibelhofer (2012: 256) have called a 'human rights governmentality', which may serve as a tool for dominating the same minorities (e.g., Muslim women) it claims to be 'rescuing'. Indeed, Mahmood opens up space for a notion of agency that is not premised on the understanding that Muslim women need to shed their 'particular' cultural and religious attachments (Bracke and Fadil 2012: 54).

The young women at the centre of this essay present themselves as practising Muslims engaged in both worldwide Islamic revival and Swedish Muslim youth activism. This category of organized Muslims receives much public attention and is often depicted as 'hyper' religious. To counter this constricted view, a growing bulk of academic work looks into less organized expressions of Muslim life and identity (Jeldtoft and Nielsen 2011; Otterbeck 2011; Jeldtoft 2012). This is a constructive approach, but it is nonetheless important to keep in mind that the boundary between 'organized' and 'non-organized' is anything but rigid, and that people in both categories also share conditions with many other religious people in modernity, such as the diversified turn from traditional religious authority to the emphasis on subjective experience (Heelas and Woodhead 2005; Furseth 2006). The young women studied here are organized, devout Muslims, yet they call for recognition as autonomous subjects who personally choose to engage in their faith. In accord with Mahmood's work on the 'politics of piety', they establish their pious self-formation in terms of personal agency, that is, as a matter of an individual decision and considerable achievement that gives them religious merit and self-esteem (Mahmood 2005: 171, 174). This vocation includes resistance to power and struggle for change; it also calls for deep involvement in affirmative synthesizing processes.

Following these premises, this chapter will illustrate how young women move beyond dominant, bipolar discursive practices that deny them simultaneous identification as Muslims and Swedes, or as subjects and moral agents. It will show how, through their Islamic faith and youth organization, young women enter a third space where new positions are shaped, displayed and alternatively framed. This study has isolated a Swedish Muslim subject position attuned with nation-bound identity politics and an Islamic universal location, both potentially destabilizing conventional fixities.

Sweden's Young Muslims

Muslim immigration to Sweden became significant after the Second World War. From the fifteen people defining themselves as Muslims in a 1930 census, the estimated number has grown to 350,000–400,000 in a country with a total population of 9 million. Of these, approximately 100,000–150,000 belong to Muslim congregations entitled to receive state support (Larsson 2009: 56; SST 2012). The various Muslim communities exhibit significant heterogeneity along class, ethnic, rural, urban and sectarian affiliations, and variations also occur insofar as differing social, cultural and integration policies influence each community in its present society. Yet Haideh Moghissi (2006) distinguishes an emerging group identity among people originating from Muslim societies. In an anthology titled *Muslim Diaspora,* she and the contributors demonstrate how this collective sense of constituting a minority is based less on historical commonalities and 'more on the urgent contemporary and common concerns and grievances that these diaspora communities experience in relation to the "host" countries in which they now live' (Moghissi 2006: xiv).

Moghissi stresses the experience of being attacked by the larger society as the impetus propelling younger generations to resort to a heightened Muslim identity that 'does not represent increasing adherence to Islam as a religion, but to Islam as an ideology of resistance and the only force that at present seems to effectively challenge global power structures and domination systems' (Moghissi 2006: xvi). The present study of young women's negotiations of subjectivity requires additional readings of this ideological dimension. My analysis is informed by research on the contemporary Islamic revival that implies not only resistance, or 'affective empowerment' among peers (Grossberg 1997: 31, 72; Karlsson Minganti 2007, 2008), but certainly also a dimension of religious conviction.

Dating back to the 1970s, a global Islamic revival sustains the strengthening of Islamic piety, identity and ethos. Saba Mahmood (2005) has clarified that political and militant Islamic movements make up but a small part of this piety movement, which she describes broadly as a religious ethos or sensibility that has developed within contemporary Muslim societies, characterized by an increased number of mosques and rising attendance by men and women alike, increased production and consumption of religious media and literature, intellectuals who comment on the world from a religious perspective, and adherence to everyday codes of dress and behaviour (Mahmood 2005: 3–4). The Islamic revival reaches out to audiences around the globe, not least through migration and the Internet. It has particular implications for Muslim immigrants and their children in the Western diaspora, possibly attracted by the deterritorialized aspect of global Islam (Schmidt 1999; Roy 2004; Bunt 2009).

The religious revival of young Swedish Muslims involves processes of individualized piety as well as organized group action. This chapter draws on material collected during fieldwork among the members of the Sunni-dominated national umbrella organization Sveriges Unga Muslimer (SUM; Sweden's Young Muslims) and some of its local youth associations between 1998 and 2002, with complementary collections from 2009 to date (see, e.g., Karlsson Minganti 2007, 2011). Established in 1991, SUM today claims 2,800 members and over forty local youth associations in towns all over the country.[1] Although it has links to regular Muslim organizations, it cannot be defined as a mere 'youth section' of any of them. SUM is an autonomous establishment reflecting generational divergence and a sense of belonging to a 'new' generation of Swedish Muslims. It attracts adolescents and young adults, many of whom were born in Sweden, though others arrived recently. In this essay I will quote from in-depth interviews with six women under fictive names: Amal, Latifa, Leyla, Noor, Samira and Suad.

Figure 2.1. Participants at the annual conference of Sweden's Young Muslims, Stockholm 2012. Copyright: SUM

While SUM embraces members from all over the world these six women were born in West Asia and North and East Africa. Having come to Sweden as children (4–11 years of age), they were educated in public school and speak fluent Swedish. They were all over 18 years of age when they first became part of this study, and they have often functioned as leaders for younger members (Karlsson Minganti 2011).

The majority of the interviewees and the other members of SUM grew up in Sweden, where they are affected by powerful discourses that deny them simultaneous identification as Muslims and Swedes. In the post–9/11 climate, in which Muslims are constantly portrayed as having some 'indefinable propensity to barbarism' (Moray and Yakin 2011: 31), young women and their peers have become increasingly dissociated from modernity and

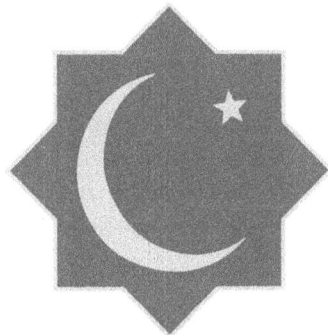

sveriges unga muslimer

Figure 2.2. The logo of Sweden's Young Muslims. Copyright: SUM

democracy, which in Sweden are the core elements of the construction of national belonging and full citizenship (Hübinette and Lundström 2011; see also Andreassen, this volume; Keskinen 2012). Further affecting the women and their peers are Islamic interpretations claiming that integration into non-Muslim societies is against Islam. Rather than delve deeper into the complexity of such divisive views, I point to the fact that some influential religious authorities *do* legitimize integration. One main actor of importance for the young women is the Geneva-born professor of theology at Oxford University Tariq Ramadan, who is a grandson of Hassan al-Banna, the Egyptian founder of the Muslim Brotherhood. Ramadan declares Islam to be universal and adaptable to any context and encourages Muslims to participate at all levels of European societies. Much of his work aims at deconstructing the sense of 'otherness' that is still reproduced within Muslim contexts (e.g., Ramadan 1999).

Influenced by the corpus of teachings produced by scholars such as Ramadan, the members of SUM claim their simultaneous identification as Swedish and Muslim is in line with authoritative Islamic doctrine. SUM may not always emphasize Ramadan's teachings as a leading example, but the young activists' website presentation reflects his stance:

> SUM works for Muslim youth to learn to know Islam and strengthen their Muslim identity. We work from a balanced and tolerant Islamic perspective based on the Koran, Sunna and Idjma. We strive to maintain the heritage of Islam and humanity even as we remain open to the possibilities and challenges of the present time. As our members are a natural part of Sweden, we promote their positive participation, responsibility, and engagement in the society on the local, national and international levels. It is important that our members feel safe in their Swedish Muslim identity.[2]

This quotation accords not only with Islamic thinkers like Tariq Ramadan but also, in a sense, with Bhabha's notion of the third space as a creative, critical space that neither rejects nor overemphasizes the existing bipolar discourses but allows new positions to emerge. The quotation presents a new Swedish Muslim position beyond conventional Muslim and Swedish identities. The very designation Sweden's Young Muslims highlights this new position intimately related to 'the heritage of Islam and humanity', which alludes to a universal Islamic identity transcending diasporic ties. As will be discussed below, such a new position has the potential to keep a reflexive third space open as long as it is not 'reclaimed, disciplined, or incorporated by one of the dominant discourses' (Ababneh 2006: 9).

Shaping Islamic Identity

A closer look into the young women's adoption of a new Swedish Muslim subject position reveals that it is not a matter of simple adherence to two traditional ethnicities, but rather of highly reflexive negotiations in a third space that result in new identifications beyond such boundaries. The paramount identification builds on their explicit priority of faith: they are shaping a trans-boundary *Islamic* identity. Exploration of the various aspects that concur to form an Islamic identity first demands a grasp of the uncertainty that still accompanies this new faith-based position. Despite its legitimization by Tariq Ramadan and other religious authorities, youths struggle continuously with the question of how exactly this positions should be occupied. What virtues must they cultivate? What ideals and values should they strive for?

Like other young people, the interviewees and their peers live in a society characterized by 'reflexive modernity' (Beck et al. 1994); that is, they are increasingly aware of the forces behind socialization and positioning in the social structure. This experience is intensified by living as a minority in a society where religion has little bearing on social authority and institutions. Rather than happening 'naturally', as everyday common sense, religion becomes the responsibility of the individual. For instance, the young women have to actively seek out halal meat, since most meat sold in Sweden is not halal. They have to remember the schedule for the daily prayers and motivate themselves to temporarily withdraw from other, 'normal' ongoing activities.

Moreover, outside their home environments the young women meet with alternative ideas that make them increasingly self-reflexive. All of the women interviewed were born into families that somehow identify as Muslim. Their upbringing socialized them into a firm belief in God and the basic pillars of Islam. For this, the women express deep gratitude. However, their narratives tend to critique the elder generation for not adequately substantiating Islam in accordance with their everyday experiences and increased reflexivity. Religion is no longer tacit common sense for them; they now look for explicit elaboration on Islamic faith and identity.

Another condition in the Swedish context further elucidates this process of enunciating faith-based identity. The young women themselves are constantly asked to elaborate on 'what Islam says' and 'what Muslims do'. Researchers have pointed to the absurdity of the demand that young people provide theologically qualified explanations for social and political circumstances in countries of which they have no experience (Otterbeck 2000: 115; Jacobsen 2002: 106–9). Yet it is made of the women again and again: Suad recalls being singled out as 'the Muslim' of the class, while Amal thinks that 'it takes up all my time to tell about Islam, or about my opinion, rather than just studying or having fun with my friends'. This representative position, ascribed to the young women by various non-Muslims (e.g. teachers, schoolmates, journalists), seemingly leaves space for them to express subjective opinions. It is, however, a space that is limited by the phenomenon that Nadia Jul Jeldtoft (2012) has studied in terms of a 'hyper-visibility' and 'hyper-religiosity' of Muslims, which academic and public debates reproduce in contrast to 'secular normality'. This subordinates Muslims to non-Muslims, so that Muslims feel a need to articulate their religious identity comprehensibly and respectfully.

Moreover, the young women face divisive discourses and discrepancies between what they are taught at home, among peers and in society at large, particularly concerning issues of gender and belonging. Their bodies become sites of signification and contestation. On the one hand, they are affected by the construction of a Swedish national self based on the notion of 'our' equality, contrasted to the oppressive Muslim other. On the other hand, discourses of women as carriers of Muslim identity place heavy demands on their modesty and chastity. Altogether these discourses leave little space for the women to express subjective experiences but increase their wish to gain deeper knowledge and take a personal stance. The pressing questions of *why* and *how* to live Islam are evident in the following statement by Leyla:

> We have always been Muslims, so to speak. We were born Muslims, so then one is Muslim. But I am. … I was brought up in a more cultural way. Like, when I began to wear the hijab my hair was visible. But then, when I checked in the Koran and so on, I thought like: 'Do I wear a hijab? Why should I wear it at all?' I had just put it on without questioning. But now lately, I have thought: 'Why should I wear a hijab? And if I do, I should do it properly.' I have kind of searched for an answer myself to *why* I should wear it, and *how* I should wear it, and not only donning it in a traditional way.

The quotation points to a key scenario in the women's narratives about their development as Muslims: (1) being born in a Muslim family with Islam as the tacit common sense; (2) going through a teenage crisis upon growing up and meeting with alternative norms and practices outside the home sphere; (3) being religiously awakened by enrolling in Muslim youth associations and, consequently, in the global Islamic revival (Karlsson Minganti 2007, 2010). This scenario coincides with a common Islamic narrative suggesting that: (1) all human beings are originally born Muslims; (2) later they are led astray from 'the straight path of Islam'; (3) some are finally back on track to Islam as 'converts' or 'reverts', or, as the women themselves would define it, as 'practising Muslims' of 'true Islam'.

Indeed, 'practising Muslim' is the emic definition that the young women give for their new devout position – a Muslim who continually practises Islam with a reflexive understanding of the pious meanings, forms and motives of the practices. Consequently, the women construct themselves in opposition to 'non-practising Muslims', understood as having an unreflexive relation to the religion into which they were born, or as having been led astray from the straight path of Islam. They associate the unreflexive Muslim with passive adherence to ethnic customs in the country of origin. When the women attempted to verbalize this category, they used the term 'cultural Muslim'. Contrary to this figure, the 'practising Muslim' manages to distinguish between cultural traditions and Islam. As Amal phrased it, in concurrence with Leyla above: 'In my home country women wear their headscarves with their hair sticking out. It's their tradition, but it's not in accordance with Islam.'

The young women themselves carefully seek knowledge on why and how to don the hijab in accordance with what they perceive to be 'true' Islam. They are critical of women who exhibit the hijab merely as an ethnic marker, and of Muslims who visit the mosque only during festivities and not as part of their everyday observance of Islam. Saba Mahmood highlights this specific critique as a vital part of the contemporary Islamic revival:

> The ritual acts of worship in the popular imagination have increasingly acquired the status of customs or conventions, a kind of 'Muslim folklore' undertaken as a form of entertainment or as a means to display a religio-cultural identity. According to them [the pious Egyptian women in Mahmood's study], this has led to the decline of an alternative understanding of worship, one in which rituals are performed as a means to the training and realization of piety in the entirety of one's life. (Mahmood 2005: 48)

The interviewees' religious activism and everyday practice aim to restore this alternative pious understanding of worship. Elaborating on this revivalist critique in a European context, Olivier Roy has developed the notion of a 'Muslim neo-ethnicity' (Roy 2004: 124–37). He points to its diasporic origin and its intimate link to the generic category of 'the Muslim', which discursively substitutes 'the Stranger' or 'the Immigrant' as a negative stereotype in non-Muslim minds. Roy's use of 'neo' implies the construction of a new identity position to which earlier ethnic or national origins are no longer relevant, while 'ethnicity' indicates that he understands religion to refer less to faith and spiritual life than to an inherited set of cultural patterns (Roy 2004: 124). On the one hand, this dominant perception of a single Muslim culture shared by all Muslims regardless of origin seems absurd to the young women and their peers, who struggle daily to manage the differences induced by their various backgrounds and generation gaps. Nonetheless, the idea of Muslim unity makes sense to them for several reasons: (1) increased transnational conversations through migration and the media make the search for a single 'true' Islam more reasonable than fragmented adherence to particular traditions; (2) non-Muslim actors constantly interpellate the youths themselves into the definite subject position of 'the Muslim'; (3) identification with the whole Muslim *umma* (community) of Sweden, or of the world at large, forms a pertinent basis for identity politics.

Then again, an important difference separates the idea of Muslim 'neo-ethnicity' from the women's self-categorization as 'practising Muslims', namely, the pious dimension theorized by Mahmood. The designation 'practising' indicates that the women refrain from understanding Islam as an inherited set of cultural patterns. Rather, they are involved in the de-ethnicization/de-culturalization of Islam, that is, the recovery of Islam as a 'pristine' and omnipresent religion. Again quoting Amal: 'There are women who wear hijab to show that they are Muslims. But they do not pray and do not behave in accordance with Islam. So, their wearing the hijab is not worth anything before God.' And Leila: 'For instance, if I wear a headscarf in order to have everyone thinking, 'Wow, you are cool!', then it does not count, so to speak. No, you really need the intention to wear it because it is prescribed in the Koran and because God wants you to.'

Through their religious activism and everyday practice, the interviewees intend to restore this pious understanding of worship. They prioritize a universal faith-based Islamic identity over association with ethnicity and culture, whether based on family origin or the Western stereotypical idea of one monolithic Muslim culture. At the same time, they work to associate themselves with Swedish society. SUM, like many other Muslim youth organizations in Europe, is society-oriented and comprises relatively progressive and inclusive forms of Islam.[3] Concisely, the women and their peers work to be recognized as 'practising Muslims' of 'true' Islam, moreover as Swedish Muslims, that is, ordinary citizens, only of different faith.

Displaying Islamic Identity

Identity is displayed in dialogue with the wider society, and SUM has become an important platform representing Swedish Muslim youth.

This section illustrates their attempts to move beyond the fixities ascribed to them and into a third, 'Islamic' space where they can negotiate subject positions such as 'Swede', 'Muslim', 'youth' and 'woman'.

As a national organization, SUM aims to gather a wide range of young people who, in one way or another, identify as Muslims. The organization has a relatively permissive attitude towards the different orientations among its members. This inclusive approach derives from explicit awareness that the majority of young Muslims in today's Europe perceive themselves as unknowledgeable about Islamic doctrine and little motivated to practise religious rules, not to mention lacking a sense of belonging and guidance. SUM has undertaken to transmit Islam to the young generation while still leaving space for variations in mode and degree of religious observance. Moreover, the activists acknowledge the situational and relational dimensions of identity and the taking of multiple subject positions. It is, for instance, possible to enjoy a raï music concert and momentarily identify with the North African diaspora, then join in a Muslim association meeting and thus the Islamic revival, and at the end of the day appear as a 'traditional' youth at the family dinner table (Vertovec and Rogers 1998: 3). In this way, SUM's approach to its members coincides with Bhabha's notion of a third space that does not reject the seemingly contradictory positions available.

Many of the women are, through their families, loosely or closely associated with liberation movements with ethnic profiles, though they simultaneously prioritize universal Islamic identity and solidarity. Certainly they share with young Muslims elsewhere anxieties about 'the future, political repression, foreign occupations and wars, corrupt governments, poverty, restrictions on their movement and choices, racism … to name just a few' (Herrera 2005: 4). Many see the display of Islamic identity as a way of resisting injustice. But caution is warranted in placing Muslim youth in the 'rebel' position, since this is all too often attached to 'sticky' emotions such as rage and vindictiveness (Ahmed 2004: 131–32). As aptly encapsulated by Linda Herrera, young Muslims' expressions of angst and anger, which sometimes turn into violence and radicalism, are only one aspect of the story. The 'problem-oriented' focus (common to youth research in general) needs to be redirected towards recognition of Muslim youth as 'agents of change, creators and consumers of new technologies, trendsetters in the arts, music, fashion, and innovators of new forms of political organization and social movements towards greater social and economic justice' (Herrera 2005: 4).

For instance, many members of SUM are also organizing in environmental movements, and some of them have taken part in the formation of 'Islamic environmentalism' (Schwencke 2012). Similarly, many are active producers and consumers of 'Islamic fashion' (Karlsson Minganti 2013; Moors and Tarlo 2013). The interviewees relate the colours, forms and fabrics of their dress to various ideas of beauty, modesty, piety and politics. They are in fact involved in developing 'new styles of Islamic fashion or hybrid forms of fashion that include Islamic elements ... through a creative fusion of multiple sources of inspiration' (Moors 2005: 59). A number of young women, like Iman Aldebe and Mejsa Chaaraoui, have succeeded as designers in Sweden (Karlsson Minganti and Österlind forthcoming).

For some youths it seems urgent to be part of a well-defined, officially registered organization like SUM that displays both a nation-bound Swedish Muslim identity and a trans-boundary Islamic identification in dialogue with wider society. In reality SUM is a platform for what could be called identity politics: 'an intersection of *group* identity and politics, which can lead to social change' (Phoenix 2000: 1097). Part of the women members' identity politics is to counteract predetermined social discourses that deny their subjectivity. They contest the discourse that refuses to acknowledge them as Swedes by stamping them as unfit for modern democracy. At the same time they challenge the discourse that refuses to acknowledge them as proper Muslim girls because they do not live up to certain cultural traditions. To clarify her experience of such dichotomous framing, Noor evoked the initial phase of her wearing hijab.

> I was supposed to wear a headscarf. It has always been important to my father that we maintain our roots. But I took it off. I wore it when I left home and then I sneaked into some stairway and took it off before arriving at school. That was a really hard time. I guess one could call that a crisis, when I didn't know what to do. On the one hand it worried me that my family might see me in town or somewhere without the headscarf. And on the other hand I didn't want my schoolmates to see me with the headscarf. This was the kind of anxiety that I would feel all the time during that period.

This narrative – common among the women in this study – indicates how women's bodies become sites of contestation of gender and belonging. As Rikke Andreassen aptly describes it (this volume), in today's Scandinavia the veiled bodies of individual women are turned into representations of collective Muslim female oppression and thus arouse emotions of anger, fear and disgust. Simultaneously, the collective maintenance of ethnic 'roots' tends to position women as symbolic reproducers of the group and its boundaries (Yuval-Davis 2011). This situation leads back to the initial questions this chapter poses: Is there any space for the young women to express subjectivity? Is there any recognition of them as subjects?

The analysis shows that the women take initiative to move beyond restricted views on Swedish versus Muslim belonging and take on a third, Islamic position instead. Their narratives reveal a link between this alternative location and the tactical distinction between religion and culture, 'true' Islam and local custom. Noor tackled her troublesome situation by involving herself in an alternative 'Islamic' sphere, where she elaborated her religious faith and came to appreciate hijab as a personal choice. In this way, she and the other women activists of SUM can now publicly declare that 'true' Islam concedes women the right to voluntarily don the hijab, and that the religion is hence in line with Swedish norms for gender equality. Simultaneously they counter practices they deem un-Islamic, such as coercion, supposedly maintained by 'cultural Muslims'. For instance, while discussing female genital cutting and physical abuse of women, Latifa stated that 'this is a matter of so-called Muslims doing stupid things, and then the Swedes cannot understand that this is actually not Islam'. She and the other women were convinced of the possibility of ending Islamophobia by disseminating knowledge about what they themselves perceive as the critical difference between 'true religion' and 'cultural misconceptions', 'real' and 'so-called' Muslims. In fact, this informative task has become a central objective within SUM and its affiliated local youth associations.

Like many other religious revivals, this one challenges established authorities. The younger generation of Muslims, dissatisfied with conventional interpretations of Islam, ask for elaborated, more individualized approaches to religion. A common impression is that 'adherence to Islam requires a personal knowledge of Islamic ethical and juridical traditions and that the individual cannot rely on the viewpoints of others in regard to doctrinal issues' (Hirschkind 2006: 111). Hence, organizations like SUM offer courses in religious reasoning; media technologies also facilitate the dissemination of religious knowledge among lay people. Migration and the enhancement of communication technology have increased both the quest and the opportunity for debates on a 'peer' basis, enabling new religious leaderships to find their audiences. This process potentially sidesteps conventional authorities (e.g., theological scholars, men, parents), resulting in increased interpretive authority among young people and women – in SUM as well as in Muslim communities abroad (Jonker and Amiraux 2006; Jouili and Amir-Moazami 2006; Karlsson Minganti 2007, 2011; Bano and Kalmbach 2011).

This increase in authority paves the way for women to have religious careers, as well as stronger positions in various negotiations, for instance, in resisting family members' attempts to control their daily lives, be it a matter of the division of labour, the right to pursue public Islamic activism or the choice of a future spouse. With solid references to the Koran, to its reinterpretation by renowned religious authorities and to her own piety, Noor managed, despite initial opposition from her family, to achieve her aims in several areas, for example, participating in mixed-gender activities organized by SUM and becoming engaged to a 'brother in Islam' of a different ethnic background.

Having increased their religious knowledge and authority, these women are furthermore legitimized to publicly represent Islam, not just as passive symbols for group affiliation or alienation, but also as active subjects assigned the important task commonly known as *dawa* (call to Islam). *Dawa* is oriented towards the self, but also towards other Muslims and non-Muslims alike, so it can be undertaken in a 'missionary' spirit with the goal to awaken or convert. For the young women in diaspora, however, it is largely a matter of making themselves and their religion understandable. Contrary to the coercive position of 'the Muslim', accountable for 'what Islam says' and 'what Muslims do', the concept of *dawa* offers a positive understanding of this representational task: it endows the young women with religious merit, self-esteem and opportunities to make Islam comprehensible to others in a way that reflects their subjective views.

A crucial part of the women's performance of *dawa* is to challenge the negative stereotype of Muslim women as passive victims of religious oppression. Indeed, Amal, Noor and the other women acknowledge cultural patterns of suppression, but they call attention to Islam in terms of liberation, and to SUM as a space that enables women to present themselves as free subjects: Why should they be seen as poor, suffering girls, when in fact anyone can see them at cafés and universities, in TV studios and other public media, involved in martial arts as well as numerous topical societal projects? Contrary to the victim image, they promote a self-image of cheerful, educated, independent, 'normal' women who are welcome to educate themselves and others, and to act as leaders and decision-makers. They have sat on boards and committees and also served as chairpersons. They work as public debaters, lecturers and guides in mosques, and cooperate with other religious and non-religious organizations such as charities, anti-discrimination leagues and temperance societies.

Opposing the exclusionary discourse that denies Swedish identity to veiled women by stamping them as unfit for a modern democracy, the young women promote an alternative view of hijab by highlighting it as a voluntary practice. This narrative emphasizes that free choice is a basic moral category and pressure disqualifies religious merit. The women do not deny that some of them were subjected to various forms of pressure when they initially donned the hijab, from both families who wanted to see it on and non-Muslims who wanted to see it off. Like Noor above, Samira was critical of her parents for pressuring her and wished they had given her time to reflect and only afterwards make an independent choice:

> I would have liked to learn more about Islam first, to understand more and be stronger in my faith, to be prepared somehow and then put it on. … But *now* the hijab is my own choice, because I have chosen to keep it on. And now I know why I wear it. I know what it implies and I wear it out of conviction. … If you are forced to don the hijab before the time is right you might not behave appropriately and then you can make it lose its value. Also, people might think that it is a garment only for oppressed, broken girls. It is important to understand the difference between Islam and what people and societies choose to do. But many Swedes don't and instead become upset with women in hijab.

Latifa expressed herself in the same vein:

> This image of Muslim women today, it is actually horrible. In fact, the other day a girl asked me: 'Are you allowed to watch TV?' I just went: 'Yes?!' Like as if I'm not normal. Like: 'Poor you, do you have to wear this veil? Did your parents force you? And you are never allowed to go outside of home. You can never. …' You know, like that. So I want to counter that image, to demonstrate that I am an individual! No one owns me! I am myself, a human being. I have freedom. I *myself* have chosen to put on this hijab. I *myself* have decided to follow Islam. I do it because I feel that it is useful. Because, I feel that the hijab it, kind of, makes up me. It is *it* that makes up myself, you see.

The claim to personal subjectivity through the declaration of Islam as a voluntary choice can be read as part of active identity politics. Nadia Jul Jeldtoft (2012), whose research focuses on non-organized youth, is also open to the possibility of conceptualizing this process as individual tactics. Regardless, our interlocutors have in common their involvement with ideals of the liberated subject that are celebrated in Western cultural imaginaries. In fact, 'we can speak of personal autonomy, personal freedom, and free choice as forms of symbolic capital in Western contexts' (Jeldtoft 2012: 232). Expressing individual autonomy and adapting universalist and highly inclusive approaches to Islam means inhabiting the norms of secular sensibilities, making young Muslims more likely to be associated with the 'modern', normalizing non-Muslim majorities.

However, the women's words should not be reduced to a Westernized and secularized discourse. They do indeed draw on their understanding of what Islam is and what the Koran says; secularized and religious discourses may exist side by side and interact in complex ways. Hence, the claim to subjectivity via emphasis on free choice can also be read in terms of piety, as part of the ethical self-formation of a pious Muslim subject. Saba Mahmood argues against the trend of downplaying Islamic revivalist movements as mere expressions of identity politics. For instance, she points to the common scholarly view that interprets hijab as an expression of resistance against Western politico-cultural domination but disregards any religious implications (Mahmood 2005: 24). Her theorization clarifies the intimate link between the practice of hijab and the cultivation of pious virtues: 'Significant in this program of self-cultivation is that bodily acts – like wearing the veil or conducting oneself modestly in interaction with people (especially men) – do not serve as manipulable masks in a game of public representation, detachable from an essential interiorized self. Rather they are the *critical markers* of piety as well as the *ineluctable means* by which one trains oneself to be pious' (Mahmood 2005: 158).

The set of virtues cultivated in the gendered practice of the hijab is easily associated with traditional aspects of female passivity (such as chastity and patience); hence the women's affirmation of agency may be hard to grasp. However, the women appreciate their religious practice as a process of continuous voluntary decisions to *persist* in their cultivation of piety. As Noor put it:

> This development from a practising to a non-practising Muslim starts with small things. Perhaps you open your hijab a little bit because you think, 'Oh, it doesn't matter. It's so warm'.... Women who wear the hijab are very, very strong. It includes so many hardships.... If you don't have a strong *iman* [faith] it comes off immediately. But I know that it will pay off in the long run, even if it doesn't seem so right now. I know that this is right and that this is the truth. There are people who think that hijab is about the surface. That it is not so important. But the main thing is faith. Otherwise you begin to waver and think about taking it off. So you really need to be convinced in order to maintain this [touches her *hijab*] and to strengthen your *iman* every day, every week.... You know: you must make *jihad* [struggle] against your own *nafs* [ego].

The interviewees consider the process a struggle against family tradition, non-Muslim aversion and personal ego. Mahmood underscores that the individuals themselves experience this positive self-formation of pious subjects as crucial evidence of personal agency – a considerable investment and achievement that results in religious merit and self-esteem (Mahmood 2005: 171, 174). For that reason, the young women's narratives of voluntarily displaying Islamic identity cannot be read only as a way of living the Western notion of the autonomous self, which conditions the recognition of subjectivity and full citizenship in today's Sweden. They should also be read as the ethical self-formation of pious Muslim subjects in modernity. This claim leads into the final section, which reflects on alternative, more productive ways of framing Muslim women's subjectivity in third space.

Framing Islamic Identity

The young women explore, mould and communicate religious identity. The national organization SUM offers space for such processes. As argued so far in this article, SUM provides a 'third space' for critical and reflexive forms of engagement in between unfavourable 'Swedish' and 'Muslim' forces. Homi Bhabha's concept of the third space challenges the idea of stable, authentic cultures, identities and subjectivities pitted against each other and forcing individuals to make anguished choices. Think, for example, of Noor's account of being torn between her Muslim community members' demands that she wear the hijab as a marker of ethnic dignity and 'Swedish' demands that she take it off to prove her eligibility for full citizenship – a troublesome situation that she addressed by involving herself in an alternative 'Islamic' sphere, where she elaborated her religious faith and came to appreciate *hijab* as a personal choice.

In the light of my findings, I claim that the young women enter a third Islamic space in between allegedly fixed and essential boundaries of Muslim and Swedish identity, not because of categorical rejection of one or the other, but as the outcome of critical and creative reflections and negotiations. In this third space, they can question the norms of parents and religious authorities without automatically adapting to any trend in broader society. They can also present themselves as Swedish citizens of Islamic faith. According to Bhabha, this alternative position emerges from a third space of cultural hybridity that 'gives rise to something different, something new and unrecognizable, a new area of negotiation of meaning and representation' (Bhabha 1990: 211).

In this final part of the chapter, I will discuss how the women engaged in SUM manage the potential of this third space and how we may frame it in an academically productive way. If we accept Bhabha's notion of the third space as a 'moment in which hybridity is not reclaimed, given a name, disciplined, or incorporated by one of the dominant discourses' (Ababneh 2006: 9), then what happens when the women's third space is associated with Islamic or Swedish Muslim identity? If the third space allows the women to conceptualize and practise their own experiences in opposition to hegemonic identities, what happens when hybridity is articulated, allowing discourses and identities to start (re)producing their authority anew? Finally, is it really only a matter of how 'they' manage third space potentiality, or rather how 'we' all handle and condition it?

These questions connect with the notion of identity politics. Above I have quoted from SUM's online self-presentation, which states that the organization works to strengthen its members' Swedish Muslim identity and to maintain the heritage of Islam. Joining an organization with the explicit aim of upholding a (religious) identity is a step into what could be defined as identity politics: 'an intersection of *group* identity and politics, which can lead to social change. Identity politics arises when oppression becomes the focus of a strong separate group identity around which support, political analysis, and action are developed' (Phoenix 2000: 1097).[4] However, identity politics is a contradictory concept: 'On the one hand, it can perpetuate the status quo by treating social categories as natural, static, and based on characteristics unique to a group – that is, by being essentialist. On the other hand, it can disrupt the status quo by providing a basis for new political definitions and new struggle' (Phoenix 2000: 1097). In brief, three general dilemmas of identity politics appear relevant to the analysis here: (1) identity claims always build on a constitutive exclusion of an (internal or external) other; (2) fixed identity categories make up the basis for oppression and new political power simultaneously; (3) the identity political process creates shared goals out of the fragmented realm of personal subjectivity.

Starting with the latter problem, I refer to Avtar Brah: 'The political process of *proclaiming* a specific collective identity entails the *creation* of a collective identity out of the myriad collage-like fragments of the mind. The process may well generate considerable psychic and emotional disjunction in the realm of subjectivity, even if it is empowering in terms of group politics' (Brah 1996: 124, emphasis in original). The women in this study did declare themselves empowered by their engagement in Islamic organizational life, and they actively work for Islam and Swedish Muslim citizenship. As discussed above, one of their highest priorities is to combat the stereotype of the victimized Muslim woman. In Brah's words, they wish 'to make a distinction between "Muslim woman" as a discursive category of "representation" *and* Muslim women as embodied, situated, historical subjects with varying and diverse personal or collective biographies and social orientations' (Brah 1996: 130). Still, involvement in identity politics sometimes requires downplaying subjective ambivalence and desires on behalf of collective interests.

This is a vital point in various postcolonial and feminist theoreticians' critiques of identity politics. For example, Nira Yuval-Davis (2011) illuminates how the notion of groups as homogeneous entities often leads to a reification of the group that hinders investigation of the diverse experiences and positioning within it. She offers cogent ethnographic examples of communities (e.g., nations or religious communities) constructed as masculine entities, with male domination over agendas and public relations. Exemplifying this situation is a case of reported gender discrimination at the new Stockholm Grand Mosque that drew the young women of this study into conflict-ridden identity politics of gender, religion and diversity.

In June 2000, just a week after its inauguration, the new Stockholm Grand Mosque was reported for gender discrimination. The report was filed with the government agency Jämställdhetsombudsmannen (Office of the Equal Opportunities Ombudsman, EOO)[5] by a woman member of the Swedish parliament, who was reacting to the gender separating order in the mosque, which has a special entrance and balcony for women. Her report was titled 'Open to everyone but on different terms', in reference to the congregation's generous attitude towards Muslims of diverse cultural and social backgrounds as well as other potential visitors. From a perspective favouring accommodation of social, cultural and religious diversity, the mosque fulfilled the ideal of equality. Now the politician was requesting the EOO to review the gender division in the mosque, which she regarded as potentially discriminating against women due to unequal distribution of access, visibility and voice.

The EOO never complied with the request, claiming it was beyond the scope of its mission, defined as 'increasing equality in working life'.[6] However, in an open letter addressed to the politician in question,[7] representatives of several Muslim women' organizations explained that whereas no principle prevents women from praying alongside men in the main prayer hall, the tradition of separating the two genders in prayer dates back to the days of the prophet Muhammad. They underlined their perception of this gender division as a voluntarily chosen order that facilitates a focus on God in prayers. Today, they wrote, this gender division can be organized architecturally to give women a separate space, free of 'disturbances', from which they can 'see and hear everything going on in the mosque'. The young women in my study agreed with the open letter, arguing that the prevailing gender order was voluntary, practical and, above all, in line with God's will.

The women's response to the reporting of the mosque indicates that core aspects of their religious belief are not easily regarded as negotiable. However, considering their determined negotiation to avoid restraining conditions in the familial and societal spheres, it might seem surprising that they did not seize the chance to discuss possible gendered restrictions within the frame of Muslim congregational life. Knowing that they could deliberate on this topic within the confines of SUM and its local associations, this was definitely a good opportunity for them to bring this multifaceted debate into public light. To better understand the women's priorities in negotiating gender dynamics within the Muslim community, I propose use of the concepts of *frontstage* and *backstage* actions (Karlsson Minganti 2007, 2011). According to Goffman (1959), frontstage actions aim at presenting a coherent self before a broader audience, while keeping all incoherence backstage. In critical frontstage situations, as in the case of the gender discrimination report filed against the Stockholm Grand Mosque, the young women did not prioritize debates on alternative gender orders but stood together with traditional religious authorities to protect the prevailing order. However, in less formal situations – that is, backstage among peers – these women engage in reflexive deliberations and test alternative norms and practices. For example, when Suad's youth association opted to remove the curtain dividing girls and women from the male teachers and peers, she appreciated the decision as an improvement: 'I mean, you actually don't learn well if you are only listening. One also wants to see the speaker and to be able to put direct questions.'

The case of the reporting of the Stockholm Grand Mosque illustrates that identity politics potentially risks downplaying subjective complexity in favour of definite collective interests. It carries an additional risk of cementing positions and hierarchies, not least those based on gender. The case at hand demonstrates the intersectional tension between the young women's position as Muslims and Muslim women specifically. In situations that reify and polarize identities, assumed attacks against 'our' women and gender order are taken as attacks on the entire nation (Yuval-Davis 2011). To illustrate this point, let us consider yet another case where the issue of women's position in mosques was put to test. On 18 March 2005, Professor Amina Wadud, the author of Muslim feminist classics such as *Quran and Woman* (1999) and *Inside the Gender Jihad* (2006), stood in front of a mixed-gender congregation in New York to lead the prayers and deliver the Friday sermon. Muslim men and women all over the world perceived this event as radical and condemned it. One of the arguments against Wadud's conduct was that it was a provocation leading to *fitna* (chaos). Here *fitna* referred not only to sexual disorder: by publicizing the issue of gender and leadership, Wadud was, her accusers claimed, actually bringing *fitna* in terms of discord to the entire Muslim community, thus weakening Islam. This argument was supported by the perception of feminism (which Wadud was held to represent) as a Western phenomenon and part of the struggle for Western hegemony (Hammer 2011).

The responses to Wadud's conduct, and to the reporting of the Stockholm Grand Mosque, go to the heart of religious belief. However, if religious beliefs are seen as objects of interpretation, and mosques and Muslim organizations as sites of contestation of such interpretations, then Wadud's position can be seen as one alternative minority position within contemporary Islam, raising another question: What happens to the young women's potential third space in between hegemonic discourses, when alternative minority interpretations are framed within a clash-of-civilization discourse and women are framed as crucial symbols for the continuity of the community?

Sara Ababneh (2006) has analysed a similarly conflict-ridden situation using Bhabha's notion of cultural hybridity as resistance to hegemonic discourses. Her study draws on a campaign to make women wear the hijab during the Palestinian Intifada, so that the headscarf would signify not only women's religious devotion but also their commitment to the Palestinian national struggle. Like the young Swedish Muslim women in a diasporic context, many Palestinian women persisted in challenging the conceptualization of a reality that assumed binary opposites. By carving out a third space not yet disciplined or incorporated by any of the dominant discourses, the women articulated and practised their own experiences in opposition to hegemonic nationalist or Islamist discourses. Both diaspora and the Intifada can be understood as hybrid moments spurring a reshuffling of power relations and the emergence of alternative positions. However, as Ababneh effectively argued, a hybrid third space faces the threat of shutdown, and of its own development into a dominant discourse. Hybrid third spaces guarantee neither their own continuity nor empowerment to those involved: 'Ambivalence alone does not dismantle dominant power structures, as long as the dominant discourses continue to portray themselves in terms of fixity' (Ababneh 2006: 22–23).

Like some women of the Palestinian hijab campaign, the young Swedish Muslim women are constantly regulated by hegemonic discourses and display a tendency to turn the third space into fixity. Identification with universal Islam can be used to deconstruct antagonisms, but also to criticize others and create new polarizations. This happens through reification of the transnational Muslim *umma* (community) in terms of nationhood and the Muslim 'people', and the dichotomous clash-of-civilizations discourse. But it can also happen through the reification of 'authentic' Islam and 'real, practising Muslims' versus 'so-called, cultural Muslims' and non-Muslims. Hence, young women might not only dissociate themselves from rigid ethnic dress codes (such as forced donning of the hijab), but also voluntarily shift from hybrid, personal styles of clothing towards an Islamic uniform with attendant pressures on its wearer. Associating coercion with 'cultural Muslims', they do not always engage in self-reflexive deliberations over their own 'encouragement' of other women (e.g., younger girls in the youth associations) to veil. For instance, some of the women in my study did not consider obligatory hijab in a Muslim scout uniform to be a form of coercion.

Having made these critical remarks on the potential for essentialist outcomes of the women's engagement in identity politics, I now arrive at a conclusion based on that side of identity politics that works more in favour of a reflexive and creative third space, that is, 'identity politics as a basis for new political definitions and new struggle' (Phoenix 2000: 1097). I argue that in order to support such efforts, debates on women's construction of an Islamic identity must adopt a new structure more productive than just addressing the simplistic question whether it is either 'segregating or integrating', 'oppressive or emancipatory' (Jacobsen 2011a; Bracke and Fadil 2012; Jeldtoft 2012).

Divisive frameworks draw our attention to the essentialist tendencies among Muslims, for instance, the young women's promotion of a uniform with obligatory hijab. This focus obscures such crucial aspects as their simultaneous construction of an ethics around the concept of *niyyah* (conscious intention), which actually encourages an open attitude to women who do not veil. This ethics code prescribes that all pious actions be performed not only voluntarily but with the conscious intention to please God. Because intentions are concealed in the individual's heart and soul, hijab is ultimately a private matter between a woman and God. When slander and pressure obstruct her free choice, they disqualify the religious significance of the practice. To catch sight of such ethics, the analysis needs to take complexity into consideration, calling on the interplay of processes of both reification and destabilization within lived Islam.

An analysis of women's Islamic identity that fails to account for complexity further runs the risk of being influenced by dominant debates, which revolve around the presumption that veiled women neither willingly nor consciously subject themselves to this sartorial practice, and that 'our' secular liberal societies can offer 'them' emancipated gender identity and agency (Bracke and Fadil 2012: 54). As Bracke and Fadil have persuasively argued, this leaves the women, and other advocates of their rights, with the task of demonstrating that 'Muslim women who veil are "active agents" of their destiny' and do 'in fact conform with these liberal requirements and can perfectly integrate into the public space which is defined according to these liberal terms' (Bracke and Fadil 2012: 52). To avoid this influence, the authors 'try to account for the possibilities of overcoming these discursive conditionalities and the capacity of rendering other forms of agency intelligible' (Bracke and Fadil 2012: 36). For instance, the politics of piety advanced by Saba Mahmood builds on agency in terms not restricted to resistance and subversion. In addition to that, consider the SUM women's approval of eliminating gender-separating curtains in classes despite their simultaneously call to maintain gender-separate seating on other occasions because 'it feels good' and 'SUM and the mosques make up the only spaces today that allow us to assemble like this'. Subjectivity is constructed not only by inhabiting one particular subject position, but by moving between different positions or inhabiting them simultaneously.

The analysis of young women's negotiations of subjectivity and identity is thus no simple question of examining how 'they' manage their opportunity to speak. It also concerns how 'we' all contribute to conditioning this capacity. It is not only a question of how 'they' manage the third space, but how 'we' all contribute to keeping it open. Formal attempts to ban the hijab and public reporting of mosques for gender discrimination exemplify how the issue of women's rights collapses into presumptions of: (1) 'our Swedish gender equality' versus 'their Muslim gender oppression'; (2) Muslim women's need to shed their particular attachments (culture, religion, family and so forth); (3) Swedish society's need to reform the sensibilities and commitments of its Muslim inhabitants. The resulting climate, instead of maintaining a third space of respectful and inclusive communication, grounds the exclusion that the young women of this study have set out to combat.

The women strive for recognition as full subjects and citizens. SUM and its local associations have developed into a platform – indeed a third space – for this struggle. It has already produced a member of the Swedish Parliament for the Green Party (Mehmet Kaplan)[8] and an elected European Muslim Woman of Influence 2010 (Barni Nor).[9] Its young female members are gradually revealing themselves to a broader public as precisely outgoing, leading, versatile activists and citizens. Identity politics has a side that essentializes and reproduces domination, especially when actors in conflictual 'frontstage' situations feel a need to close ranks and thereby risk postponement of alternative power relations within the community. But identity politics certainly also has

Figure 2.3. Doing citizenship. A Forix Suburban Parliament weekend course on the theme 'We and the Power', 2011. Copyright: SUM

its innovative 'third space' potential. SUM leaves the door open for its members to join, or even launch, other movements felt to be compatible with Islam whose agendas are not dominated by Muslim identity politics, for example, the Swedish Temperance Movement, The Sisters' Shelter Somaya, Forix Suburban Parliament, or Swedish Muslims for Peace and Justice.[10] This third space will generate 'other ways of knowing' that challenge white privilege and patriarchal power.

Notes

This chapter was made possible by support from the Swedish Research Council, the Bank of Sweden Tercentenary Foundation and the Swedish Council for Working Life and Social Research.

1. Retrieved 6 November 2013 from http://www.ungamuslimer.se/index.php ?option=com_content&view=article&id=173&Itemid=912
2. Retrieved 6 November 2013 from http://www.ungamuslimer.se/index.php ?option=com_content&view=article&id=173&Itemid=912. All quotations in this article have been translated from Swedish into English by the author.
3. Much of Olivier Roy's theorization in *Globalized Islam* (2004) is applicable to this study, but his focus on 'radical neo-fundamentalists', who in many

ways resist identification and integration with any nation-state, diverges from the society-oriented activists in focus here.

4. For further reading on identity politics among young Muslims in Europe, see Jonker and Amiraux (2006), and in Scandinavia, see Schmidt (2012).

5. On 1 January 2009, EOO was merged with the Diskrimineringsombudsmannen (the Equality Ombudsman), a government agency that 'seeks to combat discrimination on the basis of gender, transgender identity or expression, ethnicity, religion or other belief, disability, sexual orientation or age'. Retrieved 4 January 2013 from http://www.do.se/en

6. Report from the Stockholm Grand Mosque to the EOO: registration number 515/00. EOO's decision to dismiss the case: 515/00 appendix 3.

7. Letter dated 28 June 2000, published on the Internet homepage *Living Islam*. Retrieved 6 November 2013 from http://www.abc.se/~m9783/misf_sv.html

8. Retrieved 6 November 2013 from http://www.mp.se/om/mehmet-kaplan

9. Retrieved 6 November 2013 from http://www.strategicdialogue.org/EMWI 2010.pdf

10. See http://www.somaya.se; http://www.forix.se; http://www.muslimerfor fred.org

References

Ababneh, S. 2006. 'Changing Power Structures: The Possibilities and Limits of Hybrid Resistance', *International Studies Association Conference, San Diego CA*. Retrieved 4 January 2013 from http://citation.allacademic.com/meta/ p_mla_apa_research_citation/0/9/9/9/2/pages99926/p99926-1.php

Ahmed, S. 2004. 'Affective Economies', *Social Text* 79 22(2): 117–39.

Bano, M. and H. Kalmbach (eds). 2011. *Women, Leadership and Mosques: Changes in Contemporary Islamic Authority*. Leiden: Brill.

Beck, U., et al. 1994. *Reflexive Modernization: Politics, Tradition and Aesthetics in the Modern Social Order*. Oxford: Polity.

Bhabha, H.K. 1990. 'Interview with Homi Bhabha: The Third Space', in J. Rutherford (ed.), *Identity: Community, Culture, Difference*. London: Lawrence and Wishart, pp. 207–21.

———. 1994. *The Location of Culture*. London and New York: Routledge.

Bilge, S. and P. Scheibelhofer. 2012. 'Unravelling the New Politics of Racialised Sexualities: Introduction', *Journal of Intercultural Studies* 33(3): 255–59.

Bracke, S. and N. Fadil. 2012. '"Is the Headscarf Oppressive or Emancipatory?" Field Notes from the Multicultural Debate', *Religion and Gender* 2(1): 35–56.

Brah, A. 1996. *Cartographies of Diaspora: Contesting Identities*. London and New York: Routledge.

Brah, A. and A.E. Coombes (eds). 2000. *Hybridity and Its Discontents: Politics, Science, Culture*. London and New York: Routledge.

Bunt, G. 2009. *iMuslims: Rewiring the House of Islam*. Chapel Hill, NC: The University of North Carolina Press.

Castells, M. 1996. *The Rise of The Network Society, The Information Age: Economy, Society and Culture*. Vol. I. Oxford: Blackwell.

Farahani, F. 2007. *Diasporic Narratives of Sexuality: Identity Formation among Iranian-Swedish Women.* Stockholm: Acta Universitatis Stockholmiensis.

Frisina, A. 2006. 'The Invention of Citizenship among Young Muslims in Italy', in G. Jonker and V. Amiraux (eds), *Politics of Visibility: Young Muslims in European Public Spaces.* Bielefeld: transcript, pp. 79–101.

Furseth, I. 2006. *From Quest for Truth to Being Oneself: Religious Change in Life Stories.* Frankfurt am Main: Peter Lang.

Goffman, E. 1959. *The Presentation of Self in Everyday Life.* New York: Doubleday.

Goldstein-Kyaga, K. and M. Borgström. 2009. *Den tredje identiteten: Ungdomar och deras familjer i det mångkulturella, globala rummet.* Huddinge: Södertörns högskola.

Grossberg, L. 1997. *Dancing in Spite of Myself: Essays on Popular Culture.* Durham, NC: Duke University Press.

Hall, Stuart, 1990. 'Cultural Identity and Diaspora', in J. Rutherford (ed.), *Identity: Community, Culture, Difference.* London: Lawrence and Wishart, pp. 222–37.

Hammer, J. 2011. 'Activism as Embodied Tafsīr: Negotiating Women's Authority, Leadership, and Space in North America', in M. Bano and H. Kalmbach (eds), *Women, Leadership and Mosques: Changes in Contemporary Islamic Authority.* Leiden: Brill, pp. 457–80.

Heelas, P. and L. Woodhead. 2005. *The Spiritual Revolution: Why Religion is Giving Way to Spirituality.* London: Blackwell.

Herrera, L. 2005. 'Editorial', *ISIM Review* 16: 4.

Hirschkind, C. 2006. *The Ethical Soundscape: Cassette Sermons and Islamic Counterpublics.* New York: Columbia University Press.

Hübinette, T. 2004. 'Adopted Koreans and the Development of Identity in the "Third Space"', *Adoption & Fostering* 28(1): 16–24.

Hübinette, T. and C. Lundström. 2011. 'Sweden after the Recent Election: The Double-Binding Power of Swedish Whiteness through the Mourning of Loss of "Old Sweden" and the Passing of "Good Sweden"', *NORA* 19(1): 42–52.

Hutnyk, J. 2005. 'Hybridity', *Ethnic and Racial Studies* 28(1): 79–102.

Jacobsen, C.M. 2002. *Tillhørighetens mange former: Unge muslimer i Norge.* Oslo: Unipax.

———. 2011a. 'Troublesome Threesome: Feminism, Anthropology and Muslim Women's Piety', *Feminist Review* 98(1): 65–82.

———. 2011b. *Islamic Traditions and Muslim Youth in Norway.* Leiden: Brill.

Jeldtoft, N.J. 2012. *Everyday Lived Islam: Religious Reconfigurations and Secular Sensibilities among Muslim Minorities in the West.* Copenhagen: Copenhagen University.

Jeldtoft, N. and J. Nielsen. 2011. 'Introduction: Methods in the Study of 'Non-organized' Muslim Minorities', *Ethnic and Racial Studies* 34(7): 1113–19.

Jonker, G. and V. Amiraux (eds). 2006. *Politics of Visibility: Young Muslims in European Public Spaces.* Bielefeld: transcript.

Jouili, J. and S. Amir-Moazami. 2006. 'Knowledge, Empowerment and Religious Authority Among Pious Muslim Women in France and Germany', *The Muslim World* 96(4): 617–42.

Karlsson Minganti, P. 2007. *Muslima: Islamisk väckelse och unga kvinnors förhand-lingar om genus i det samtida Sverige.* Stockholm: Carlsson.

———. 2008. 'Becoming a 'Practising' Muslim: Reflections on Gender, Racism and Religious Identity Among Women in a Swedish Muslim Youth Organisation', *Elore* 15(1): 1–16.

———. 2010. 'Islamic Revival and Young Women's Negotiations on Gender and Racism', in S. Collins-Mayo and P. Dandelion (eds), *Religion and Youth.* Farnham: Ashgate, pp. 115–21.

———. 2011. 'Challenging from Within: Youth Associations and Female Leadership in Swedish Mosques', in M. Bano and H. Kalmbach (eds), *Women, Leadership and Mosques: Changes in Contemporary Islamic Authority.* Leiden: Brill, pp. 371–91.

———. 2013. 'Burqinis, Bikinis and Bodies: Encounters in Public Pools in Italy and Sweden', in A. Moors and E. Tarlo (eds), *Islamic Fashion and Anti-Fashion: New Perspectives from Europe and North America.* London and New York: Bloomsbury, pp. 33–54.

Karlsson Minganti, P. and L.K. Österlind. forthcoming. 'New Faces of a New Phase. Politics of Visibility among Young Muslim Women', in J. Björklund and U. Lindqvist (eds), *New Dimensions of Diversity in Nordic Culture and Society.* Newcastle upon Tyne, UK: Cambridge Scholars Publishing.

Keskinen, S. 2012. 'Limits to Speech? The Racialised Politics of Gendered Violence in Denmark and Finland', *Journal of Intercultural Studies* 33(3): 261–73.

Khan, S. 2002. *Aversion and Desire: Negotiating Muslim Female Identity in Diaspora.* Toronto: Women's Press.

Larsson, G. 2009. 'Sweden', in G. Larsson (ed.), *Islam in the Nordic and Baltic Countries.* London: Routledge, pp. 56–75.

Mahmood, S. 2005. *Politics of Piety: The Islamic Revival and the Feminist Subject.* Princeton, NJ: Princeton University Press.

Moghissi, H. 2006. 'Introduction', in H. Moghissi, *Muslim Diaspora: Gender, Culture and Identity.* New York: Routledge, pp. xiv–xxv.

Moors, A. 2005. 'Muslim Fashions – Fashionable Muslims', *ISIM Review* 16: 59.

Moors, A. and E. Tarlo (eds). 2013. *Islamic Fashion and Anti-Fashion: New Perspectives from Europe and North America.* London and New York: Bloomsbury.

Moray, P. and A. Yaqin. 2011. *Framing Muslims: Stereotyping and Representation after 9/11.* Cambridge, MA: Harvard University Press.

Mørck, Y. 1998. *Bidestregsdanskere: Fortællinger om køn, generationer og etnicitet.* Copenhagen: Forlaget Sociologi.

Otterbeck, J. 2000. *Islam, muslimer och den svenska skolan.* Lund: Studentlitteratur.

———. 2011. 'Ritualization among Young Adult Muslims in Malmö and Copenhagen', *Ethnic and Racial Studies* 34(7): 1168–85.

Phoenix, A. 2000. 'Identity Politics', in C. Kramarae and D. Spender (eds), *Routledge International Encyclopedia of Women: Global Women's Issues and Knowledge,* vol. 3. New York: Routledge.

Ramadan, T. 1999. *To be a European Muslim: A Study of Islamic Sources in the European Context.* Leicester: Islamic Foundation.

Roy, O. 2004. *Globalised Islam: The Search for a New Ummah.* London: Hurst.

Runfors, A. 2009. 'Avoiding Culture and Practicing Culturalism. Labelling Practices and Paradoxes in Swedish Schools', in S. Alghasi, T. Hylland Eriksen and H. Ghorashi (eds), *Paradoxes of Cultural Recognition. Perspectives from Northern Europe.* Aldershot: Ashgate, pp. 133–44.

Schmidt, G. 1999. 'Sveriges Förenade CyberMuslimer: Blågul islam på internet?', in I. Svanberg and D. Westerlund (eds), *Blågul islam? Muslimer i Sverige.* Nora: Nya Doxa.

———. 2004. 'Islamic Identity Formation Among Young Muslims in Denmark, Sweden, and the United States', *Journal of Muslim Minority Affairs* 24(1): 31–45.

———. 2012. ''Grounded' Politics: Manifesting Muslim Identity as a Political Factor and Localized Identity in Copenhagen', *Ethnicities* 12(5): 603–22.

Schwencke, A.M. 2012. *Globalized Eco-Islam: A Survey of Global Islamic Environmentalism.* Leiden: Leiden University.

SST (Swedish Commission for Government Support to Faith Communities), 2012. 'Statistik 2010'. Retrieved 4 January 2013 from http://www.sst.a.se/statistik/statistik2011.4.4bf439da1355ecafdd2243b.html

Vertovec, S. and A. Rogers. 1998. 'Introduction', in S. Vertovec and A. Rogers (eds), *Muslim European Youth: Reproducing Ethnicity, Religion, Culture.* Aldershot: Ashgate, pp. 1–24.

von Brömssen, K. 2003. *Tolkningar, förhandlingar och tystnader: Elevers tal om religion i det mångkulturella och postkoloniala rummet.* Göteborg: Göteborgs universitet.

Wikström, H. 2007. *(O)möjliga positioner: Familjer från Iran & postkoloniala reflektioner.* Göteborg: Göteborgs universitet.

Wolf, M. 2008. 'Interference from the Third Space? The Construction of Cultural Identity through Translation', in M. Muños-Calvo et al. (eds), *New Trends in Translation and Cultural Identity.* Newcastle upon Tyne: Cambridge Scholars.

Yükleyen, A. 2012. *Localizing Islam in Europe: Turkish Islamic Communities in Germany & the Netherlands.* Syracuse, NY: Syracuse University Press, pp. 11–20.

Yuval-Davis, N. 2011. *Politics of Belonging: Intersectional Contestations.* London: Sage.

3

Political Muslim Women in the News Media

Rikke Andreassen

Introduction

For over a decade, Muslim women's veils and headscarves have been an integral part of the Danish news media's portrayals of female 'visible minorities'[1] (immigrants and their descendants). Veiled women have visually dominated the images of visible minority women in the news media, and the practice of veiling and headscarves has been fiercely debated verbally. During the 2000s, one woman and her headscarf (hijab) made headlines. Her name is Asmaa Abdol-Hamid. In 2006, Abdol-Hamid became the first veiled Danish TV-hostess and in 2007 she ran for Parliament. This chapter analyses the media debates about Abdol-Hamid and her headscarf. These debates function as a window onto a broader understanding of how media construct and contest categories of ethnicity/race, gender, sexuality and nationality. They further illustrate how representations of veiled Muslim women play important roles in the construction of Danish nationality, especially construction of the Danish nation as an ethnically/racially white nation. Regarding the many feminists who have participated in discussions about headscarves, the chapter shows the close tie between headscarf debates and struggles between different feminists about the right to define feminism. It also throws light on the media's treatment of Abdol-Hamid and other female Muslim candidates during the 2007 election season. Drawing upon Sara Ahmed's notions of politics of emotion and 'stickiness' (2004), the chapter illustrates the different approaches taken towards Abdol-Hamid and other Muslim female candidates, as opposed to white ethnically Danish Parliament candidates, due to the signs that 'stuck' to her hijab. Journalists repeatedly asked her the same questions as if they did not believe her answers, asking her over and over again about her attitudes towards sexual minorities in particular. I analyse this investigation and point out how sexual tolerance is constructed as a white and ethnically Danish phenomenon in politicians' speeches as well as the media.

This chapter highlights individual minority women's attempts to participate in Danish national politics. These attempts can be interpreted as manifestations of the women's wish to exercise their political rights and fulfil their dreams; however, the women's right to participate in politics, and hence move freely in the society, seems to be limited by several external forces directed at maintaining a clear division between what could be called the 'diaspora community' and the 'Danish mainstream majority society'. The Danish news media form one of these forces, as do smaller groups of fundamentalist Muslims that have demonstrably hindered the women's political participation. The chapter shows how enforcement of 'us' versus 'them', embodied in a strict division between the diaspora community and the majority society, impedes the women's free political movement, regardless of whether the women themselves support such a division between 'their' diaspora community and 'our' majority society.

Asmaa Abdol-Hamid and Danish Public Service TV

In March 2006, the Danish public service TV station, *Danmark's Radio* (DR), hired Asmaa Abdol-Hamid, a young Danish Muslim woman of Palestinian origin, as a hostess for a presenter of a debate programme called *Adam & Asmaa*. Abdol-Hamid was hired together with the ethnically Danish journalist Adam Holm, who is an atheist. DR gave a reason for the programme: 'The cartoon crisis has disclosed a wide gap between the Western and the Islamic world. *Adam & Asmaa* is a series of debate programs which will cover both sides of the comprehensibility gap' (DR press release March 29, 2006). With this reasoning, DR participates in constructing 'the Western and the Islamic world' as opposites.

The hiring of Abdol-Hamid sparked an outcry from the newly established feminist organization Women for Freedom, which demanded her removal.[2] On 2 April 2006, Women for Freedom sent out a press release that harshly criticized DR for hiring Abdol-Hamid: 'Asmaa Abdul Hamid [*sic*] is known as an Islamic fanatic and a supporter of Sharia. ... DR is a public service station, and it is important that TV-hostesses are objective and don't become a space [*sic*] where fanatic attitudes can be expressed and honoured. Attitudes that, in this situation, are a serious threat against, among others, women's rights' (Women for Freedom press release April 2, 2006).The press release was cited in all major news media, and Women for Freedom used the plentiful media attention they gained thereby to express their dislike for Islam and headscarves, interpreting the latter solely as oppressive of females.

The following day another feminist organization, the Feminist Forum, supported DR's hiring of Abdol-Hamid in a press release. They wrote: 'The Feminist Forum congratulates DR on their hiring of Asmaa Abdol-Hamid as hostess for the debate program *Adam & Asmaa*. With this hiring DR participates in strengthening both gender and ethnic equality in Denmark' (The Feminist Forum press release April 3, 2006).[3] The following week, several debates between Women for Freedom and the Feminist Forum took place in various national newspapers and on television news programmes.[4]

The debates reflected disagreement about how to interpret headscarves and veiling. Women for Freedom argued that veiling should be seen as female oppression, while the Feminist Forum argued that veiling is a multifaceted practice that cannot be simply interpreted as oppression. Furthermore, they argued that Women for Freedom had no right to dictate the standards for female emancipation. Women for Freedom, on the other hand, called the Feminist Forum naïve, arguing that a DR hostess should signal neutrality and not agitate for a specific religion. The Feminist Forum countered that there is no such thing as a neutral space and that the debate about veils on TV was a nationalist debate about who was allowed to represent Denmark.

On 18 April 2006, Women for Freedom presented DR's (then) news director, Lisbeth Knudsen, with a document signed by 500 people criticizing the hiring of Asmaa Abdol-Hamid and demanding her dismissal.[5] Lisbeth Knudsen replied that she was not planning to remove Abdol-Hamid, but the signatures did make an impression (DR press release April 21, 2006.)

Struggles to Define Feminism

The feminists' debate about Abdol-Hamid's headscarf is not simply about the headscarf. On a superficial level, it concerns how to interpret the headscarf, and more precisely whether headscarves should be viewed as oppression of females or as a multifaceted practice that can be liberating as well as oppressive. But other issues are at play in the debate, for it can also be seen as a struggle over how to define feminism. Both Women for Freedom and the Feminist Forum define themselves as feminist, and both present their version of feminism as a right version. The two organizations' disagreement can therefore be interpreted as a conflict over how to view feminism. The headscarf debate illustrates an ongoing struggle about whether feminism should be viewed from a postcolonial perspective – the viewpoint the Feminist Forum represents – or as a universal right, the viewpoint behind Women for Freedom's arguments. Seen in this perspective, the debate about veiling becomes a platform on which struggles to define feminism take place. In the debate, feminism can be seen as a floating signifier with no specific meaning ascribed to it. The different arguments about headscarves as oppressive or liberating are inputs in an ongoing disputation about the definition of feminism in which different actors actively strive for hegemonic acceptance of their definitions (Laclau 1990: 28, 1993: 281ff.; Laclau and Mouffe 1985).

Feminist Debates About Veiling and Headscarves

Danish feminists have been discussing headscarves and minority women's rights for several years. The first larger debate took place in 2001 (Andreassen 2007: 106ff.; Hervik 2002: 191ff.), sparked by an article by journalist and writer Helle Merete Brix, who accused the Danish women's movement of letting visible minority women down. The article opened by asserting, 'It is embarrassing that the Danish women's movement remains completely silent about the fact that numerous female citizens in the country are living under oppressing patriarchal norms from seventh-century Arabia' (Brix 2001).[6] Commentators in the debate, including well-known Danish feminists, levelled accusations drawn from their often implicit negative attitudes towards Islam and headscarves. Writer Hanne Vibeke Holst, for instance, argued: 'To me, the headscarf is a profoundly revolting way of limiting girls' and women's free actions, bodily as well as mentally' (Holst 2001).[7] The politician Mai-Britt Iversen, representing the Social Democrats in Aalborg city council, agreed with Holst when she (Iversen) told readers about an experience she had with the headscarf: 'I met two totally veiled girls who had problems playing. It was a frightening sight not only because of the clothing but because of the oppression behind it' (Iversen 2001).[8]

In these three citations, emotions are at play. It is 'revolting' and 'frightening' how visible minority women (apparently) are oppressed by headscarves and veils, and it is 'embarrassing' that (ethnically Danish) women (apparently) do not do anything about it. Headscarf-covered women and girls trigger strong emotions in Denmark. Sara Ahmed argues that emotions produce surfaces and boundaries; they circulate between bodies and align different subjects (e.g. veiled visible minority women) with each other; they also make those subjects into sources of other people's feelings (Ahmed 2004: 6, 9, 46ff.). Here individual women (who happen to be veiled) become bodily representatives of a collective female oppression that is both frightening and revolting. The individual visible minority women are constructed as the source for, and reason behind, the ethnically Danish feminists' fear and revolt: emotions produce boundaries between 'us' and 'them' – and 'they' cause 'our' fear and revolt.

The article in which these quotes appeared were published in the centre-left national newspaper *Politiken*. The national right-wing newspaper *Jyllands-Posten* contributed to the debate with a lengthy article based on interviews with ethnically Danish feminists about their lack of support for visible minority women and about Islam as a misogynist religion. The piece began with a rhetorical question: 'Who fights for the veiled woman passing by on the street with her eyes on the ground and the prospect of forced marriage, and who sees the debate about career options as utopian?' (Ammitzbøll 2001).[9] According to the article, veiling, forced marriage and lack of a career all result from Islam's 'different view of women' (Ammitzbøll 2001).[10] One of the interviewees was Ulla Dahlerup, introduced as 'Ulla Dahlerup, nation-wide known "redstocking" (*rødstrømpe*) activist all the way back to the 1970s, (who) has almost given up trying to help immigrant women in contemporary Denmark' (Ammitzbøll 2001).[11]

As Dahlerup explained in the *Jyllands-Posten*-article: 'Back in 1992, I contacted a Pakistani women's group in [the Copenhagen area] Noerrebro and it was a dreadful let-down. Later I tried to make connections in other situations but the women do not want help. They view "red stockings" (feminists) with horror and see us as satanic women. The cultural gap is simply too wide' (Ammitzbøll 2001).[12] Earlier that same year, Dahlerup had come out with the book *Denmark dit land – dit valg*, published by the right-wing, populist, nationalist Danish People's Party (Dansk Folkeparti). The book can be characterized as one long argument against Muslims and against making Denmark a multicultural society. The *Jyllands-Posten* article did not mention Dahlerup's cooperation with the Danish People's Party, nor did its author, Pernille Ammitzbøll, reflect on the fact that Dahlerup's hostility to visible minorities, in particular Muslims, may have deprived her opinion of nuance. Dahlerup's tie to the Danish People's Party became still closer in September 2003, when she was the runner-up to become the party's candidate for the European Parliament election held 13 June 2004.[13]

The debate included a few letters to editors from ethnically Danish feminists who claimed to have helped or collaborated with visible minority women, but overall the newspapers allotted little space to these counter voices. For instance, they did not print letters to the editor that tried to add nuance to the debate or tried to criticize Ammitzbøll's article; instead, they devoted space to items presenting the headscarf as a symbol of female oppression.[14]

The anti-headscarf attitudes that Women for Freedom expressed in 2006 were therefore not new to the Danish context. Rather, they echoed years-old attitudes and interpretations of headscarves and veiling.

Hegemonic Feminism or Diverse Feminisms

The majority of Danish feminist participants in the headscarf debates belong to the older generation of feminists. The contretemps between Women for Freedom and the Feminist Forum can be interpreted as a generational debate. Women for Freedom consists mainly of white, middle-class, heterosexual, ethnically Danish women aged 50 and over, whereas the Feminist Forum is composed of younger women in their mid-20s to mid-30s. They too are mainly, though not only, white, middle-class and ethnically Danish, but the high percentage of lesbian and queer women in the Feminist Forum distinguishes it from Women for Freedom. Age-related attitudes are a clear tendency in the Danish debates about headscarves and veiling. Older women argue that headscarves are female oppression and favour restrictions on the use of headscarves in public spaces like TV, schools and Parliament, whereas younger women contend that headscarves are not necessarily female oppression and oppose banning headscarves and veils from public institutions and spaces. To be sure, this generational conflict is not unambiguous; indeed there are older women who argue in favour of Abdol-Hamid and her headscarf as well as younger women who argue against having her as a TV hostess.[15]

Developments in the women's movement and feminism (Andreassen 2007: 141ff.) may partly explain the conflict between Women for Freedom and the Feminist Forum. In Denmark, the women's movement was quite strong during the late 1960s and the 1970s, when it centred on two issues: women's right to bodily self-determination, and women's economic independence via entrance into the workforce. The first issue related to the right to abortion, which was obtained in 1973. The second issue was influenced by demographic developments linked to a dramatic increase in women's employment in the 1960s and 1970s. In 1965, 34 per cent of women aged 15 to 66 were employed outside the home. This number increased to 55 per cent in 1975, 65 per cent in 1985, and 72 per cent in 1995. The number remained around 73–74 per cent in subsequent decades (Dahlerup 1998: 158; Danish National Statistics).[16] Employment, and thereby financial independence, has been an ideal for women's movement outside Denmark as well. Indeed, women's paid employment has been a symbol of women's liberation among Western, white, middle-class women since the publication of Betty Friedan's *The Feminine Mystique* (1963). Similarly, the right to abortion was a fundamental part of many women's movements in the 1970s.

The women's movement(s) in the 1970s, also known as second wave feminism, has been criticized as white, Western, middle-class and heterosexual, and as presenting the issues central to heterosexual, white, middle-class, Western women as universal to all women (Collins 1990; Maart 1992; Anzaldua 1990). These critiques pointed out that lesbian women felt their oppression was not mainly rooted in the lack of access to abortion but in society's lack of acceptance of their sexuality. Women of colour pointed out that not only patriarchy but racism too played into their oppression. In the United States, when white, middle-class women began entering the workforce in the 1960s and 1970s, women of colour increasingly began working as domestic workers in these white women's homes, performing the domestic duties the white women were no longer able to perform as they were busy being emancipated by joining the workforce. The women of colour were also working, but doing low-paid domestic work for white, middle-class people was not necessarily their way to emancipation. Their liberation lay not simply in employment but rather in gaining civil rights and getting fair pay for their work.

Western second wave feminism was further criticized from a postcolonial perspective by feminists from so-called developing countries. They argued that Western women's feminism was not universal; rather, it was Western-centric and as such maintained hierarchical power relations between the Western world and the so-called developing world, positioning women from the latter countries lower in the hierarchy by asserting that they were oppressed, unlike Western women, who had been emancipated. Postcolonial feminists also accused Western feminists of regarding women from so-called developing countries as a homogeneous group and ignoring their plurality and diversity. Western women's feminism was thereby a continuation of the colonial relationship between the Western world and the so-called developing world, participating in constructing the two as binary oppositions, and attributing positive characteristics (women's emancipation) to the former and negative characteristics (women's oppression) to the latter (Mohanty 1991).

In a Western context, criticisms of second wave feminism have appeared mainly in the United States, Canada and Britain. Here this criticism, among others, has led to nuanced understandings of women's emancipation. Emancipation is no longer understood as a homogeneous, universal phenomenon, and the road to liberation is known to differ from woman to woman depending on her situation, including her ethnicity/race, sexuality, class, geographical place and so forth. The criticism has had an impact; one result is that North American feminist discourses often acknowledge that feminism and women's liberation are multifaceted concepts that must be contextualized.

The situation in Denmark is quite different. Here, criticisms of second wave feminism have seldom been popularized in academia, among activists or in mainstream society. Rather, the interpretation of women's emancipation from the 1970s tends to (hegemonically) dominate. During the debate about Abdol-Hamid as TV hostess, for instance, a well-known feminist published a feature article in *Politiken* that characterized immigrant women as one homogeneous group of oppressed women, rhetorically asking: 'Isn't a woman's right to education, the earning of her own money and the right of self-determination over her body the cornerstone of women's emancipation?' (Hansen 2006).[17]

Seen in this light, the discussion between Women for Freedom and the Feminist Forum challenges the hegemonic view of feminism and women's liberation. The debate is about how to define feminism. Women for Freedom represent second wave feminism when they argue that headscarves are solely oppressive of females and that women's emancipation should be understood as universally homogeneous. Asmaa Abdol-Hamid challenges this view by claiming she is a feminist and her headscarf a tool of liberation. Similarly, the Feminist Forum challenges the hegemonic view by insisting that the practice of veiling is multifaceted, and that there are different ways of being a feminist and different roads to emancipation; that is, it argues that white, middle-class, heterosexual, Christian, ethnically Danish feminists do not have a monopoly over the signified meaning of being a feminist, or over the means of reaching liberation. The debate about Abdol-Hamid and her headscarf became a platform supporting challenges to hegemonic understandings of feminism.

The hijab debates that dominated much of the discussion about minority women in the 2000s seem to have disappeared recently, replace by new debates about niqabs and burkas, veiling that fully covers women (Andreassen 2011, 2012; Siim and Andreassen 2010).

A Veiled Candidate Running for Parliament

In April 2007, Asmaa Abdol-Hamid's hijab made headlines again when she decided to run for Parliament as a member of the socialist Red-Green Alliance (Enhedslisten), the most left-wing party in Denmark.[18] Had she been voted in, she would have been the first Muslim woman, and the first woman with a headscarf, in Parliament. Her candidacy caused an outcry. A member of the Danish People's Party, Søren Krarup, compared the headscarf to a Nazi swastika, saying on DR1's prime-time news programme *TV-Avisen* (19 April 2007), 'I have argued that the headscarf is a totalitarian symbol and therefore it is equal to other totalitarian symbols that we know from Communism and Nazism'.[19]

The debate continued the following day. The host of DR1's *TV-Avisen* introduced a news clip about the debate as follows:

> The veil debate has exploded because the politician Asmaa Abdol-Hamid from the Red-Green Alliance announced that she will run for Parliament and that she will wear her headscarf in Parliament. This announcement has made Søren Krarup compare the symbol of the Muslim headscarf with a Nazi swastika. The leader of the Danish People's Party, Pia Kjærs-gaard, has maintained that she agrees with Krarup's message. Today more fuel has been added to the fire with prominent members of the Danish People's Party attacking Asmaa. (20 April 2007)[20]

A voice-over continued:

> New serious reactions to Asmaa Abdol-Hamid's headscarf came in to-day's issue of *Nyhedsavisen* [a national newspaper distributed free of charge]. Here the Danish People's Party's member of the European Par-liament, Mogens Camre, has argued that she [Abdol-Hamid] needs psy-chiatric treatment, and the party's spokesperson on EU issues, Morten Messerschmidt, has declared that all Muslims who confess to the Islamic ideology are losers. (20 April 2007)[21]

Two things are noteworthy in this introduction. First, the TV presenter underscores the dramatic aspects of the conflict with the words 'the veil debate has exploded', indicating that the debate is so harsh it is like an explosion. Second, the voice-over depicts Abdol-Hamid as the reason for the conflict: it arose because she was running for Parliament and re-fused to remove her headscarf. Thus Abdol-Hamid was made respon-sible for the conflict and the fact of the conflict exploding. Alternatively, the news media could have explained the conflict by referring to the Danish People's Party's intolerance of women with headscarves.

During the election campaign of October and November 2007, the news media treated Abdol-Hamid differently from other candidates. Journalists repeatedly asked her the same questions, as if it were legiti-

Figure 3.1. Asmaa Abdol-Hamid and the media during the 2007 election.
Photo: Freddy Hagen

mate not to accept her answers. She was mainly asked about her headscarf, the death penalty, gender equality and LGBT rights. Regardless of
her repeated answers that she was against death penalty, was a feminist and favoured LGBT rights, it was apparently deemed legitimate to
keep asking her these questions – in other words, to doubt the answers
she gave. No ethnically Danish candidates were asked specifically and
repeatedly about their views on the death penalty, feminism or sexual
minorities' rights. The myth that Muslims speak with two voices appeared to dominate news journalism during the election campaign.

Playing the Race Card

The news media's treatment of Asmaa Abdol-Hamid can be characterized as a media campaign against her. Interestingly, it was not only the
right-wing press that attacked her but also the left-wing press. For instance, the then chief editor of the national left-wing newspaper *Information*, Bent Winther, asked – or demanded – that Abdol-Hamid resign
her candidacy. He wrote in an editorial titled 'Dear Asmaa':

> The situation for the party you have joined is serious. According to polls,
> the Red-Green Alliance's voter turnout will be close to the minimum per-
> centage of votes necessary to be represented in Parliament... If there is

any chance of replacing (Prime Minister) Anders Fogh Rasmussen after the next election – which I assume you, Asmaa, also find important – then this chance will be missed if the Red-Green Alliance does not make it into Parliament. In order words, if the Red-Green Alliance does not begin moving away from the low level of voter support, it is the best guarantee of four more years with the Liberals (*Venstre*) and the Conservatives. And this is where you come into the picture, Asmaa. Everything indicates that a substantial part of left-wing voters have turned against the Red-Green Alliance because of your candidacy. So dear Asmaa Abdol-Hamid … please resign as a candidate for the Red-Green Alliance. (Winther 2007)

Winther's patronizing rhetoric echoes the hierarchical relation between the older, white man – who presents himself as wiser – and the younger, racial/ethnical minority woman, presented as less wise. He continues:

In the future election campaign your candidacy will be used to the maximum by the parties who wish to continue the Liberal-Conservative Government… A substantial part of the Red-Green Alliance's future election campaign will be about the death penalty, stoning of women, *sharia* legislation, gay rights and gender equality. Areas where the Red-Green Alliance traditionally has had strong viewpoints, viewpoints which are directly opposite to the attitudes being – maybe unfairly – ascribed to you. (Winther 2007)[22]

Winther's argument runs along the lines of 'blame the victim' rhetoric. He is asking Abdol-Hamid to take responsibility for other people's prejudice against her, as well as for the attitudes that others are ascribing her.

During the election campaign, right-wing parties did use Abdol-Hamid as an argument against the left wing and Social Democratic opposition. The Liberal party's election campaign chief strategist, then Minister of Employment Claus Hjort Frederiksen, said that the leader of the Social Democrats, Helle Thorning-Schmidt, was dependent on 'the controversial Muslim candidate' and asked, 'How much is Helle Thorning-Schmidt willing to compromise in order to get Asmaa's vote?' (Hüttemeier and Børsting 2007).[23] In this way Hjort Frederiksen tried to discredit the opposition by arguing that a vote for the opposition was a vote for 'the controversial Muslim candidate'. It should be added here that it is common knowledge that the Red-Green Alliance will never get a seat in Danish government – they will support a Social Democrat-led government, but they will never be offered an opportunity to take part in this government. This mirrors the situation after the national election of 2011, where the Social Democrats, the Center Liberals (Radikale) and the Socialist Party (Socialistisk Folkeparti) form the government with the support of the Red-Green Alliance. In 2007, the then leader of the centre-right party New Alliance (Ny Alliance), Naser Khader, argued that if the Social Democrat-led opposition gained power it would imply the imams' gaining power: 'With the red bloc (the opposition) you also get Asmaa and all the imams" ('Khader' 2007). Asmaa Abdol-Hamid had clearly distanced herself from imams and her party was a secularist party, unlike the majority of Danish parties, which wish to maintain Denmark as a non-secular state whose constitution secures strong ties between church and state. Pia Kjærsgaard, the leader of the Danish People's Party, also used Abdol-Hamid as a way to discredit the opposition in a televised debate between party leaders, when she asked Helle Thorning-Schmidt whether she (Thorning-Schmidt) could work together with a fundamentalist Islamist, implying that a vote for the opposition was a vote for a fundamentalist Islamist (TV2 programme *Partilederrunde* Nov. 17, 2007).

Despite Asmaa Abdol-Hamid's continuously distinguishing herself from Islamic fundamentalism during the election campaign and affirming her support of her party's views and politics, several politicians labelled her a fundamentalist and/or Islamist. Attacking visible minorities as part of an election campaign, also known as 'playing the race card', makes issues of race, ethnicity, and religion into discussion topics during election campaigns to get votes. The race card was also played in the Danish parliamentary elections of 2001 and 2005 (Andreassen 2005: 202). Abdol-Hamid was also connected visually to Islamic fundamentalism. For instance, a photograph of her with the Red-Green Alliance's logo in front of a flaming bonfire and the text 'A vote for Asmaa is a vote for Al-Qaeda' circulated on the Internet during the election campaign.[24]

From Freedom of Speech to Forced Speech

Abdol-Hamid did not get into Parliament. She was number five on the Red-Green Alliance's list of candidates, and the party got only four candidates into Parliament. She chose not to run for Parliament in the 2011 election.

Abdol-Hamid was not the only Muslim woman running for Parliament in 2007. Özlem Sara Cekic, a Danish woman of Kurdish-Turkish origin, ran for the Socialist Party, and Yildiz Akdogan, also of Turkish origin, ran for the Social Democrats, and the two became the first Muslim women in the Danish Parliament. Neither of these candidates gained as much attention as Abdol-Hamid, maybe because neither wore a headscarf. All three candidates had to contend with journalists who wanted to discuss Islam instead of politics. Cekic is a nurse and has been active in health politics for several years, yet she was not always allowed to campaign on health issues, as she was constantly asked about her religion and her arranged marriage (Mygind 2007). Indeed, these female candidates often had to answer questions about Islam, arranged marriages, headscarves and so forth before they got to talk about their politics. A possible conclusion is that young Muslim women who run for Parliament face longer odds than ordinary ethnically Danish candidates. They must deal with questions unrelated to their politics and contend with assumptions regarding their religion. Journalists' presumptions about Muslim women seem to be barriers the women need to overcome before they can perform as political candidates. Sara Ahmed explains how emotions move through sticky associations between signs, figures and objects (Ahmed 2004: 46). In the media coverage of Abdol-Hamid, the hijab – the visual sign of Abdol-Hamid's affiliation with Islam – became a sticky sign connoting female oppression, the death penalty and homophobia. Regardless of Abdol-Hamid's verbal statements, these associations stuck to her body and person. This type of emotional economy disabled the women's political performances. Their bodies – associated with 'the other' and 'non-democratic traditions' – could not become aligned with 'the Danish democracy'; hence, they were not able to perform the political 'we'.

The newspaper *Politiken,* often considered one of the most immigrant- and minority-friendly newspapers in Denmark, ran an interview with Cekic in which the attitude towards Muslim women, especially Abdol-Hamid, was clear. The journalist Kjeld Hybel described how, sitting in Cekic's house, he was 'scanning the room for suspicious items looking for signs of excessive Islamism' (Hybel 2007). He continued: 'I was thinking about Asmaa Abdol-Hamid, who has made us all, or at least the media, look suspiciously at all Muslims women who are getting near Parliament. We judge them all in relation to Asmaa: So, you are a Muslim and that means that you are in favour of whipping women who are not faithful to their husbands? That you want to send homosexuals directly to Hell? Chop off the hands of pickpockets? Exchange the Constitution with *Sharia*?' (Hybel 2007).[25]

Although Abdol-Hamid had never argued in favour of whipping or harsher punishment for criminals; although she had – repeatedly – argued in favour of homosexuals' rights and – repeatedly – stated that she supported the Constitution, here she is associated with homophobia and fundamentalist interpretations of Islam. Hybel's piece aligns 'Muslim women' together, so that the emotional economy accompanying Abdol-Hamid and causing the death penalty, female oppression and homophobia to stick to her sticks to Cekic as well (Ahmed 2004: 46ff., 90; Hvenegaard-Lassen 2008). Hybel's interview with Cekic reveals his own prejudice against Islam and Muslim women. Large parts of his article consist of his descriptions of how he thinks Muslims are, and it devotes little space to Cekic's political views. The article illustrates how journalists' prejudice hinders a young Muslim woman's access to the Danish media – and hence to the Danish democracy.

This suspicion of Muslims and the demands that a Muslim candidate answer questions about Islam, arranged marriages, death penalty, gender equality and LGBT rights are part of the overall increasing demands on Muslims after 9/11. Journalists in Europe and North America have increasingly confronted leaders of Muslims organizations, as well as individual Muslims, about their views on terror and violence, and Muslims seem to be required to publicly affirm their dislike for terror and violence each time Muslim terrorists commit a violent act. Similarly, Danish Muslim women report that they, as individual women, are confronted by ethnically Danish individuals and journalists who demand their responses to issues of terrorism, arranged marriages, forced marriages, honour killings and so on – that is, issues that popularly are connected to Islam (Andreassen 2007: 131f.).

There seems to be a need not simply to analyse situations involving freedom of expression, as has often occurred since the infamous Danish cartoon crisis (2005- 2006), but also to analyse situations of forced expression. Muslims, and maybe especially Muslim women, are forced to answer questions differently than the majority population is. They

Figure 3.2. Asmaa Abdol-Hamid and the media during the 2007 election. Photo: Freddy Hagen

are forced to deal with questions that may largely reflect the interviewer's own assumptions and prejudices about Islam and Muslim women more than the actual situation of the individual Muslim woman's life.

Female Muslim Candidates in the 2011 Election

After serving for four years in Parliament, both Özlem Cekic (Socialist Party) and Yildiz Akdogan (Social Democrats) again ran for Parliament in the Danish election of autumn 2011. This time, it was not only the Danish news media that created roadblocks for the women's election campaigns, but also small groups of fundamentalist Muslims. The women's election posters were vandalized, and especially Akdogan's posters were defaced with large stickers. The red- and orange-coloured stickers showed a hand upholding a book surrounded by burning flames, accompanied by the text: 'Legislation belongs to Allah. Democracy is hypocrisy. Hypocrites go to hell.'[26]

Being of Turkish origin, Akdogan campaigned, among other places, in the Copenhagen neighbourhood of Tingbjerg, a low-income area with a high percentage of immigrants and their descendants among its inhabitants. Here groups of younger Muslim men confronted her, verbally attacking her and accusing her of being a 'bad' Muslim for acting against the will of Allah and supporting democracy instead of the idea of a Caliphate, among other things; they also condemned her marriage to an ethnically Danish man and her support for LGBT rights. They surrounded her physically to continue their verbal attacks on her, making it very difficult for her to converse with other people, her potential voters, in Tingbjerg (DR P1, *Sådan er sofavælgerne*, 14 Nov 2011).

Regardless of their many differences, both the news media and the fundamentalist Muslims created imaginary divisions between the majority society and the diaspora community, thus cementing the 'us' versus 'them' division. Whereas the news media excluded the Muslim women, especially Abdol-Hamid, from the national Danish community and hence placed them in an (imaginary) diaspora community characterized by values fundamentally different from (imaginary) Danish values, the fundamentalist Muslims forced Akdogan 'back into' the diaspora community.

The women themselves, however, seemed to move freely between their diaspora communities and the Danish majority society – or rather, their performances seem to indicate that the division between the Danish majority society and diaspora communities does not always exist. The three Muslim women running for Danish Parliament inhabited and

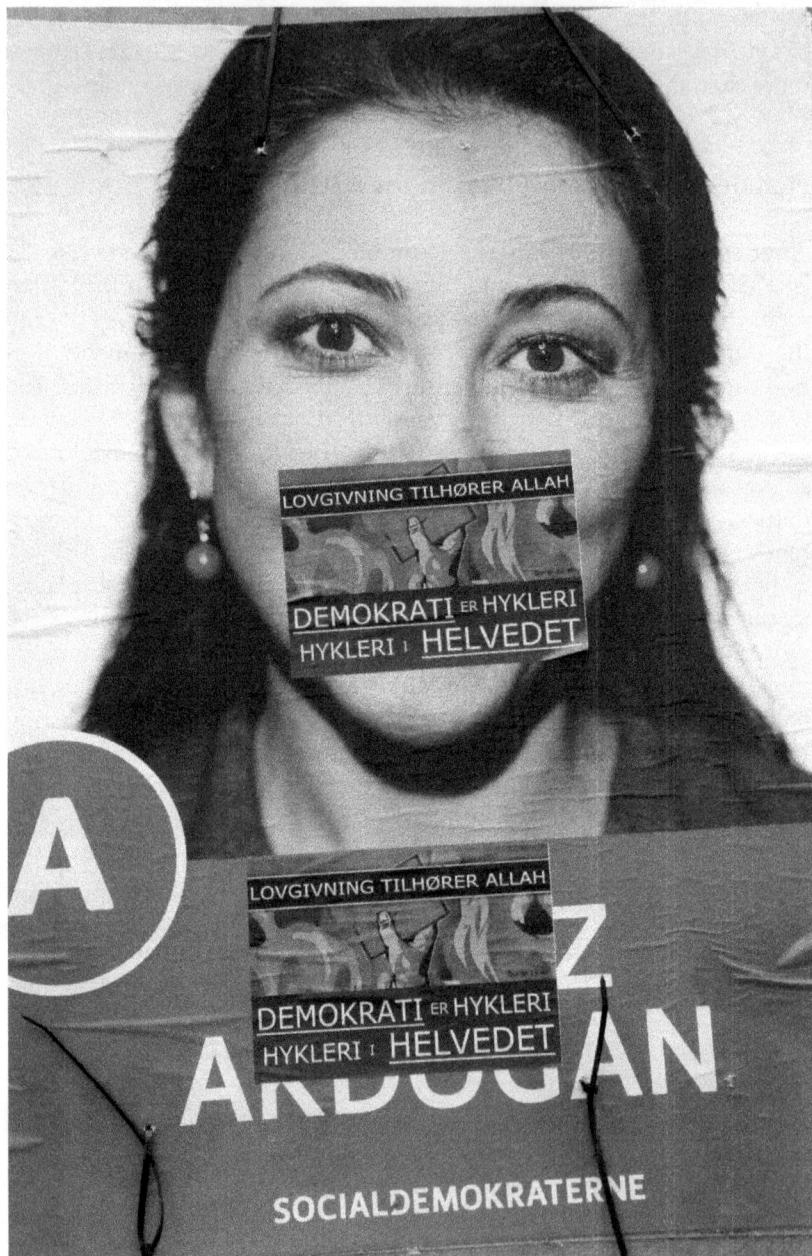

Figure 3.3. Yildiz Akdogan's campaign poster, vandalized during the 2011 election. Photo: Akdogan

performed in several arenas, and their occupation of space indicates that the arenas overlapped or even merged. Considering solely the women's performances and utterances, the spheres of diaspora community and majority society have merged. The women label themselves 'Danish Muslims' and insist they are both Danish and Muslim, both descendants of immigrant parents and integrated parts of the Danish majority society. However, they were not allowed to define their spaces and spheres of belongings: other factors, utterances and actions – by the news media or fundamentalist religious groups – crucially impacted the women's ability to participate in the majority society, and these external factors often impeded the women's movements and desire to belong.

Sexual Minorities

One of the issues Abdol-Hamid was repeatedly asked about was her attitude towards homosexuality and sexual minorities' rights. She answered repeatedly that she was in favour of minority rights and against discrimination. After her nomination as candidate to Parliament, she explicitly stated: 'I am not in favour of death penalty, and this is regardless of what kind of society we are talking about. Let me make this clear: I am in favour of equal rights for all people, and I therefore do not care what sexuality people have' (Johansen 2007).[27]

During the election season, Abdol-Hamid campaigned at LGBT clubs; sexual minorities were on her campaign staff, and right before the campaign, in an interview she gave in the national LGBT magazine *Panbladet,* she said: 'I have friends who are homosexual... So let me state again: I am in favour of equality' (Skjoldager 2007).[28] The only anti-LGBT rights statement Abdol-Hamid has made was back in 2004, before she became a member of the Red-Green Alliance. Here she asserted that she was against allowing single parents to adopt or receive fertility treatment, and that she did not believe homosexuals should be allowed to adopt (Risbro 2007).[29] It must be pointed out that Danish homosexuals gained the right to adopt only in 2010, and that lesbians and single straight women won the right to fertility treatments in 2006. In other words, for several years there was political consensus that the rights to adopt and resort to reproductive assistance should be reserved for heterosexual couples in Denmark. In the past few years, several politicians, Abdol-Hamid included, have changed their views in this area; consequently single and lesbian women were granted the same reproductive rights as heterosexual women engaged in heterosexual relationships in 2006.[30]

Despite these facts, the news media continuously treated Abdol-Hamid as though she disliked homosexuals and opposed granting them equal rights. Homosexuality and sexual minorities' rights have never been dominant issues in Danish elections, and very few politicians have branded themselves as 'gay-friendly' or have had sexual minorities' rights on their political agenda. But with Muslim candidates running for office, homosexuality apparently became a hot topic. The journalist Niels Krause-Kjær, a regular blogger at the conservative newspaper *Berlingske Tidende*, argued that Abdol-Hamid's headscarf or prejudice against Muslim women had nothing to do with the media's treatment of her, just as no prejudice against her as a veiled Muslim woman influenced her election results. He wrote: 'She [Abdol-Hamid] was of course asked the same questions again and again! About her attitude towards death penalty. Towards homosexuals... She was judged because of her attitudes. ... It had nothing to do with 30 grams of textile [the headscarf]' (Krause-Kjær 2007).[31] Analysis of the media coverage of Abdol-Hamid during the election makes clear that Abdol-Hamid was not judged by her positions but by what people presumed her positions to be, that is, by the associations that 'stuck' to her hijab. In the same vein, Krause-Kjær based his interpretation of her election results on his prejudice against her as a veiled Muslim woman, not on what she actually had said during the campaign.

During the previous Danish national election in 2005, LGBT Denmark (association for lesbians, gays, bisexuals and transgendered) had conducted a survey among candidates for Parliament to measure their attitudes towards sexual minorities' rights. The results showed that many candidates did not favour equal rights for minorities in the areas of reproduction, marriage, family formations and discrimination (LBL 2005). However, the media did not question any of these candidates about their attitudes towards sexual minorities during the election campaign of 2005. Similarly, none of the ethnically Danish candidates were questioned about their support – or lack of support – for sexual minorities' rights during the election campaigns in 2007 and 2011. Apparently only Muslim candidates, especially the one with a headscarf, had to answer questions about sexual minorities and discrimination.

The Colour of Hate Crimes

This mirrors a media tendency to interconnect discrimination against sexual minorities and visible minorities, especially Muslim visible minorities. Since a small group of visible minority men of Middle Eastern origin attacked the Copenhagen LGBT Pride Parade in 2001, the news media have often portrayed visible minorities and Muslims as hostile towards homosexuals (see also Andreassen 2012).

Politicians and journalists have repeatedly mentioned the attack on the Pride Parade when talking about homophobia and hate crimes. No research has been done on hate crime in Denmark, so very little is known about the perpetrators of hate crimes against sexual minorities. Despite the lack of factual knowledge in this field, several politicians have connected homophobia and hate crimes with visible minorities. The former Copenhagen municipality politician Klaus Bondam, who is openly gay and represents the Social Liberals (Radikale Venstre), a party known for progressive stances on minorities' rights, has blamed visible minorities for hate crimes against homosexuals. In a public speech in 2005, he said:

> Lately there has been an increase in harassments [against homosexuals] committed by second-generation immigrants.... They sit in their cars [in front of gay clubs] and wait for us to enter the streets.... They lie in wait with clubs and baseball bats.... We have struggled for many years and have gained some great settings for our existence and then these young people come and destroy our freedom. I grieve to hear that this is happening in our city – where the entrance into the nightlife should be connected with happiness, passion, energy and a zest for life. Now it becomes connected with fear.... We will not accept this.... The escalating incidents in Copenhagen are yet another example of many years of unsuccessful integration politics. (Bondam 2005)[32]

According to Bondam, homosexuality, which he reduces to white men's frequenting of gay clubs, has become associated with fear. Fear as an emotion has a function, Ahmed argues: 'fear does something; it re-establishes distance between bodies whose differences is read off the surface, as a reading which produces the surface' (Ahmed 2004: 63). Here fear produces distances and differences between racial/ethnic minorities and ethnic Danes. The fear becomes associated with the coloured body, as it, in Bondam's interpretation, is second generation immigrants (coloured males) who are threatening white homosexuals; here it is also assumed that the homosexual community is mainly white, consisting of ethnic Danes and that immigrants and their descendants are not a part of the homosexual community.

Similarly, the Danish People's Party leader Pia Kjærsgaard has blamed visible minorities for ruining the gay and lesbian community's activities. In her weekly newsletter, she wrote about the Copenhagen area Noerrebro, which has a high concentration of immigrants and descendants among its residents:

Today Noerrebro has changed.... The tolerance is gone. And one of the main reasons why is that Noerrebro has become a Muslim enclave. And where Islam goes in, tolerance goes out.... Last summer, a procession called Gay Pride was harmed. It is gays and lesbians in a festive manifestation. It is a little wild but rather harmless. But the Muslim brotherhood out there did not think so – and the homosexuals had to run the gauntlet.... We [the Danish People's Party] will work towards getting Noerrebro back. So the tolerance and broad-mindedness can again exist there. (Kjærsgaard 2003)[33]

Bondam's and Kjærsgaard's descriptions present acceptance of homosexuality as an integrated feature of Danish society and describe ethnic Danes as tolerant towards sexual minorities. Homophobia and hate crimes against sexual minorities are thereby constructed as features of the ethnically/racially and religiously diverse society. Bondam connects hate crime and integration politics when he argues that the visible minorities' attack on sexual minorities was caused by their lack of integration into Danish society. In Denmark, integration is often understood as assimilation; hence Bondam is saying that if the visible minorities had been more like the majority population, that is, more like white ethnic Danes, then hate crimes against homosexuals would not occur. Kjærsgaard similarly portrays ethnic Danes as tolerant towards sexual minorities. She intends to work towards getting Noerrebro back to an era before immigrants arrived, which – she claims – was an era of tolerance towards sexual minorities. It should be pointed out that Kjærsgaard's party, the Danish People's Party, has traditionally voted against legal improvements of sexual minorities' rights and has never branded itself as in favour of sexual minorities' rights. Rather, the Danish People's Party appears to underscore sexual minorities' rights and defend sexual minorities in situations where the defence of sexual minorities is rhetorically useful in an anti-immigration agenda.

Both Bondam and Kjærsgaard reserve the practice of hate crime to visible minorities' attitudes towards sexual minorities. Their arguments imply that white ethnic Danes are not homophobic. But according to the LGBT Denmark, this is not the case:

[We] cannot support the argument that hate crimes should be committed only by youth with another ethnic background than Danish. Just as we cannot say that hate crimes are only committed by majority Danes. We are not arguing that there is not any youth with another ethnic background – because there is. But we also know that some Danish young men, at some educational institutions, among others in the capital, arrange raids and form 'beating teams' and seek out homosexual areas in order to find random homosexuals whom they attack. (LBL 2005)[34]

Furthermore, young ethnic Danes are not necessarily tolerant of sexual minorities. A recent survey showed that 53 per cent of ethnically Danish young men and 21 per cent of ethnically Danish young women find it unacceptable for two people of the same sex to engage in sexual activities with one another (Knudsen 2007).

Nationality

Impressions and understandings of categories like nationality, ethnicity/race, gender and sexuality are not constructed in a vacuum. They intersect with, influence and construct each other, just as they intersect with other categories and with various understandings of societal contexts. The construction of homophobia as an ethnic/racial issue, and hence white Danishness as the embodiment of tolerance, is an illustration of how nationality, ethnicity/race and sexuality intersect. Negative descriptions of immigrants and descendants as homophobic create a positive impression of ethnic Danes. These descriptions construct sexual tolerance as an integral part of Danish culture and Danishness. The thusly created opposition between Danish tolerance and immigrants'/descendants' intolerance implies an ethnic/racial opposition: white ethnic Danes are tolerant, whereas immigrants and descendants of colour are intolerant. Sexual tolerance becomes nationalized and ethnified/racialized.

Nationality is imagined and continuously constructed (Anderson 1991 [1983]). Most classical work on nations and nationalism (Anderson 1991 [1983]; Hobsbawm 1990) do not deal with gender and sexuality, so gender and sexuality perspectives are often absent from traditional theories of nationalism. Feminist scholars, however, have shown that nationality must be understood in connection with gender and sexuality (Lutz et al. 1995). Women reproduce nations on various levels: biologically, culturally and symbolically (Warring 1998: 200f.). Women not only literally give birth to future generations of the nation; they are also seen as symbolic border guards, embodiments of the nation's collectivity and the nation's cultural reproducers (Lutz et al. 1995: 9). As Ruth Harris argues:

> Women have been located, not only as 'biological reproducers' but also as 'reproducers of the boundaries of ethnic/national groups', as 'transmitters of its culture' as well as ideological discourses used in the constitution, reproduction and transformation of ethnic/national categories. ... Women are often the signifiers of communities not only ideologically and

discursively but also with their bodies ... as a powerful instrument of so-cial closure. ... All forms of closure presuppose ways of defining belong-ing and 'otherness'. ... [Women] represent the boundary between 'us' and the 'Other'. (Lutz et al. 1995: 91)

Because women have been perceived as the embodiment of a na-tion's honour and functioned as the boundary defining who belonged to the nation and who did not, rape has been used as a strategic tool in times of war or conflict. Similarly, visible minority men's rape of white ethnically Danish women has been interpreted and described as an at-tack on the Danish nation and the Danish ethnicity/race (Andreassen 2006). I would like to take this argument further and argue that not only women but also other 'weak' representatives of the ethnic/racial group can embody the nation in an ethnified/racialized construction of a national community.

The news media's treatment of Asmaa Abdol-Hamid as homopho-bic and the debates about hate crime and homophobia illustrate how constructions of Danish nationality must be understood in relation to constructions of ethnicity/race and sexuality. The hate crimes against homosexuals are presented as violations against not only the sexual minorities attacked but also against Danish culture and Danish society. In these representations, it seems that homosexuals – whom the news media mainly present as white gay men – represent the nation, much in the way women have traditionally done. Because the homosexual – that is, the white gay man – has become a representative of Denmark, an attack on him is an attack on the nation. This ethnified/racialized nar-rative seems to equate harming the white gay male body with harming the whole nation (Andreassen 2012).

Meanwhile, homosexuals have often been excluded from the national community and have had limited citizenship rights and welfare state rights (Evans 1993; Hines 2009). Homosexuals have been excluded and othered because of their sexuality. They are the 'other' against which mainstream heterosexual society can construct itself. But in these de-bates, as in the media's treatment of Abdol-Hamid, the homosexuals' whiteness and ethnic Danishness seem to prevail over their sexuality. The whiteness of the gay male body trumps the alienation of the minor-ity sexuality. These debates construct Danish nationality around inclu-sion of the homosexual (white gay man) against the exclusion of hate crime perpetrators of colour.

These narratives also evince a traditional patriarchal understanding of protection in play. Central to patriarchy is the belief that men – and in welfare states, also the state – take care of and protect the weak, typically women and children. But in the representations of hate crimes, the group of weak subjects who need protection is enlarged to include homosexuals. Thus the (patriarchal) state must protect women, children and homosexuals. Here the white gay man becomes a fragile being who needs the state's protection.

Benedict Anderson separated nationalism and racism in his classic work on nationalism *Imagined Communities* (1991 [1983]) by arguing that nationalism thought in terms of historical destinies while racism dreamt of eternal contaminations (Andersen 1991 [1983]: 149). This separation is problematic in narratives where national inclusion and exclusion are ethnified/racialized. The media's treatment of Abdol-Hamid and the representation of hate crimes imply a national inclusion based on ethnicity/race instead of legal belonging to the nation state. The traditional separation between nationality and racism, as argued by Anderson, must therefore be nuanced when applied to a contemporary Nordic context.

The news media's focus on Abdol-Hamid's presumed homophobia functions as an exclusionary tool. She and her presumed homophobia are presented as non-Danish, which excludes her from the national community. Tolerance is constructed as a Danish value, and tolerance towards sexual minorities is constructed as an integrated part of Danish society and ethnically Danish citizens' values and beliefs. Abdol-Hamid holds Danish citizenship, has lived most of her life in Denmark, speaks Danish fluently and identifies as Danish, yet the news media describe her as different from 'Danes' and from 'Danish values'. Her presumed homophobia is a key factor in creating this image of her as non-Danish. Both constructions – Muslims as homophobic and ethnic Danes as tolerant – are imaginary. But they work differently: the former contributes to a negative image of Muslims as intolerant and backwards, and the latter to a positive image of ethnic Danes as tolerant and progressive. Both play into the construction of binary oppositions between the visible minority population and the ethnically Danish majority population – between a diaspora community and the mainstream society. Furthermore, they play into the exclusion of Muslims and visible minorities from the Danish national community: Abdol-Hamid is being forced 'back into' her diaspora community, characterized by homophobia, even though she verbally argues against that position and bodily tries to inhabit the space of the majority Danish society. These debates turn tolerance of sexual minorities into a nationalist tool of inclusion and exclusion in the rhetoric used against visible minorities and against Islam.

Maintaining Power Structures

Traditionally, one of the tasks of journalism has been to challenge existing power relations, but the media also participate in creating power on various levels. One way the news media construct power is via journalists' and politicians' arguments that sexual minorities are tolerated in Denmark. No journalists challenged this assumption in the coverage of Abdol-Hamid's presumed homophobia, and the assumption appears to have hegemonic status in the news media. The treatment of Abdol-Hamid functioned as a tool to maintain this hegemony. The news media are supposed to be a watchdog, but their coverage of Abdol-Hamid has failed to challenge the existing ethnic/racial power relations in Denmark. In this coverage, where ethnicity/race, religion, gender and nationality intersect, the news media have not performed as the fourth estate of the Danish realm.

Notes

1. In this chapter, 'visible minorities' designates migrants and their descendants. Danish news media and politicians use various terms to refer to migrants and descendants, e.g., 'immigrants', 'ethnic', 'ethnic minority', 'second-generation immigrants', 'foreigners', and 'Muslims'. These terms are often used synonymously and are often connected to certain political understandings. The term 'visible minorities' is useful because it acknowledges the variety among migrants and descendants and is unconnected to any specific political understanding of migrants and descendants. Furthermore, it underscores racial aspects of migration that are seldom verbalized in a Nordic context.
2. Women for Freedom was established 8 March 2006.
3. Original text: 'feministisk forum ønsker DR2 tillykke med ansættelsen af Asmaa Abdol-Hamid som vært på debatprogrammet Adam og Asmaa. Hermed er DR med til at styrke både den kønsmæssige og etnicitetsmæssige ligestilling i Danmark.'
4. I was a member of the Feminist Forum at the time and participated in these debates.
5. Many of the signatures lacked the signers' full names and addresses.
6. Original text: 'Det er pinligt, at den danske kvindebevægelse forholder sig fuldstændigt tavst til det faktum, at mange kvindelige medborgere i landet er underlagt undertrykkende patriarkalske normer fra det 7. århundredes Arabien.'
7. Original text: '…sløret for mig at se er en dybt oprørende måde at hæmme pigebarnets og kvindens frie udfoldelse på, såvel kropsligt som mentalt.'

8. Original text: 'Der mødte mig to totalt indhyllede småpiger, der med be-svær legede. Et uhyggeligt syn ikke udelukkende på grund af tøjet, men på grund af den undertrykkelse, der ligger bag.'

9. Original text: 'Hvem kæmper for den tilslørede kvinde, der går forbi på gaden med blikket i jorden og udsigten til at blive tvangsgift og for hvem debatten om karrieremuligheder virker utopisk?'

10. Original text: 'et andet kvindesyn.'

11. Original text: 'Ulla Dahlerup, landskendt som rødstrømpeaktivist helt tilbage i 1970, har nærmest helt opgivet at hjælpe indvandrerkvinderne i Danmark.' 'Redstocking' has been a common label for feminists since the 1970s in Denmark. The Danish women's movement took the name in the early 1970s, inspired by the New York feminist group that published the *Redstockings Manifesto* in 1969, calling on women to fight patriarchy with phrases like 'Women are an oppressed class' and 'Male supremacy is the oldest, most basic form of domination. All other forms of exploitation and oppression (racism, capitalism, imperialism, etc.) are extensions of male supremacy.' The name Redstockings was inspired by the disparaging sixteenth- and seventeenth-century label for intellectual women, 'Blue-stockings', which the late 1960s feminists modified to feature the colour of left-wing politics and revolution.

12. Original text: 'I 1992 forsøgte jeg at kontakte en pakistansk kvindegruppe på Nørrenbro, men jeg fik en spand koldt vand i hovedet. Siden har jeg forsøgt i andre sammenhænge at skabe kontakt, men de kvinder vil ikke hjælpes. De ser på rødstrømper med forfærdelse, og betragter os som sata-niske kvinder. Kulturkløften er simpelthen for stor.'

13. Dahlerup received 43,746 personal votes, which was not enough to get her a seat. The Danish People's Party's one seat went to the front-runner Mogens Camre, who with 53,714 personal votes regained his seat in the European Parliament.

14. See, e.g., the Feminist Forum website, which makes available the text of a letter to the editor of *Jyllandsposten* regarding the debate that was sent but not published: http://www.feministiskforum.dk/tekster/Modbilleder.html

15. Professor Birte Siim from Aalborg University and the leader of Danish Cen-tre for Information on Gender, Equality and Diversity (Kvinfo), Elisabeth Møller Jensen, both of the older generation of feminists, have publicly ar-gued in favour of Asmaa Abdol-Hamid, and the leader of Organization for Immigrant Women's Rights (IKIR), Nahid Riazi, representing the younger feminist generation, has argued against Asmaa Abdol-Hamid and against having veiled women as hostesses on public service TV stations.

16. For comparison, in the 2000s the total percentage of all employed people aged 15–66 was ca 78–79 per cent. Statistics on employment rates are based on so-called frequency of employment (*erhvervsfrekvens*), which includes people who are actively working or actively seeking employment – i.e., the employment rate includes people who are between jobs.

17. Original text: 'Er kvinders fri ret til at uddanne sig, tjene penge og ret til at be-stemme over egen krop måske ikke grundhjørnesten i kvindefrigørelsen?'.

18. For further analysis of the media coverage of Abdol-Hamid during the Danish national election, see also Rikke Andreassen 2010.

19. Original text: 'Jeg har sagt, at sløret, tørklædet, er et totalitært symbol, og dermed er det ligestillet med de totalitære symboler, vi kender fra henholdsvis kommunisme og nazisme'.

20. Original text: 'Tørklædedebatten eksploderer, fordi politikeren Asmaa Abdol-Hamid fra Enhedslisten meddeler, at hun stiller op til Folketinget, og at hun i Folketinget vil bære sit muslimske hovedtørklæde. Den udmelding får Søren Krarup til at sammenligne symbolet i det muslimske tørklæde med nazisternes hagekors. Dansk Folkepartis leder Pia Kjærsgaard fastslår, at hun er enig i budskabet. Nu er der kommet ny benzin på bålet. I dag kommer flere fremtrædende Folketingspolitikere fra Dansk Folkeparti med nye udfald mod Asmaa'.

21. Original text: 'De nye kraftige reaktioner på Asmaa Abdol-Hamids tørklæde kom i dagens udgave af Nyhedsavisen. Her siger DFs medlem af Europa parlamentet Mogens Camre, at hun trænger til psykiatrisk behandling, og EU-ordfører Morten Messerschmidt erklærer, at alle muslimer som bekender sig til den islamistiske ideologi er tabere.'

22. Original text: 'Situationen for det parti, du har meldt dig ind i er alvorlig. I meningsmålingerne ligger Enhedslisten nu og roder omkring spærregrænsen.... Hvis der overhovedet skal være en mulighed for at skifte Anders Fogh Rasmussen ud efter næste valg - hvilket jeg tror, du mener, er vigtigt, Asmaa - ja så er det uden for rækkevidde, hvis Enhedslisten ender med at ryge ud af Folketinget. Men andre ord, hvis Enhedslisten ikke får rykket sig fri af spærregrænsen, så er det den bedste garanti for fire år mere med Venstre og Konservative. Og det er her, du kommer ind i billedet. Alt tyder nemlig på, at en betydelig del af venstrefløjen har vendt partiet ryggen på grund af dit kandidatur. Så kære Asmaa Abdol-Hamid...vil du ikke godt trække dig som folketingskandidat for Enhedslisten.... I en kommende valgkamp vil dit kandidatur blive udnyttet til det yderste af de partier, som ønsker en fortsættelse af VK-regeringen ... vil en stor del af valgkampen for partiets vedkommende ende med at handle om dødsstraf, stening af kvinder, sharia-lovgivning, homoseksuelles rettigheder og kvinders ligestilling. Emner, hvor Enhedslisten og venstrefløjen traditionelt har haft stærke synspunkter, som står i direkte modsætning til de holdninger, som du - måske uretmæssigt - tillægges.'

23. Original text: 'den kontroversielle muslim'; hvor meget er Helle Thorning-Schmidt parat til at sælge ud for at få Asmaas stemme?'.

24. The image can be found at http://chromatism.net/current/images/asmaastemme.jpg. A blog debate in the newspaper *Nyhedsavisen* (Malacinski 2007) linked to the image. The producer of the image is unknown.

25. Original text: 'jeg sidder og scanner rummet for mistænkelige genstande, at jeg leder efter tegn på overdreven islamisme.... Jeg tænker på Asmaa Abdol-Hamid, som har fået os alle, eller i det mindste pressen, til at skæve mistænksomt til alle muslimske kvinder, der nærmer sig Folketinget. Vi måler dem alle i forhold til Asmaa: Nå, så du er muslim, javel, og det betyder velsagtens, at du går ind for piskeslag til kvinder, der er deres mænd

utro? At du vil sende de homoseksuelle lige lukt i helvede? Hugge hænderne af all lommetyve? Skifte Grundloven ud med Sharia?'.

26. Original text: 'Lovgivningen tilhører Allah. Demokrati er hykleri. Hyklere i helvede'. Posters for the male Muslim politician Kamal Qureshi (representing the Socialist Party) were also vandalized by both extreme right-wingers and extreme Islamists.

27. Original text: 'Jeg er ikke tilhænger af dødsstraf, og jeg er ligeglad med, hvilket samfund vi snakker om. Og lad mig slå fast, at jeg synes, at der skal være lige forhold for alle, og at jeg derfor er ligeglad med, hvad seksualitet folk har.'

28. Original text: 'Jeg har venner, der er homoseksuelle.... Men jeg kan da godt sige det igen: Jeg går ind for ligeberettigelse'.

29. Original text: 'at hun er imod at enlige skal have lov at adoptere eller have lov til at blive kunstigt befrugtet. Desuden afslørede Asmaa Abdol-Hamid, at hun ikke mener, at homoseksuelle skal have lov at adoptere'.

30. Furthermore, it should be added that 20 per cent of Danes favour the death penalty, and that these 20 per cent feature a much higher percentage of right-wing than left-wing voters and a very high percentage of voters for the Danish People's Party (Rassing et al. 2007).

31. Original text: 'Ja, det tror da pokker, at hun blev spurgt igen og igen! Om sit forhold til dødsstraf. Til homoseksuelle.... Hun blev bedømt på sine holdninger.... Det havde intet med 30 gram tekstil at gøre.'

32. Original text: Gennem den seneste tid har der været en optrapning af chikane fra anden generationsindvandrer...De sidder simpelthen i deres biler og venter på, at vi kommer ud på gaden... De ligger på lur med køller og baseball bats...Nu har vi i så mange år kæmpet og opnået nogle fantastiske rammer for vores udfoldelse, og så kommer disse unge mennesker og ødelægger vores frihed... Jeg græmmes over at høre om, at dette sker i vores by, hvor det at kaste sig ombord i nattelivet, bør være forbundet med glæde, lidenskab, energi og livslyst. Nu bliver det pludselig forbundet med angst.... Vi vil ikke acceptere det.... De eskalerende hændelser i København med hate crimes af denne slags, er endnu et udtryk for mange års fejlslagen integrationspolitik.

33. Original text: 'I dag er Nørrebro totalt forandret.... Tolerancen er væk. Og en af de væsentlige årsager hertil er at Nørrebro er blevet en muslimsk enklave. Og hvor islam går ind, går tolerancen ud.... Forrige sommer gik det ud over et optog, der kalder sig Gay Pride. Det er bøsser og lesbiskes festlige manifestation. Det er lidt vildt - men det er ganske harmløst. Det synes det muslimske broderskab derude ikke - så de homoseksuelle måtte løbe spidsrod ... vi [vil] ... arbejde på at få Nørrebro tilbage. Så tolerance og frisind atter kan gøre sit indtog nord for Dronning Louises Bro.'
    The attack on the Pride parade was in 2001, not 2002 as Kjærsgaard writes.

34. Original text: 'LBL [LGBT Denmark] har nemlig intet belæg for at sige, endsige påstå, at hate crimes alene begås af unge mænd med anden etnisk baggrund end dansk - ligesom vi heller ikke kan sige, at hate crimes alene begås af unge mænd med majoritetsetnisk dansk baggrund. Vi siger ikke, at der

ikke blandt gerningsmændene findes unge med anden etnisk baggrund - for det gør der. Men vi ved også, at der blandt visse unge danske mænd, på nogle uddannelsesinstitutioner i bl.a. hovedstadsområdet, aftales raids og sammensætning af 'tæskehold', som opsøger det homoseksuelle miljø for at udse sig tilfældige homoseksuelle, som de efterfølgende overfalder.'

References

Ahmed, S. 2004. *The Cultural Politics of Emotion.* Edinburgh: Edinburgh University Press.

Ammitzbøll, P. 2001. 'Sover du, søster', *Jyllands-Posten,* 24 June, 1/2.

Anderson, B. 1991 [1983]. *Imagined Communities: Reflections on the Origin and Spread of Nationalism.* New York and London: Verso.

Andreassen, R. 2005. *The Mass Media's Construction of Gender, Race, Sexuality and Nationality: An Analysis of the Danish News Media's Communication about Visible Minorities from 1971 to 2004.* Ph.D. dissertation, University of Toronto, 2005.

———. 2006. 'Intersektionalitet i voldtægtsnarrativer', *Kvinder, køn og forskning* 2–3 (December): 93–104.

———. 2007. *Der er et yndigt land. Medier, minoriteter og danskhed.* Copenhagen: Tiderne Skifter.

———. 2010. 'Sing a Song but Stay Out of Politics: Two Cases of Representation in the Danish Media', in E. Eide and K. Nikunen (eds). *Media in Motion: Cultural Complexity and Migration in the Nordic Region.* Farnham: Ashgate, pp. 163–81.

———. 2011. 'Gender as a Tool in Danish Debates about Muslims', in J. Nielsen (ed.), *Islam in Denmark: The Challenge of Diversity.* Lanham, MD: Lexington Books, pp. 143–60.

———. 2013. (forthcoming). 'Take Off That Veil and Give Me Access to Your Body: An Analysis of Danish Debates about Muslim Women's Head and Body Covering', in M. Schrover and D. Moloney (eds), *Shifting Control: Gender and Migration Policy, 1917–2010.* Amsterdam: Amsterdam University Press.

Anzaldua, G. (ed.). 1990. *Making Face, Making Soul.* San Francisco: Aunt Lute Books.

Bondam, K. 2005. Speech, 24 June. Retrieved 1 April 2009 from http://www.lbl.dk/nyheder/arkiv/2005/juni/artikel/klaus-bondams-tale-ved-lbls-sankt-hans-baal-paa-helgoland.html

Brix, H.M. 2001. 'Uhuu…hvor er I henne, feminister?', *Politiken,* 26 May, 3/6.

Collins, P.H. 1990. *Black Feminist Thought: Knowledge Consciousness and the Politics of Empowerment.* Boston: Unwin Hyman.

Dahlerup, D. 1998. *Rødstrømperne. Den danske Rødstrømpebevægelses udvikling, nytænkning og gennemslag 1970–1985,* vol. 1. Haslev: Gyldendal.

Evans, D. 1993. *Sexual Citizenship: The Material Construction of Sexualities.* London: Routledge.

Friedan, B. 1963. *The Feminine Mystique.* New York: W.W. Norton.

Hansen, J. 2006. 'Baby, bøn og burka', *Politiken*, 15 May.

Hervik, P. 2002. *Mediernes muslimer. En antropologisk undersøgelse af mediernes dækning af religioner i Danmark.* Copenhagen: Nævnet for Etnisk Ligestilling.

Hines, S. 2009. '(Trans)Forming Gender: Social Change and Transgender Citizenship', in Oleksy, H. *Intimate Citizenship: Gender, Sexuality, Politics.* London: Routledge.

Hobsbawm, E.J. 1990. *Nations and Nationalism since 1780: Program, Myth, Reality.* Cambridge: Cambridge University Press.

Holst, H.V. 2001. 'Det nødvendige oprør', *Politiken*, 2 June, 3/6.

Hüttemeier, C. and M. Børsting. 2007. 'Venstre: S er afhængig af Asmaa', *Politiken*, 25 October.

Hvenegaard-Lassen, K. 2008. 'The Danes are an open and tolerant people, who help other people in need. Gender and integration in Danish political discourse'. *Post-immigration Minorities, Religion and National Identities Conference*, Bristol, UK, 14–15 November 2008.

Hybel, K. 2007. 'Hvorfor er dette billede en sensation?', *Politiken*, 2 December, 14–23.

Iversen, M. 2001. 'Gu' er det vores ansvar', *Politiken*, 2 June, 3/6.

Johansen, R. 2007. 'Asmaa opstilles som nummer 7', *DR Online*, 27 April

'Khader: Med den røde blok får du Asmaa og alle imamerne'. 2007. *Politiken*, 7 November.

Kjærsgaard, P. 2003. 'Pias ugebrev', 11 November. Retrieved 1 April 2009 from http://www.danskfolkeparti.dk/Giv_os_N%C3%B8rrebro_tilbage....asp

Knudsen, L.B. 2007. *Ung2006. 15–24 åriges seksualitet. Viden, holdninger og adfærd.* Copenhagen: Aalborg Universitet and Sundhedsstyrelsen.

Krause-Kjær, N. 2007. 'Myten om Asmaa', *Berlingske Tidende*, blog, 2 November.

Laclau, E. 1990. *New Reflections on the Revolution of Our Time.* London: Verso.

———. 1993. 'Power and Representation', in M. Poster (ed.), *Politics, Theory and Contemporary Culture.* New York: Columbia University Press.

Laclau, E. and Chantal M. 1985. *Hegemony and Socialist Strategy: Towards a Radical Democratic Politics.* London: Verso.

LBL. 2005. 'Hate Crime – Hvem er gerningsmanden?', *Jyllands-Posten, JP-København*, 9 July.

Lutz, H., A. Phoenix and N. Yuval-Davis. (eds.). 1995. *Crossfires: Nationalism, Racism and Gender in Europe.* London: Pluto Press.

Maart, R. 1992. 'Consciousness, Knowledge and Morality: The Absence of the Knowledge of White Consciousness in Contemporary Feminist Theory', in D. Shogan (ed.), *A Reader in Feminist Ethics.* Toronto: Canadian Scholars' Press, pp. 129–49.

Malancinski, L. 2007. 'Asmaa går ind i plakatkrigen'. *Nyhedsavisen*, 25 October. Retrieved 1 April 2009 from http://avisen.dk/asmaa-gaar-plakatkrigen-251007.aspx

Mohanty, C.T. 1991. 'Under Western Eyes', in C.T. Mohanty et al. (eds.), *Third World Women and the Politics of Feminism.* Bloomington: Indiana University Press, pp. 51–75.

Mygind, J. 2007. 'Jeg gider ikke tale om religion', *Information*, 2 November.

Rassing, C., J. Buksti. and J. Thulstrup. 2007. *Danskerne 2007 – om overdreven bekymring*. Copenhagen: Institut for Konjunktur-Analyse.

Risbro, J. 2007. 'Asmaa er stor tilhænger af kongehuset', *TV2 Fyn*, 30 April.

Siim, B. and R. Andreassen. 2010. 'Debatter og reguleringer af muslimske tørklæder: Religiøse symboler og populisme', *Politik* 13(4): 15–24.

Skjoldager, M. 2007. 'Asmaa stiller op i homoblad', *Politiken*, 29 October.

Warring, A. 1998. *Tyskerpiger under besættelse og retsopgør*. Copenhagen: Gyldendal.

Winther, B, 2007. 'Kære Asmaa', *Information*, 1 September.

Websites

DR's website: http://www.dr.dk

  http://www.dr.dk/dr2/Adam+og+Asmaa/ (retrieved 1 February 2012).

  http://www.dr.dk/DR2/Adam+og+Asmaa/20060421143549.htm (retrieved 1 February 2012).

Danish National Statistics: http://www.statistikbanken.dk (retrieved 1 February 2012).

The Feminist Forum's website: http://www.feministiskforum.dk

  http://www.feministiskforum.dk/tekster/asmaa.pdf/tekster/asmaa.pdf (retrieved 1 February 2012).

  http://www.feministiskforum.dk/tekster/Modbilleder.html (retrieved 1 February 2012).

http://chromatism.net/current/images/asmaastemme.jpg (retrieved 1 February 2012).

Women for Freedom's website: http://www.kvinderforfrihed.dk

  http://www.kvinderforfrihed.dk/index.php?option=com_content&task=view&id=17&Itemid=2) (retrieved 1 December 2010).

LGBT Denmark's website: http://www.lbl.dk:

  http://www.lbl.dk/fileadmin/site/politik/folketinget/Valg2005.pdf (Politicians' values on homosexuality during election 2005; retrieved on 1 February 2012).

4

FINDING THEIR OWN WAY BETWEEN REVOLUTIONARY ADULT FEMINISM AND WELL-BEHAVED VEILED GIRLHOOD

Female Migrants in Denmark

Malene Fenger-Grøndahl

'Have Danish feminists let their foreign sisters down?' This question has regularly resurfaced in Danish political debate and Danish media, and different answers have been suggested by politicians, chairpersons of women's organizations and feminists of different ages. The debate has generally focused on what responsibility Danish women (mainly white and Christian or non-religious) have regarding the living conditions and individual rights of immigrant women, especially Muslim women. This chapter does not answer that question – one that, I would dare to suggest, does not make much sense and, for that and other reasons, has no clear answer. But the question will serve as a point of departure for the description and analysis that I will present in this chapter.

As a Danish journalist and writer primarily specializing in immigration issues, religion and integration, I have done research in the field of refugees and asylum seekers in Denmark, ethnic minorities in Denmark and other European countries, and the role of religion, culture and sexuality in political debate and the identity-making processes of minority groups. The role of gender is of course also a very relevant component in this field, and I have touched upon it in various parts of my research. In this chapter I will draw on my own research and the research done by primarily Danish scholars in the fields of immigration, religion and sociology, to point out how the dominant Danish self-understanding affects the perception and treatment of immigrant women, and how their possibilities for carving out new identities change in the course of the Danish political debate and the general self-understanding.

The essay will describe in brief the experience of a refugee woman from Chile who was granted political asylum in Denmark shortly after the military coup in Chile on 11 September 1973, before moving almost thirty years forward to consider the effects of the terrorist attacks of 11 September 2001 on the political agenda and the media debate about Islam and Muslim women. Then I will give some examples of how the growing focus on Islam as a potential threat and specific ideas of gender roles among Muslims have worked together with earlier – and new – ideas of feminism to create both barriers and possibilities for migrant women, and Muslim women in particular. Finally, I will summarize how female migrants have reacted to the above-mentioned developments, carving out new identities and strategies to cope with the expectations they have met from different parts of society. This should lead to an understanding of why the question of Danish feminists' possible failure to support female migrants seems to resurface in slight variations over and over again.

On 11 September 1973, a military coup in Chile forced the socialist president Salvador Allende from power and installed a military dictatorship headed by General Augusto Pinochet. In the wake of the coup, tens of thousands of people who had supported the president were persecuted, arrested, tortured and killed. Hundreds of thousands fled, and of these, around 800 ended up in Denmark between 1973 and 1975. Here they were granted political asylum and hence permitted to stay, receiving a limited amount of money and social assistance as well as language teaching and job training. The torture survivors among them, however, were not offered any kind of rehabilitation or treatment, as Danish health authorities at the time had virtually no knowledge of the devastating consequences of torture. Also, the Danish Refugee Council, which was to receive and aid the refugees, had almost no experience in dealing with refugees who were mostly political activists staying in Denmark with the overarching purpose of fighting the military dictator from abroad and supporting comrades and family who were still imprisoned or missing. Nor did the Danish authorities and the Danish Refugee Council have a strategy for receiving and supporting female migrants with backgrounds in both socialist activism and a patriarchal culture with traditional gender roles. At the same time, though, the migrants were welcomed by political grass-roots activists in Denmark who were engaged in solidarity work for Latin America and thus shared many Chilean refugees' visions and ideals – but not their experiences and cultural traditions.

Among the female Chilean refugees arriving in the unprepared Danish society was Maria Sonia Moraga, one of the cases presented in a book about the Danish history of refugees from 1954 to 2004 (Fenger-Grøn and Grøndahl 2004). Maria was one of the victims of the Chilean military dictatorship's suppression of political opposition. Before the coup she was active in the socialist party and spent most of her time engaged in political work. The main goal of her activism was to create a more democratic, more socially and economically equal society, and Maria worked hard to raise the political awareness of poor agricultural labourers and help them organize. She was brought up in a relatively conservative family, and her parents were worried about her safety and about the rumours that might spread because Maria travelled alone and stayed out at night with no husband to take care of her. Partly to gain more freedom of movement, partly out of fascination with the charisma and enthusiasm of one of the male leaders of the party, she asked this leader, Hector, to marry her. He accepted her courtship, and for some years they shared visions, work and everyday life and had two children, a son and a daughter.

After the coup, Maria was arrested twice. The second time she was tortured and forced to promise that she would work as an agent by informing the police force about the activities of her former comrades. Instead, Maria told her party comrades about her situation, and to prevent her from revealing crucial information, they planned her escape, kidnapped her and transported her to the Italian Embassy in Santiago, from where she was taken to Denmark. That was in October 1974.

In Denmark, Maria at first felt as if she had lost all direction in her life: she was in a kind of vacuum, and her identity as political activist, Chilean woman, mother and wife seemed to fall apart. Her physical and mental state was very bad because of the months spent in prison and the torture she had suffered. The Danish Refugee Council offered to place her children, two-year-old Isabel and four-year-old Rodrigo, in a child care centre north of Copenhagen, while Maria stayed at a Copenhagen hotel that housed a group of refugees. She accepted the offer, and for a couple of months she was alone. When she got her children back, she realized they had already adapted to the new situation, learning quite a lot of Danish words and forgetting most of their Spanish. She felt inadequate as a mother, and soon came to feel a failure as a wife, as she had lost contact with her husband, Hector. The two were reunited a couple of years later when he arrived in Denmark, scarred by torture and imprisonment and so changed that Maria felt she did not recognize the man with whom she had spent years of political activism. In Chile, as a member of the socialist party, she had been a member of a strong community where all shared the same goal: a fair socialist society. She also had shared this goal with her friends, her father and her husband. And with her mother and the rest of the family she shared the traditions around cultural festivals and religious feasts.

In Denmark all of this seemed far away, and she felt scared and alone. The feeling of loneliness was lessened, however, by the fact that the Chilean refugees were generally welcomed by a large part of the Danish population who had seen the news from Santiago on television. As early as October 1973, the Danish government decided to look positively on all applications from Chileans asylum seekers. Changes on the political agenda in Denmark favoured the Chileans, too. Left-wing parties and grass-roots movement were quite strong, and the strong anti-Americanism among left-wing politicians and activists was further strengthened in September 1974, when news broke that that CIA had spent 50 billion Danish Kroner on undermining Chile's former president Allende and supporting the right-wing military coup plotters. This awakened even greater sympathy towards the Chilean refugees, not least because they were mostly socialist and communist activists.

Even before Maria arrived in Denmark, members of some Danish left-wing parties had formed a new group called Chilekomiteen and engaged themselves in the cause of the Chilean refugees. Whereas the Danish authorities and the Danish Refugee Council had difficulties dealing with the refugees' strong wish to return to Chile and concentrate on political activism while staying in Denmark, the grass-roots movements were more open towards the refugees' wishes. They understood why the activists spent hours each day listening to the radio, seeking information about their friends and family members in Chile, and why even small details in political opinion could spark fierce discussion among refugees.

Meanwhile, some Danish activists were very keen to share their feminist ideas with the Chilean refugees. Having expected these left-wing activists to agree with them on the issue of gender equality, they were surprised to discover that many of the refugees were still very much influenced by traditional gender roles and Latin-American machismo. In Chile even the most left-wing socialist and communist parties were generally led by men, the women mainly taking lower positions in the hierarchy. Men made the speeches and were supposed to take responsibility for protecting female members of the party. Maria's marriage to Hector had partially resulted from the general idea that women needed someone to protect them. Also, most female refugees had been dependent on the incomes of husbands, fathers and brothers while living in Chile.

All this changed in diaspora in Denmark. Whereas female refugees were 'embraced' by their Danish 'sisters' and 'brothers', male refugees were regarded with suspicion and sometimes even strong aversion because they did not fit into the Danish conception of gender equality.

They were expected to give way to the women by stepping aside to let their female counterparts take part in political activism on the same level as them. Many male refugees found these expectations difficult if not impossible to live up to, and they felt humiliated by their inability to regain their former importance in a political movement, due to both the gender equality issue and their lack of linguistic capabilities in Danish and English. Many did not want to learn Danish, as they expected – or at least hoped – to return to Chile soon, and for the same reason they did not want to start over with higher education. Thus male architects, engineers and the like witnessed the erosion of their status and importance as political activists, breadwinners and members of society. This made their dream of repatriation even stronger.

For female Chilean refugees, the situation was almost the opposite. Most of them did not have higher education and did not expect life in diaspora to give them education, economic independence or high-ranking positions in a political movement. For many, life in diaspora opened unexpected new doors, giving them a chance to learn new skills, receive formal education and become economically independent. They could gain new ground and at the same time more or less continue their job as mothers. Many struggled to learn a new language and had a hard time adjusting to Danish society and its changing norms, which differed greatly from what they were used to in Chile. But generally they were happy to have the chance to get jobs in new sectors that grew rapidly these years: as more and more Danish women entered the labour market, more and more people were needed to clean houses and care for children and elderly people, work the female Chilean refugees performed very competently. Meanwhile, many of them were influenced by the Danish left-wing and feminist agendas. Women their own age urged them to demand more freedom and equality in their marriages, often telling them to divorce husbands who refused to allow them more freedom or assume their responsibilities when it came to child care and housework.

Some Chilean women found this far too much, wondering why issues of gender equality and free sexuality were so important to the Danish feminists when in Chile, both men and women were imprisoned and tortured and thus were far from even thinking about how to deal with gender roles in everyday life. Others took to divorce rather quickly, inspired by their Danish feminist friends and frustrated with the way some seemed to cling to the dream of returning to Chile, even after it should have been clear to everybody that this aim would be unrealizable for many years to come. The difficulties of finding a new way of living together as a family after years of torture and imprisonment also played a role in many divorces between couples from Chile. Many years later, some Chilean women regretted that they had not had more patience with their husbands, having let themselves become overexcited by the agenda of the Danish left-wing parties and feminist groups.

In this regard, Maria was somewhat special, as she had already been aware of the gender equality issue while in Chile. She mainly married to gain more freedom, and while incarcerated in a women's prison became more conscious of the importance of strong solidarity among women. Many of her co-inmates had been raped and humiliated by male prison guards, which brought Maria to realize that suppression and political liberation was also a matter of gender. Meeting the same idea among Danish women, regardless of age, language and cultural barriers, gave her a sense of belonging that she otherwise struggled to gain in a country where she did not know the culture or speak the language well.

Maria took different jobs as an unskilled labourer and worked hard. Even though her employers did not always treat her well, she was happy to earn her own money, and it made sense to her to try to create a new life for her and her two children in Denmark. Her marriage with Hector, on the other hand, was unhappy, and when she revealed some of their problems to her Danish friends, they encouraged her to divorce her husband and liberate herself through the Western concept of feminism. But Maria hesitated. For many years she accepted Hector's increasingly depressed and passive attitude and his outbursts of rage, knowing that he was marked by torture and imprisonment and understanding that his pride as a man and a human being was hurt because he had no role to play in a political movement in Denmark and could not even fulfil his role as a breadwinner. Only after fifteen years in diaspora did Maria and Hector divorce. Since then, Maria has often wondered if she should have made this decision much earlier. Once general amnesty was granted to allow political refugees to return to Chile, Hector decided to move back.

A few years later, Maria's daughter Isabel – now an adult – decided to do the same. Though disappointed about her daughter's decision to leave the country where she had fought to create better living conditions for her, Maria was also proud of her daughter's courage and even smiled upon recognizing the mild irony that her daughter was now liberating herself by leaving her mother and moving back to her country of origin.

Maria's son, on the other hand, had difficulty finding his way in life. In his late teens he started hanging out with other young male immigrants who felt alienated and unwanted in society. He started using drugs, and soon Maria realized her son was a drug addict. After several years spent trying to get him out of his addiction, at last she succeeded. Soon afterwards her son converted to Islam, seeking moral and practical guidelines for his life in an Islamist group called Hizb ut-Tahrir, which at the time was known for its ability to get young men of immigrant background back on track after years as drug addicts or members of criminal gangs. Maria, for her part, was happy to see her son saved from drug addiction, but at the same time she was sorry to see him embracing a religion she found too rigid and old-fashioned. She particularly regretted that he had joined Hizb ut-Tahrir, which was also known for its rather illiberal interpretation of the Quran and either separating men and women at meetings or holding meetings in study groups for men and for women.

A somewhat ironic coincidence was that Maria and her children's life in diaspora began at a turning point for gender and integrations issues in Danish political life. Shortly after her arrival in Denmark, she heard of Chilean men being denied access to meetings in the Danish women's movement, a big shock to both male and female Chilean refugees. And she remembers that many Chileans were shocked at the open debates about homosexuality and the Danish law permitting abortion. Some thirty years later, Maria sees how female refugees and immigrants of Middle Eastern and African (mainly Somali) origin fight for their right to wear the veil publicly and to organize separate meetings, swimming lessons and the like for women. She also sees how some young female Muslim immigrants claim to wear the veil as an expression of individual freedom. She is herself active in the movement Women in Black, which organizes demonstrations and campaigns in solidarity with suppressed women and female victims of war worldwide. She is a bit bewildered as how to react to young Muslim women in Denmark, who claim that their fight for freedom is a fight for religious rights and a fight for the right to cover up.

Especially since 9/11 Maria sees how Muslim immigrants are often suspected of being aspiring terrorists or at least of supporting terrorism. She notices that both politicians and citizens of various political orientation encourage Islamists, like the members of Hizb ut-Tahrir, to leave Denmark if they disagree with the laws, regulations and order of Danish society. She sees a parallel with the discussions going on after her arrival in Denmark in the 1970s, when right-wing groups cited Chilean refugees' arrival in Denmark as 'proof' that capitalism had shown its superiority to socialism and communism. In the autumn of 1976, for example, the weekly magazine *Minut* ran an article under the headline 'Red Refugees Do Not Want to Go to the Soviet Union' that stated that 'socialism is something that is discussed, not a reality that people want to live.' The piece accused the refugees of ruining their own homelands with socialist activism while also bad-mouthing the Western capitalist countries where they sought refuge.

In 2003, Maria took part in anti-war demonstrations in the wake of the start of the war on Iraq. She believes the terrorist attacks of 9/11 are now misused as a pretext to declare war on innocent civilians, and she finds it a strange coincidence that the Chilean coup that ultimately brought her to Denmark took place on exactly the same date twenty-eight years earlier.

Now, over a decade since the beginning of the war in Iraq and still longer since the 9/11 attacks, the headscarf issue and the debates about Islam, Islamism and its perceived threat to democracy and Western concepts of a liberal and free society are still quite heated. Issues of Islam and Islamism, and of Muslim women's position both globally and in Denmark, often rank high on the political agenda as well. They resurface in discussions of developments in Iraq, Afghanistan, Egypt, Libya and Tunisia, and often factor into discussions of gender equality, integration of immigrants and secularism versus religious freedom.

In general, both female and male Muslim newcomers to Denmark and children of Muslim immigrants are expected to fit into a new political agenda that views Islam as a threat to democracy and gender equality. The tests and teaching materials presented to newcomers in Denmark as part of their 'integration process' contain questions about gender equality and sexual liberty as well as about whether the newcomer intends to respect the norms of gender equality and to respect the Danish constitution over religious codes of conduct. Most of these regulations were formulated with specific reference to perceived and real problems of violence against, and suppression of, girls and women in migrant families. Examples of violence, forced marriages and social control of girls have generally been at least partly explained with reference to the negative impact of 'Islamic culture', Muslim traditions, suppression of women in Muslim societies and the like.

Some immigrants and refugees of Muslim background agree with this and see Denmark as a free haven, which they will fight to preserve as a place where religion in general and Islam in particular should not have a say in public affairs. This applies for some Iranian refugees in Denmark who fled the suppressive so-called Islamic regime in Iran. For most Muslim immigrants and their children, though, being Muslim is an important part of their identity, and unlike the very few exceptions, such as the members of Hizb ut-Tahrir, they see Islam, democracy and modernism as compatible dimensions of their life in Denmark.

Yet over and over again, these Muslims meet with scepticism and direct or indirect allegations about Islam and democracy being incompatible. Even mainstream media journalists sometimes present Islam and democracy, or Muslim identity and Danish identity (or 'Danishness'), as contradictory. One example is a survey commissioned by the Danish Broadcasting Corporation that made television news in 2005 after the infamous 'cartoon crisis' was ignited by twelve cartoons of the Prophet Mohammed published in the daily newspaper *Jyllands-Posten* in March 2005. The survey question was: 'Do you think that the Mohammed cartoons have deepened the divide between Danes and Muslims?'

Many Muslims in Denmark regard this question as based on an absurd argument that the categories Danish and Muslim are equal and oppposed to one another. Many Muslim immigrants are already Danish citizens, and thus officially both Muslim and Danish, and often the younger generations were born in Denmark and have lived most or all of their lives there. Others are converts to Islam, but we will leave them out of the discussion here. A large number of the 200,000 or so Muslims living in Denmark would describe themselves as both Muslim and Danish, or maybe as Muslim Danes with Arabic, Somali, Kurdish, Turkish, Pakistani or Iraqi background. But at the same time they feel that they do not have the right of self-definition. One example of this is given in the book *Muslimsk-Dansk dagbog - 19 dagbøger fra Muhammed-krisen* (Muslim-Danish Diary: 19 Diaries from the Mohammed Crisis), which appeared in 2006. As the title suggests, the book contains nineteen personal reflections by Danish Muslims about the cartoon crisis and its effect on their lives. One contributor, Fatma Yeliz Öktem Simsek, defines herself as an '*Aarhusianer*' (a person from Aarhus, Denmark's second biggest city) and calls herself 'Danish/Turkish/democrat/Muslim and much else'. She describes how Danish public discourse limits her right to define herself as such and states: 'I do not like when the two sides of me (the Muslim and the Danish) are made to confront. I hate that feeling. I felt the same way after September 11th. I feel the pain of being hit twice. If I think it is stupid of *Jyllands-Posten* to publish the cartoons, does it than mean that I am not a democrat? And if I understand that they have the right to publish the cartoons, does it then mean that I am not a good Muslim?'

The discussion of how Islam can or cannot be combined with democracy, gender equality and liberal freedoms is complex and will not be entered into here. Suffice it to say that the discussion has frequently topped the political agenda in Denmark since 9/11. The change in world view is exemplified by the change in the mainstream media's interest in and description of the above-mentioned Islamic group Hizb ut-Tahrir.

Just two days before the 9/11 attacks, a full-page article in the daily newspaper *Politiken* described the positive effects of Hizb ut-Tahrir's proselyting among Muslim youth in the suburbs of Copenhagen as convincing criminals to put their illegal activities behind them and engage themselves in Islamic teaching and a moral lifestyle. But after the terrorist attacks, the fear of more such attacks of same kind fostered a great media interest in identifying radical Islamist groups in Denmark, including Hizb ut-Tahrir, as a possible breeding ground for terrorism. The group's message of social responsibility was totally forgotten, and the focus was now on its radical teachings, its possible plans of a violent revolt and its 'medieval' custom of separating men and women.

The discussion about terrorism, Islamism, Islam, Muslims, human rights, religious freedom, secularism and the like has shifted its focus many times since then, but one of the prevailing issues has been that of the headscarf or the veiling of women – a debate very often placed in the context of the debate about the relationship between politics and religion in general. Several European countries have had the headscarf issue on their political agendas, with some of the same questions being debated repeatedly, though with slight differences according to the political situation and the religious landscapes in the given country, as described in the anthology *Tørklædet som tegn* (Degn and Søholm 2011). In Denmark, part of the debate concerns which political or religious messages the veil can be said to send to the public, and whether a girl or a woman is able to choose the veil of her own free will. Some see the veil as a symbol of Islamism and a culture of suppression of women, or even as a symbol of anti-democratic values. This was especially so in the case of the politician Asma Abdol-Hamid, who was a candidate for Parliament for the left-wing party Enhedslisten (see Rikke Andreassen's chapter in this book). It has often been suggested that girls or young women who wear the veil are more or less directly forced to do so by their parents, and that wearing the veil should and will limit their opportunities to work as, for example, doctors, nurses or judges. In December 2003 the Conservative Party urged local authorities and schools to adopt rules forbidding Muslim girls and young women to wear a veil at school or to work at municipal jobs. The party's spokesperson on immigration issues, Else Theill Sørensen, was quoted in the daily newspaper *Politiken* (19 December 2003) saying that, 'We cannot accept that young immigrant women's chances of integrating into the Danish society are diminished because their parents keep them in an environment based on bigotry and intolerance.'

The discourse of Muslim (veiled) girls and women being victims of suppression by elder (primarily male) generations of Muslim immigrants is quite familiar in the Danish political debate. Whereas Muslim men, perhaps parallel to the male Chilean refugees, are seen as a violent threat to the societal order and to the girls and women in their families, Muslim women – maybe partially parallel to the female Chilean refugees – are seen as victims of male dominance and religious and cultural traditions, from which Danish society (especially Danish women and even more so the feminists among them) are somewhat expected to liberate them.

Thus we return to the introductory question of whether Danish feminists have let their foreign sisters down. Most Muslim girls interviewed by Karen-Lise Johansen for her book *Muslimske stemmer* (Muslim Voices) do not find the question relevant. They do not see themselves mainly as passive victims formed by parents or other people's choices, but as free agents of their own lives, consciously balancing between different loyalties and interests to find their own way of being Muslim girls and women in Denmark. As for veiling, several of them explain that they consciously chose to wear or not wear the veil, unlike their mothers, who more or less just followed the customs and habits of their village or family. One Muslim girl explains her relationship to her parents:

> My mother doesn't wear the veil, but I have chosen to wear it, because I think that it is the right thing to do. Sometimes my parents ask me if I am really able to cope with it and follow the way I have chosen, but then I just tell them that this is how it is to follow Islam. I reflect on why I do what I do and what lies behind the religious acts. When you grow up in an Islamic country, you take things more for granted, but here I am forced to find out what my religion stands for. I don't want to just continue an empty ritual, which my parents have been taught to follow. (Johansen 2002: 66)

Several girls in Johansen's survey explain that they started wearing their veil regardless of their parents' wishes. They also describe how their parents often express scepticism and wonder or anxiety about the consequences of wearing the veil.

Muslim women wearing the veil may also meet with reactions from people who feel provoked by the veil, assuming that wearing it is some kind of anti-democratic statement. Or they might get reactions from social workers or teachers, who advise them to take off the veil to enhance their chances of getting a good education and a good job. Incidents of Somali women being told not to have too-high ambitions about education as long as they wear a veil were documented by anthropologist Christina B. Jagd in her Ph.D. thesis on Danish-Somali citizens in Denmark and their efforts to build a meaningful life in Danish society by means of paid work (Jagd 2007).

Descriptions of the girls as victims of suppression have often been the departure point for special social projects aimed at liberating or helping supposedly suppressed Muslim girls. Some of these projects have focused on directly liberating the girls by helping them leave home others have created 'free spaces' for the girls by establishing clubs where the girls can go after school to have fun with other girls, do their homework and be introduced to parts of society their parents have not introduced them to. These so-called girls' clubs have proved to work well when established in cooperation with the girls themselves and in dialogue with their parents. Often the parents' acceptance has hinged strictly on their certainty that the girls would not be exposed to alcohol or socialize with boys. As anthropologist Marianne Nøhr Larsen recounted in her book *De små oprør* (The Small Revolts), parents also often stressed that the club should not just be 'for fun' but instead help the girls with homework and prepare them for higher education. At the same time, though, the girls might, as mentioned above, be warned that wearing the veil could keep them from getting the education they want.

The warnings and pressure on the girls and women to take off the veil seems, however, to have contradictory results or none at all. Although to date there are no statistics on the numbers of girls and women wearing the veil, there is general agreement that the share of veiled Muslim girls and women is on the rise, in Denmark as in many other countries. Part of the explanation might be that some Muslim girls and women react to the often heated debate on Islam with a stronger Muslim identity, which they express visually with the veil.

The Catínet survey agency's *IntegrationsIndex* survey, conducted annually since 2002 among immigrants (mainly from Muslim countries), shows rising religiosity in the youngest group of respondents (aged 15–29), which now ranks as the most religious age cohort. Another Catinét survey, *IntrationsStatus 2007*, based on interviews with 1,002 persons (81 per cent of them Muslims), found that 42 per cent of the female Muslim migrants considered it very important to wear a headscarf, whereas 48 per cent answered that it was not important or not important at all. Of the Muslim male respondents, 66 per cent said it was not important or not important at all whether their wife wore a headscarf, whereas only 29 per cent said they found it important or very important. And just 22 per cent of Muslim men and 29 per cent of Muslim women said they found it important or very important that their daughter wear a headscarf. The survey showed that it women from Lebanon, Palestine, Somalia and Iraq were particularly likely to wear headscarves.

In general, many young female Muslims who wear the veil seem to do so not because of pressure from their parents or husband, but rather as a result of an individual decision, probably often taken as part of an identity-building process in which being Danish, modern and Muslim are keywords in the young women's self-understanding. They sometimes contrast this to their parents' identity, which is often based more on the ethnicity and nationality of the country of origin than on a global Muslim identity or a feeling of belonging to Denmark.

Sometimes the girls even, as both Johansen (2002) and Nøhr Larsen (2004) describe, use Islam as a trump card when negotiating the limits of their self-determination with their parents. They might use Islam to sway their parents' opinion on something perceived as too 'Danish', 'Westernized' or 'liberal' for a good Muslim girl, be it social activities at school or freedom to choose a spouse. It seems Muslim girls tend to prefer a Muslim spouse, but they might not want to marry a cousin or a person with the same ethnic background, whereas their parents – who may also prefer a Muslim son-in-law – primarily want their daughter to marry someone with the same ethnic and linguistic background; also, they might be accustomed to arranged marriages and expect their daughters to accept their choice of spouse. In such situations some Muslim girls point to interpretations of Islam that stress the importance of freedom of choice and emphasize that Islam is universal and not ethnocentric; thus they expose the parents' focus on ethnicity as 'un-Islamic'.

When it comes to education, some Muslim girls face difficulties getting permission to take part in social activities at school. Here, some of them might chose to wear the veil to appear 'modest' and thus protect themselves against gossip, or they might play the 'the Prophet said…' card, as explained by Hatice, a Turkish girl who, as a teenager, wanted to attend parties at her high school, but whose father would not let her take part in social activities involving alcohol. She used religious arguments and referred to her parents' wish to see the family improve their social and economic conditions:

> I explained to my father that according to Islam everybody has to seek knowledge and education, even if they have go as far as China to achieve it a saying about the Prophet refers to his telling believers to seek knowledge, even if that meant they had to go to China…). I also explained to my father that group work and social activities mean a lot in the Danish educational system. I almost gave him the impression that if I did not attend the parties, it would be the same as truancy, and so I would risk getting lower grades. He accepted that explanation. So I was permitted to attend the parties as long as I promised not to drink, and if I came home early. For me it was an acceptable compromise. And I made an equivalent compromise when I was to choose my education. It was quite clear that I would never be allowed to move from Odense to Copenhagen and live

on my own; that would simply cause too much gossip among the friends and acquaintances of my parents, if they let their daughter live on her own without keeping an eye on her. So I had to give up my dream of studying political science and instead study economics, which I could study in Odense. So the compromise was that I stayed in Odense and lived with my parents, and apart from that I really have a lot of freedom. (Mikkelsen, Fenger-Grøndahl and Shakoor 2010: 284–85)

Indeed, many girls are given quite a lot of freedom and can, for example, postpone the time of marriage as long as they fulfil the expectations of a 'good Muslim girl'. Education is thus often a tool to get more knowledge and freedom and 'win some time' before the question of marriage gets urgent. Sometimes education might even lead girls who were not previously allowed to live alone to leave their parents' home and live alone for a while. As a young woman of Pakistani origin put it, when asked about changes in family life among the Pakistanis she knows in Denmark and the different degrees of freedom granted to daughters and sons:

> For women it is different. They can't just move away from home. They are expected to stay at their parents' place until they get married, and then they move to their in-laws' or get their own flat where they live with their husband. But in some cases the girls are allowed to move away from home if they are going to study in another city. Typically, the family then arranges for the girl to rent a room at some relatives' place or find a flat that the girl possibly shares with another Pakistani girl. To move to a college is almost unthinkable for the girls. The parents are simply more insecure about letting a girl live alone and in general they don't fancy the thought of a girl being unmarried for a long time. I guess they most of all fear that she will have boyfriends or have sex before marriage. For the boys they fear instead that they will drink alcohol or not study seriously. Such worries also play a role when it comes to letting their sons or daughters move away from home or not. (Mikkelsen, Fenger-Grøndahl and Shakoor 2010: 189)

Pakistani parents' worries about their boys seem relevant in the face of recent surveys on ethnic minority youth and educational trends. A survey by Catinét (cited in Mikkelsen et al. 2010: 198–99) shows that girls in the group aged 15–19 spend more time on homework and religious activities than their male counterparts, who tend to spend more time away from home. The difference seems to get smaller the older they get, but in general, young women invest more time and resources in intellectual activities like homework, studies and reading books.

Anthropological studies in primary schools in Denmark indicate that Muslim girls are not merely forced by their parents to be good girls and good students; rather, they choose this identity because it is one of very few 'roles' that are open to Muslim girls. As the girls grow older, they have to choose among different 'roles' offered by teachers and other students. Muslim girls are simply expected to behave in a certain way, and these expectations largely fit their parents' ideas of a well-behaved Muslim girl. Dorthe Staunæs elucidates this mechanism in her book *Køn, etncitet og skoleliv* (Staunæs 2004) (*Gender, Ethnicity and School Life*) in accordance with a study done by anthropologist Laura Gilliam. Gilliam's book (2009), *De umulige børn og det ordentlige menneske; identitet, ballade og muslimske fællesskaber blandt etniske minoritetsbørn* (Badly Behaved Children and the Proper Man; Identity, Fuss and Muslim Communities Among Ethnic Minority Children), focuses on immigrant (mainly Muslim) boys in primary school, showing how teachers' negative expectations and negative, stereotypical descriptions of Muslim boys in the media form the self-understanding of Muslim boys, many of whom 'choose' to play the role of 'troublemaker'. Whereas the girls behave 'well', doing their homework and trying to live up to their parents' positive expectations, the boys 'choose' to live up to the negative expectations, thereby attracting considerable negative attention from teachers, social workers and the like, but also gaining a lot of street credibility.

The different roles and strategies adopted by girls and boys are described in the book *I Danmark Er Jeg Født...(In Denmark I Was Born...)* (Mikkelsen et al. 2010). Generally it concludes that the women are doing better than the men in terms of education. Meanwhile, the boys' many activities outside the family home give them a chance to strengthen their identity in a group of like-minded boys, and the self-esteem they acquire in this way tends to compensate for the lack of positive response in school. Furthermore, it seems that in some immigrant families, boys' ability to earn money to help raise the family's economic status in the short term counts for more than does a long education – maybe because both parents and sons lack confidence that a long education will lead to a well-paid job.

Many different factors are probably in play, but those mentioned above might be of greater importance in explaining the hard fact that with further education, girls earn better results than boys. As the publication *Indvandrere i Danmark 2009* concludes: 'During the last 10 years there has been a remarkable rise in the share of 20-year-old non-Western immigrants pursuing an education. Among the men 37 per cent are educated today compared to 30 per cent in 1999. The rise been even stronger among the female non-Western immigrants: 41 per cent are educated in 2008 compared to 23 per cent in 1999' (Danmarks Statistik 2010).

In this context it is also relevant to mention a generational change among female migrants. While only 49 per cent of female immigrants aged 30–35 are employed or seeking job, more than 75 per cent of second-generation female immigrants aged 30–35 are employed or looking for a job. Young women of immigrant origin tend not to follow in their mothers' footsteps but rather enter the labour market. When asked how they have managed to get an education and a job, these girls often even point to their mothers as their most important source of inspiration and support (Mikkelsen et al. 2010: 118–48). Migrant women's role in their daughters' educational success contradicts the idea, generally held by politicians and social workers in Denmark, that uneducated migrant women who are not employed outside the home will influence their daughters to marry at an early age and spend their lives as housewives.

Overall, the family pattern changes quite quickly among Muslim migrants, and in many ways it increasingly resembles the pattern of the majority population. Immigrants live in smaller families than before and marry at higher ages, and the divorce rate is on the rise, as is women's educational level. However, it seems that for both girls and boys, the number of 'roles' to choose from is limited if they want to balance the expectations of their own families against those of the majority society. Girls seem able to find some success by choosing the role of a well-behaved Muslim girl, whom the parents perceive as modest and loyal to the family and the majority society perceives as well behaved, though maybe also suppressed and in need of 'rescue' by Danish feminists.

In conclusion, it seems that negative perceptions of Islamic women's status and of the veil might in some ways have a negative influence on Muslim girls and women. But at the same time, they open new opportunities. Apart from the sympathy and understanding these girls will most probably receive if they actually seek their Danish sisters' help in freeing themselves from the bonds of family or religion, the image of the veiled Muslim girl can also – as we have seen – create a space for liberation through education.

Returning again to this chapter's opening question of whether Danish feminists have let their foreign sisters down, another question seems perhaps more relevant: Has Danish society let down male Muslim immigrants, as it let down male Chilean refugees forty years ago? Alternatively: Has Danish society let female migrants down by offering them only a limited number of 'roles' to play or identities to take on?

Just as relevant, however, is this question: How do female Muslim migrants (and their daughters) react to the expectations they face? Of course, the extensive research required to answer this question is not in the scope of this essay. It must suffice to mention that while some Muslim women adapt to expectations by playing the role of 'well-behaved' Muslim girls, other Muslim women challenge the expectations in different ways. For example, the above-mentioned woman of Turkish origin, Fatma Yeliz Öktem Simsek, has defended Muslim sisters' right to wear the veil, even though she does not wear it herself. A member of Parliament for the liberal party Venstre, she has for many years been engaged in the public debate about gender equality, integration and social issues, and was a leading figure in the establishment of an umbrella organization for ethnic minority women's organizations in 2009.

Another woman of Turkish origin, Yildiz Akdogan, was one of two Social Democrats of Turkish background who became the first female Muslim members of the Danish parliament from 2007 to 2011. She is active in women's issues as well as in European politics and immigration politics. In an interview (parts of which were published in Mikkelsen et al. 2010) she explained the motivation behind her political engagement:

> History shows us that we need to keep on fighting to make sure that our society will be one of solidarity and welfare. Had the women's movement not come into being, had no women taken to the streets and burnt their bras and demanded equality, we wouldn't have had formal equality before the law today. Had the workers not joined forces and fought for better conditions, then the conditions on the labour market would have been very different from what we see today. I fight to preserve the pillars of our welfare society, and then it is also of outmost importance to me to break down the cliché image of female immigrants being passive and suppressed. Regarding social politics I am preoccupied with the conditions of female immigrants. And I am very keen on finding out how to help the young men. It has dawned on me, that while we have all focused a lot on 'the poor women', then the boys have lagged behind, when it comes to education, employment etc. The question is whether we are about to create a new underclass of young men with no education. (*In Denmark I Was Born*: 408)

The case of Yildiz Akdogan might be the best answer to the question with which we started. Maybe the Danish feminists have let down the female Muslim migrants. But many of them have found their own way, carving out new possibilities and new multilayered identities. Many successful female migrants are aware that not of all their sisters are able to succeed similarly, and that they and their male counterparts too need support and help – not mainly within a feminist framework, but within one that allots space for multiple interpretations and conceptions of Islam, Danishness, womanhood and manhood. Such a framework would accommodate both the Chilean refugee woman with socialist aspirations and a background in a traditional Catholic society and the Muslim girl of Turkish or Pakistani origin with a Danish passport.

References

Danmarks Statistik. 2010. *Indvandrere i Danmark 2009*. Copenhagen: Danmarks Statistik.

Degn, I. and K.M. Søholm (eds). 2011. *Tørklædet som tegn; tilsløring og demokrati i en globaliseret verden*. Aarhus: Aarhus Universitetsforlag.

Gilliam, L. 2009. *De umulige børn og det ordentlige menneske; identitet, ballade og muslimske fællesskaber blandt etniske minoritetsbørn*. Aarhus: Aarhus Universitetsforlag.

Grøndahl, M. and C. Fenger-Grøn. 2004. *Flygtningenes danmarkshistorie 1954– 2004*. Aarhus: Aarhus Universitetsforlag.

Jagd, C. Bækkelund. 2007. 'Medborger eller modborger? Dansksomalieres kamp for at opbygge en meningsfuld tilværelse i det danske samfund – gennemt et arbejde', Ph.D. thesis. Copenhagen: Institut for Antropologi, Københavns Universitet.

Johansen, K.L. 2002. *Muslimske stemmer; religiøs forandring blandt unge muslimer i Danmark*. Copenhagen: Akademisk Forlag.

Mikkelsen, F., M. Fenger-Grøndahl and T.R. Shakoor. 2010. *'I Danmark er jeg født...' Etniske minoritetsunge i bevægelse*. Frederiksberg: Frydenlund.

Nøhr Larsen, M. 2004. *De små oprør; tanker og metoder i arbejdet med minoritetspiger*. Aarhus: Aarhus Universitetsforlag.

Staunæs, D. 2004. *Køn, etnicitet og skoleliv*. Frederiksberg: Samfundslitteratur.

5

Gendered Experiences of Homeland, Identity and Belonging among the Kurdish Diaspora

Minoo Alinia

Introduction

This chapter discusses the impact of gender on experiences of migration, on diasporic identity and the sense of 'home' and belonging. It is based on a larger study of the Kurdish diaspora, carried out in Sweden (Alinia 2004). The study's overall purpose was to investigate displacement, deterritorialization, exclusion and their impact on identity formation. Its primary focus was Kurdish diasporic experiences, identities and movements from the perspective of the people involved. Several so-called first-generation Kurdish women and men, settled mainly in Gothenburg, were interviewed about their experiences of and relation to Swedish society, their 'homeland' and the Kurdish diasporic community. The study found differences between the respondents' articulations of their experiences with regard to gender and politics. This essay focuses on the internal differences within the Kurdish diaspora in regard to gender and with a particular focus on women's experiences.

Boundaries of the Kurdish Diaspora

Seen as a complex social process, diaspora is characterized by two major elements. The first is the existential relation to a home(land),[1] a homing desire and a need for 'home' and belonging that occupies a central place in people's daily lives and identities. However, this should be understood in its context to avoid essentialization of the relation between identity and territory. Exile, exclusion and homing desire are closely related and can partly explain feelings of homing desire and homeland orientation. The second is the formation of a collective identity and collective actions around issues of home(land) and community formation (Alinia 2004, 2007). Diaspora is thereby not only characterized by homing desire and feelings of homelessness, but also includes an active identity politics, collective action and activism. In a broad perspective, all diasporic experiences imply these two central elements as characteristics of a diaspora (ibid.). Departing from Melucci's definition of social movement (Melucci 1991), diaspora can be defined as a system of action and, as such, a social movement. I regard diaspora as a social movement that can be distinguished as a transnational movement oriented towards home(land) and community formation (Alinia 2004, 2007).

Social movements challenge and exceed the boundaries of the social system within which they act and bring about social change (Melucci 1991). They imply three very closely related dimensions: solidarity, social conflict and social change (ibid.). The collective identity as a point of solidarity, or 'we-identity', is used to identify antagonists and opponents both inside and outside the movement. The apparent unity or we-identity should be seen as a result, rather than a point of departure. Collective action as the manifest level of a social movement is based, according to Melucci, at the latent level of the social networks of everyday life, where alternative meanings and identities are formed (ibid.). Thörn discerns two dimensions in the process of identity construction within social movements: an inward and an outward. Outwardly, collective identities are constructed in terms of difference and in opposition to other collectives. Inwardly, collective identities are constructed through contradictory interactions between individuals and groups that constitute different standpoints within the movement (Thörn 1997: 115). The respondents' identities, and their experiences of and relations to Swedish society and the Kurdish community, are therefore not unambiguous but ambivalent and complex.

Departing from an intersectional perspective (Collins 2009) it can be said that diaspora members are located not only in terms of ethnic category, but also in terms of gender, sexuality, class and generation, which together constitute main sources of their oppression in Sweden and also generate various kinds of subjectivity, knowledge and experience. Thus the Kurdish identity that outwardly appears as uniform and homogeneous includes many internal divisions and differences. Furthermore, these categories do not exist in a vacuum, but are included in, and interact with, social and political processes that always imply power dimensions. These categories are not isolated either, but intersect and affect each other.

Experiences of and Relation to Sweden as Citizen and Immigrant 'Other'

Political Freedom and Social Mobility

Like other immigrant groups in Sweden, Kurds have access to formal citizenship and enjoy different degrees of citizenship rights. However, the concept of citizenship becomes more complicated when we go beyond the merely administrative definition and look at the principles on which it is constructed, namely, principles of descent, *jus sanguinis*, or of territoriality, *jus solis*, that is, ethnic and civic definitions of citizenship (Hammar 1990). Furthermore, the respondents talk about Swedish citizenship in formal, legal terms to indicate that informally they are denied belonging as fully adequate citizens. The younger, so-called second generation shares these experiences (Eliassi 2010). The gap between formal citizenship and substantial citizenship shows how the boundaries of Swedishness and Swedish citizenship are constituted (ibid.).

Schierup and Ålund (2011: 56), discussing citizenship and politics of belonging in Sweden, argue that the two last decades have 'step by step, led towards neoliberal disciplinary strategies, neoconservative moral reaffirmation and the erosion of a comprehensive citizenship pact.' However, respondents' experiences are complex and multi-faceted. It is not uncommon for respondents to have experienced democracy for the first time in their lives in Sweden, something they appreciate and talk about as a positive aspect of living in Sweden. This should mainly be seen in relation to their experiences of their countries of origin, a frequent point of reference and comparison. When the respondents talk about the advantages of living in Sweden, they refer mainly to democratic rights and what they mean for their political and personal advancement. Shapol recounted her experience of living in Sweden:

> There are many things here that I really appreciate. I feel that I have improved here. We were brought up in a system where you were not allowed to think by yourself and you did not dare to express yourself. All essays that we wrote in school had to be about Saddam Hussein and the Baath party. ... Here I feel that I have advanced, my personality has improved, and I have become more mature. Maybe it is because I have become older, I don't know. ... In this society there is really freedom but it has to be used in the right way.

For his part, Goran talked about his surprise upon his first encounter with the Swedish authorities:

> In Sweden, for example, the first time when the police wanted to talk to me, they asked me if I wanted to have a Kurdish or a Turkish translator. I was very surprised that this was so important in Sweden. Later I real-

ized that here there were both Kurds and Turks. I didn't know before, to be honest.... Living in Sweden has been very good for me in order to find my identity. It is very important. Here there is more freedom to read whatever you want; to see whatever you want; to discuss. It is very important to meet whoever you want without being afraid. It is a very nice environment. It has been a very nice environment for me. It influenced me in a positive way. However, I can't say that it also influenced my relationship to Sweden in a positive way.

As citizens and quasi-citizens, regardless of their migrant position, women have certain social and legal rights in Sweden that are not always taken for granted in their countries of origin. This affects gender relations by shifting the power relations within the family in favour of women (Alinia 2004; Darvishpour 2002). Further, these rights impact women's relation to Sweden. Compared to men, women show a more positive and open relation to Sweden and are more willing to, as they say, 'adapt' to Swedish society. Another point of difference between women and men is social mobility and how they handle it. People's experience of social mobility differs depending on their social background in their homelands. However, clear distinctions mark how women and men handle the situation. Men more often suffer from downward social mobility in countries of settlement as they often lose their status as men and as the head of the family. Women also lose their positions and their social networks, both of which they regard as important, but they seem to accept this more easily – perhaps because they appreciate the rights they have gained as women. Bahar said:

> I also feel that I have lost many things, my identity, my social position, and my social networks and so on. But maybe women are more patient and can handle difficulties better than men. Women in our societies are oppressed, whereas we have more rights here. Another thing is that for women in general it is easier to adapt to new conditions, while this is very difficult for men.... Here there are positive things for women as for example in relation to divorce and children and things like that.

Women's stronger self-conception, self-confidence and feelings of continuity in their identities may be partly due to the continuity of their role as mothers and caretakers. As mothers, they have still the main responsibility for their children. This also forces them to come in contact with society, learn the language and become better informed. Motherhood can also provide a sense of continuity in their lives and identities. Men, on the other hand, tend to lose the continuity of their identity to a greater extent, as their roles and identities are mostly associated with their profession and/or their position in the family, society and politics. They are discouraged by the downward mobility they experience within both the family and society, as well as their experiences of everyday racism.

Racism and Exclusion

When talking about immigration and the movement of people, it is crucial to locate movement and identify who moves, where, why and under what circumstances (Brah 1996). The focus should be not only on mobility itself, but also its location within the regime of power and stratification in a global context. By immigrant, I mean the category of non-Western immigrants to which my respondents belong. Irrespective of gender, as immigrants they are both systematically excluded from the society and subjected to the discourses and practices of everyday racism (Statens Offentliga Utredningar 2004–2006; Jonsson 2010; Alinia 2011; Ålund and Alinia 2011; Eliassi 2010; Schierup and Ålund 2011). The juridical status of citizenship does not automatically mean that immigrants are regarded as equal members of society. Moreover, colonial conceptions of East and West, and South and North, strongly influence how the host society treats them. For example, non-Western Muslim immigrants are particularly exposed to discrimination and exclusion in Western societies (Alinia 2011, 2013; Ålund and Alinia 2011; Eliassi 2010; see also Gardell 2010; Wallach Scott 2007). Of course, hierarchies exist among non-Western migrants too, for example in terms of colour, origin or religion. Shilan (a woman) described a recurrent experience of suspicion towards immigrants; something other respondents referred to as well:

> There is to some extent mistrust towards foreigners. For example when you go into a shop you see that the assistants look at you suspiciously. They are worried and think that you will pinch something. This distrustfulness hurts, it disturbs me. They do not know you and do not know what kind of person you are. The assistant's look is like torture for me. Some old women for example do not like foreigners and show it very clearly.

Many of these interviews took place in 2002, in a political climate strongly influenced by the discourse of the 'war on terror' declared by the Bush administration, which divided the world into we and them, Christianity and Islam, civilization and barbarism. Anti-Muslim and anti-immigrant sentiments in Sweden were exacerbated in 2002 when a woman of Kurdish origin from Turkey was killed by her father, who referred to cleansing the family honour as his motive. Media and politicians widely described the crime as a cultural phenomenon among non-Western immigrants, especially those originating from the Middle East. However, it was Kurds who immediately became associated with 'honour culture' (for more discussions see Alinia 2011), a fact all respondents mentioned. Azad (a man) criticized the way the Swedish media represents immigrants: 'If a non-Swede commits a crime then they talk about Kurds, Somalis, Iraqis, Iranians, etc. When a Swede commits a crime, he has a name. They say that Kalle, Tomas etc., has done it. The individual is responsible for his/her crime, not all the Swedish nation; but if a foreigner commits a crime, the whole nation gets responsibility for it. The person has no name but he is an Arab, a Kurd, a Persian etc. This is very bad.'

Hamid said he had had many experiences of discrimination and pointed out that they increased considerably after 9/11:

> Once, a friend of mine and I went to a petrol station to rent a car. My friend asked for a car and paid one thousand crowns as a deposit. But they asked both of us to show our driving licences, our ID-cards and our Visa cards. It took a long time to check our cards. Meanwhile a Swedish woman came in and wanted to rent a car. It was very different for her. She did not need to go through so many controls and everything was completed within a short time. When I protested and asked them why they checked us so much, they said that it is the rule. I was very disappointed. I can also give you more examples. Such things happened to me before too. For example, in the bank you see that they treat you badly. I do not mean that they say bad/unpleasant things but they behave in such a way, their body language is not nice or they do not trust you or do not respect you. They ignore you and do not care if you are waiting a long time. I have seen many things like that but I have tried to ignore them. I cannot pay so much attention to these things because in that case my life will become very difficult. You cannot pay so much attention to them.

Repressing the memories of such experiences serves as a survival and protective strategy for Hamid. Whereas he did not deny that he had been exposed to discrimination and everyday racism, he said he had learned to live with it and no longer allows it to disturb his daily life. It has become, he said, a 'natural' part of his daily life. According to a report from the National Integration Office, some immigrants want to deny and repress the fact of their exposure to discrimination (de los Reyes and Wingborg 2002). The report points to a strong dislike of regarding special treatment and humiliating attitudes as discrimination. Denial of discrimination can be seen as a way of avoiding the stigma sometimes associated with the role of victim of discrimination. Acknowledging discrimination can be experienced as shameful and degrading (ibid.: 59–60), since the victim himself/herself can be blamed for it.

Experiences of and Relation to Sweden as Kurds

'Cultural Freedom of Choice'

Sweden's Kurds have enjoyed freedom in accordance with the explicit acceptance of ethnic and cultural diversity in Sweden formulated in the mid-1970s. This policy, based on 'cultural freedom of choice' (Soininen 1999: 690) with regard to cultural identity and assimilation, stipulates that all Swedish citizens, regardless of ethnic/cultural background, have equal rights and equal obligations. Multiculturalism has become an integral part of contemporary European politics, and in some places, like Sweden, it has become the official political ideology.

However, Schierup (1991) has stated that Swedish multiculturalism gives rise to a dual policy of standardization/assimilation and to 'ethnization'. On the one hand, immigrant culture and forms of political expression are processed, transformed, assimilated and standardized to make them fit for Swedish public consumption. On the other hand, individual ethnic cultural groups are defined as culturally unique and organizationally separated and set apart from each other. The multicultural policy and discourse of integration, which according to Wahlbeck (1999: 14) is the dominant pattern of inclusion in multicultural societies, can also influence immigrant minorities in such a way that 'ethnicism' (Cockburn 1998: 39) or 'ethnization' (Ålund and Schierup 1991) becomes their own dominant ideological discourse and their basic infrastructure for organizing themselves (Schierup 1991: 134; see also Alinia 2004). The concept's complex and contradictory nature rules out simplification in terms of being entirely good or bad. Respondents' experiences and views of Swedish multiculturalism confirm this complexity. Despite their critical views of Swedish multiculturalism, Shierup and Ålund (2011: 56) conceded that it 'offered an extended and substantial body of citizenship rights to "newcomers"'. However they also stated that the past two decades had witnessed erosion of these citizenship rights and 'a probable beginning of the end of Swedish exceptionalism.' (ibid.).

Evin received her education in Syria in Arabic. She cannot write or read Kurdish, her children, who are being brought up in Sweden, are learning it by attending Kurdish language classes. Evin says:

> I speak Kurdish with my children because I want them to learn it. Now after attending courses in Kurdish they have also learned to read and write Kurdish. I cannot read and write in Kurdish but my children have the possibility to learn it here in Sweden. Here you become more conscious about your culture and nationality.

The respondents' experiences of and opinions about multicultural policy are divided because of their political and ideological orientations. However, they all appreciate the political freedom and social prerequisites that they, as Kurds, have gained in Sweden. Sweden boasts the third-highest level of Kurdish cultural activities worldwide, after Iraqi Kurdistan and the Caucasian Republics (Galip 2014; Tayfun 1998; see also Alinia 2004, 2007; Emanuelsson 2005; Khayati 2008).

Gendered Racism

Kurdish male respondents report frequently experiencing the assumption that they are violent and oppressive towards their female relatives, whereas Kurdish women say they are often regarded as being passive victims of men's violence. The discourse of 'honour killing' and its culturalization of gender-based violence have contributed considerably to normalizing and legitimizing such 'gendered racism' (Essed 2005: 76), which results when racism and sexism intersect. Support from politicians, some feminists, media and scholars has lent this discourse strong dominance in Sweden (Alinia 2011, 2013; Ålund and Alinia 2011; Carbin 2010; Gruber 2007). Culturalization of violence and murder, alongside the discursive construction of gender oppression as a cultural act, delimits female subordination and male dominance, associating them with specific cultures described as threatening the Swedish culture described as gender-equal. It gives way to a conception based on it: that patriarchal structures only occur in certain cultures, within certain national boundaries and within certain communities (Mohanty 1991, 2003; Alinia 2006, 2008, 2011, 2013; Ålund and Alinia 2011; Eliassi 2010).

According to the respondents, violence in general and gender-based violence in particular are often associated with Kurds (Eliassi 2010; Alinia 2004). In their experience, Swedish media and public opinion usually represent Kurds as murderous and violent. The respondents recount how, as Kurds and immigrants, they have experienced different degrees of distance, indifference and dislike at first hand. Azad weighed in with his opinion on how Swedish society regards Kurdish women and men:

> Swedes think that all Kurds, Arabs, etc., are backward/uncivilized nations and that everyone batters their wives and that women do not have the right to say anything. They show more sympathy for women because they have a conception that all Kurdish men batter their wives. They think so. That is why they feel sorry for Kurdish women and see them as helpless victims who need help. They have such biases. They treat Kurdish women as children who know nothing and need to be helped and liberated.

The respondents' accounts show that in society's encounter with non-Western migrants, femininity and sexuality are constantly racialized as gender based violence is ascribed certain cultures and certain ethnicities (Mohanty 2003, 1991; Anthias and Yuval-Davis 1992; Alinia 2011; Yuval-Davis 1997; Eduards 2007). Shapol said:

> As soon as you say that you were married young, they say, 'Did your father force you to marry?' I had a chat with some colleagues at work. As

soon as I said that I married my husband when I was twenty-one, they suddenly felt sorry for me and said: 'Did your father force you to get married?' I said no, we also do marry because of love. They have such a notion about us, that men always decide for us women.

Another woman, Shirin, had a similar experience:

My colleagues did not expect that I could travel or have activities by my-self, because my husband would not allow me. They thought that I had to ask for my husband's permission to do things. Not all Swedes, but some, think that Kurdish women are all sitting at home and cannot speak the language, have many children, and take care of the home and children. This is how they regard Kurdish women.… My neighbour told me that she did not believe that I was Kurdish. She thought maybe I was from Chile or something like that. They don't expect you, as a Kurdish woman, to be independent.

These narratives demonstrate the conception of Kurdish women as subordinate and under the control of their male relatives and men in general, who in turn are portrayed as violent oppressors. The respondents say that they often have to defend themselves against such conceptions.

Experiences of and Relations with the Kurdish Diaspora Community

Kurds, like other non-Western immigrants in Sweden, experience exclusion from the realms of power, the Swedish national community and its everyday networks. On the other hand, diasporic communities, networks and activities offer them a 'home', a platform or a 'location' where they can orient themselves and meet the society. This gives them a we-identity, that is, a sense of belongingness and solidarity with an imagined community that exceeds many national boundaries. In many respects, these diaspora spaces are essential to people's survival (Alinia 2004, 2007, 2008).

For individuals, indulging the desire and longing for home(land) gives vent to the need to belong that arises in response to exclusion and otherness. People mobilize historical, social and political resources in their new society to make their lives meaningful and bearable. Memories, cultural traditions and resources, intellectual activities, social networking and political activities, to name but a few, are all identifiable resources in respondents' narratives and their strategies of survival and resistance. However, the collective identity that appears unified from the outside is internally divided according to people's location in categories of class, gender, sexuality, age and so on. In my interviews, I found that next to political and ideological divisions, gender was the most significant source of difference in relations with Sweden and with Kurdish diaspora communities.

Kurdish Diaspora and Gender

The respondents' political orientations and social situations are central to their experience of and relation to both Swedish society and the Kurdish community (Alinia 2004). In addition to general political orientations, however, gender significantly impacts on these processes. Women's relations to the Kurdish diasporic community are far more ambivalent than men's, and women are also more sceptical and critical of what they see as a patriarchal Kurdish community. Yet despite their often more positive and open attitude towards Sweden and their desire to be part of the society, Kurdish women still experience exclusion from society and degradation as migrants and Kurds. Instead women find a 'home' in their social networks and activities in the Kurdish community, even though they often challenge its boundaries in different ways. Not all female respondents are critical of gender relations within the Kurdish communities, but the majority are. Some men are also critical of the way gender issues have been pursued in Kurdish politics. One man, Sherko, explained:

> We have a woman, a poet, Kajal, who says that politics in our society is made by moustaches. It means that Kurdish politics have been patriarchal. Politics in our society has been a male domain. Men have done it. Here, our problem with cultural associations is that they are not places where you can make progress. These are created on the basis of male domination. They are places where men sit and play dominoes. You see that there is a male power that makes politics with a big moustache.

Women members of different associations – often divided according to countries of origin and/or political and ideological directions – also experience differences with regard to gender relations, although these differences are not fundamental. Maryam and Shirin, who together with some other women had started an association for Kurdish women, were keen to highlight gender issues that, as they saw it, had been subordinated within the Kurdish movement (see also Alinia 2013). In the late 1990s and early 2000s, the national movement dominated the Kurdish diaspora's activities, whereas women's associations were quite new in Sweden. These women said they had been criticized by Kurdish nationalists, mainly men, who accused them of dividing the Kurdish movement by raising such issues. Maryam and Shirin, and other women from their association whom I interviewed, emphasized that they identify themselves as Kurds in relation to the 'outside' world, but they define themselves as feminists and as women in relation to the Kurdish community. Maryam said:

> Many Kurdish men say that we weaken the Kurdish movement by bringing up such conflicts. Our answer to them is that Kurdistan will not be free as long as its women are not free. Men have always decided on different political issues in the Kurdish movement and now we see the result. Women have also been involved in the Kurdish movement, but political decisions have always been taken by men.

Several studies have found that politics is a significant part of the everyday life of Kurdish diaspora networks and communities (Alinia 2004; Wahlbeck 1999; Khayati 2008; Emanuelsson 2005), and as is evident from the respondents' accounts, Kurdish politics is a male-dominated arena. In the Kurdish movement, leftists and nationalists alike have seen gender equality as a by-product and a subordinated issue. Even though women have been active participants in national liberation movements, the question of sexuality and gender equality has never been recognized as a problem because it has been subject to different political ideologies and movements (cf. Accad 1991, Alinia 2013, Mojab 2001).

The struggle against national oppression is not only appreciated; it is regarded as obligatory for every citizen, whether male or female. Women's participation in the Kurdish movement, together with their insistent efforts and their 'latent feminism' (hooks 1990), has created a space and an arena for them within the movement. However, as Mojab (2001) argues, despite its formal support for women's emancipation, Kurdish nationalism has proved a major obstacle to the development of the feminist movement by relegating gender equality to the future, subordinate to the achievement of independence (Alinia 2004, 2013). To be sure, this is not specifically a Kurdish phenomenon. As Waylen puts it, the phenomenon of nationalism 'is not constructed in a gender neutral fashion' (Waylen 1996: 14; see also Yuval-Davis 1997; Eduards 2007; Connel 2009; Einhorn 2008; Nagel 2005). Though as part of the nation included in the processes of nation building, women as agents and subjects have been excluded from the discourse of nationalism (Yuval-Davis 1997; Nagel 2005; Enloe 2000). Yuval-Davis, Anthias and Campling (1989) identify five major ways in which women have been implicated in nationalism: (1) as biological reproducers of the members of national collectives, (2) as reproducers of the boundaries of national groups (through restrictions on sexual or marital relations), (3) as active transmitters and reproducers of the national culture, (4) as symbolic signifiers of national difference, (5) as active participants in national struggles (ibid.: 7; see also Enloe 2000: 54). The Kurdish case is no exception.

Despite women's positive attitudes towards Swedish society, their sense of belonging and their relations to Sweden and their countries of origin do not fit into the framework of a 'home/host dichotomy' (e.g. Alicea 1997). According to Alicea, this dichotomization, results from dichotomization and categorization of host and home in terms of modernity and tradition, progressiveness and backwardness, and so forth (ibid.; see also Bhabha 1999; Sassen 1999; Alinia 2004). The women's experiences reveal a rather contradictory, ambivalent relationship: on the one hand, their newfound economic independence and social and legal rights encourage them to be more open and receptive towards the Swedish society; on the other hand, unfavourable, oppressive racial and class conditions systematically exclude them from society and social power. Additionally, the 'home/host dichotomy' conceals the variety of family structures, benefits, resources and social networks that women experienced in their home countries. Hence the complex, multi-dimensional experiences of diasporic Kurdish women and men and their relations to Sweden, their countries of origin, and their Kurdish diasporic communities must be understood within intersecting structures of class, gender, ethnicity, sexuality and generation. This is also the only way to avoid Western-centric explanations (Collins 2009; Mohanty 2003; Alinia 2004, 2011).

Being Both a Kurd and a Woman

Although the respondents' participation in diasporic networks and movements develops at an individual level, it cannot simply be regarded as an individual phenomenon. Although motivation is individually based, it is built up and developed through interaction (Melucci 1991). Both the identity that emerges from this process and the politics to which it gives rise depend on various individual experiences mobilized in particular constructions of identity, and on the way these elements are articulated in discourse (Bowman 1994).

As a project, Kurdish identity includes a number of internal subdivisions, one of which is the identity of Kurdish women. Being a 'Kurdish Woman' is a political project, a positioning opposed to women's subordination within the Kurdish community, within their countries of origin, subordination within the Swedish society and the imposed and stigmatized migrant identity. One female respondent, Hana, stated that Kurdish women, being doubly oppressed as Kurds and as women, have two main tasks: fighting national oppression and fighting gender oppression. Most of the female respondents stressed that in relation to Swedish society they identify as Kurds, whereas in relation to the Kurdish community they identify as women.

Identifying as a Kurdish woman implies ambivalence and contradictions, which these women have to deal with. Their accounts make clear that despite experiencing exclusion and racism, they have not turned away from Swedish society. Yet it is within the Kurdish community that they find a sense of home and belongingness, even as they challenge patriarchy and gender hierarchies within it by carving out their own, often transnational, spaces and activities. These spaces, created by women for women, revolve around gender issues, helping to generate knowledge, solidarity and empowerment. Massey (1999) observes that an important aspect of space and spatiality is their connection with social power. Talking about '*spatialized* social power', she concludes that 'it is the power relations in the construction of spatiality, rather than the spatiality alone, which must be addressed' (ibid.: 291).

Notes

1. Here home(land) is used in both a symbolic and territorial sense.

References

Accad, E. 1991. 'Sexuality and Sexual Politics: Conflicts and Contradictions for Contemporary Women in the Middle East', in C.T. Mohanty, A. Russo and L. Torres (eds), *Third World Women and the Politics of Feminism*. Bloomington and Indianapolis: Indiana University Press, pp. 237–51.

Alicea, M. 1997. '"A Chambered Nautilus": The Contradictory Nature of Puerto Rican Women's Role in the Social Construction of a Transnational Community', *Gender and Society*, 11(5): 597–626.

Alinia, M. 2004. *Spaces of Diasporas: Kurdish identities, experiences of otherness and politics of belonging*. Department of Sociology Göteborg University. Göteborg Studies in Sociology No 22. Available at: http://hdl.handle.net/2077/16269.

———. 2006. 'Invandraren, Förorten och Maktens Rumsliga Förankring: Berättelser om Vardagsrasism' [The Immigrant, the Suburb, and the Spatial Anchoring of Power: Stories About Everyday Racism], in M. Kamali (ed.), *Den Segregerande Integrationen: om Social Sammanhållning och dess Hinder* [The Segregating Integration: On Social Solidarity and Its Obstacles]. Stockholm: Statens Offentliga Utredningar, pp. 63–90.

———. 2007. 'Den Kurdiska Diasporan som en Transnationell Rörelse för "Hem" och Gemenskapsbildande' [The Kurdish Diaspora as a Transnational Movement for 'Home' and Community Building], in E. Olsson et al. (eds), *Transnationella Rum* [Transnational Spaces]. Umeå: Boréa, pp. 271–97.

———. 2008. 'Ett Hem i Rörelse: Diasporisk Mobilisering i den Svenska Gemenskapens Periferi' [A Home in Motion: Diasporic Mobilisation in the Swedish Community's Periphery], *Diskriminering och Exkludering. Socialvetenskaplig Tidskrift* [Discrimination and Exclusion: Journal of Social Science] 15(3–4): 332–49.

———. 2011. 'Den Jämställda Rasismen och de Barbariska Invandrarna: "Hedersvåld", Kultur och Skillnadens Politik' [Gender-Equal Racism and Barbarian Immigrants: 'Honour Violence', Culture, and the Politics of Difference], in C. Listerborn, I. Molina and D. Mulinari (eds), *Våldets Topografier: Betraktelser Över Makt och Motstånd* [The Topographies of Violence: Reflections on Power and Resistance]. Stockholm: Atlas, pp. 287–329.

———. 2013. *Honor and violence against women in Iraqi Kurdistan*. New York: Palgrave Macmillan.

Ålund, A. and M. Alinia. 2011. 'I Skuggan av Kulturella Stereotypier: Perspektiv på Forskning om Genus, Jämställdhet och Etniska Relationer i Sverige' [In the Shadow of Cultural Stereotypes: Perspective on Research on Gender, Gender Equality, and Ethnic Relations in Sweden], *Sociologisk forskning* [Sociological Research] 2: 43–65.

Ålund, A. and C.U. Schierup. 1991. *Paradoxes of Multiculturalism: Essays on Swedish Society*. Avebury: Aldershot.

Bhabha, H.K. 1999.'Liberalism's Sacred Cow.' In Joshua Cohen, Matthew Howard, and Martha C. Nussbaum, (eds.), *Is Multiculturalism Bad for Women*, Susan Moller Okin with Respondents, pp. 79–84. Princeton, NJ: Princeton University Press.

Bowman, G. 1994. '"A Country of Words": Conceiving the Palestinian Nation From the Position of Exile', in E. Laclau (ed.), *The Making of Political Identities*. London and New York: Verso.

Brah, A. 1996. *Cartographies of Diaspora: Contesting Identities*. London and New York: Routledge.

Carbin, M. 2010. *Hedersrelaterat Våld och Förtryck – En Kunskap- och Forskningsöversikt* [A Survey of Knowledge and Research on Honour-related Violence and Oppression]. Uppsala: Nationellt centrum för kvinnofrid (NCK).

Cockburn, C. 1998. *The Space Between Us: Negotiating Gender and National Identities in Conflict*. London and New York: Zed Books.

Collins, P.H. 2009. *Black Feminist Thought*. New York: Routledge.

Connel, R. 2009. *Gender in World Perspective*, 2nd ed. Cambridge, Malden: Polity Press.

Darvishpour, M. 2002. *Immigrant Women Challenge the Role of Men: How the Changing Power Relationship within Iranian Families in Sweden Intensifies Family Conflicts after Immigration*. Stockholm: Stockholm University.

de los Reyes, P. and M. Wingborg. 2002. *Vardagsdiskriminering och Rasism i Sverige: En Kunskapsöversikt* [Everyday Discrimination and Racism in Sweden: A Survey]. Norrköping: Integrationsverkets rapportserie.

Eduards, M. 2007. *Kroppspolitik: Om Moder Svea och Andra Kvinnor* [The Politics of the Body: On Mother Svea and Other Women]. Stockholm: Atlas.

Einhorn, B. 2008. 'Insiders and Outsiders: Within and Beyond the Gendered Nation', in K. Davis, M. Evans and J. Lorber (eds), *Handbook of Gender and Women's Studies*. London: Sage, pp. 196–210.

Eliassi, B. 2010. 'A Stranger in My Homeland: The Politics of Belonging Among Young People With Kurdish Backgrounds in Sweden', Ph.D dissertation. Östersund: Mittuniversitetet.

Emanuelsson, A.C. 2005. *Diaspora Global Politics: Kurdish Transnational Networks and Accommodation of Nationalism*. Göteborg: Göteborg University.

Enloe, C. 2000. *Bananas, Beaches, and Bases: Making Feminist Sense of International Politics*. Berkeley: University of California Press.

Essed, P. 2005. 'Vardagsrasism' [Everyday Racism], in P. de los Reyes and M. Kamali (eds), *Bortom Vi och Dom: Teoretiska Reflektioner om Makt, Integration och Strukturell Diskriminering*. [Beyond We and Them: Theoretical reflections on power, integration and structural discrimination]. Stockholm: Statens Offentliga Utredningar, pp. 71–95.

Galip, Ozlem. 2014. 'Where is Home? Re-visioning "Kurdistan" and "Diaspora" in Kurdish Novelistic Discourse in Sweden', in Alinia, et al. (eds), The Kurdish Diaspora: Nordic and Transnational Ties, Home and Politics of Belonging. Special issue, *Nordic Journal of Migration Research*.

Gardell, M. 2010. *Islamofobi* [Islamophobia]. Stockholm: Leopardförlag.

Gruber, Sabine (2007) *I skolans vilja att åtgärda "hedersrelaterat" våld: etnicitet, kön och våld*, Rapport 2007:1, Centrum för kommunstrategiska studier, Linköpings universitet. [Dealing with honour related violence in schools: ethnicity, gender, and violence. Report 2007: 1, Centre for municipality studies, Linköping University].

Hammar, T. 1990. *Democracy and the Nation State*. Aldershot: Avebury.

hooks, b. 1990. *Yearning: Race, Gender, and Cultural Politics*. Boston, MA: South End Press.

Jonsson, S. 2010. *Rapporter Från Sopornas Planet: Kritiska Essäer* [Reports From Refuse Planet: Critical Essays]. Stockholm: Norstedts.

Khayati, K. 2008. *From Victim Diaspora to Transborder Citizenship: Diaspora Formation and Transnational Relations Among Kurds in France and Sweden*. Linköping: Linköping University.

Listerborn, C., I. Molina and D. Mulinari (eds). 2011. *Våldets Topografier: Betraktelser Över Makt och Motstånd* [The Topographies of Violence: Reflections on Power and Resistance]. Stockholm: Atlas.

Massey, D. 1999. 'Spaces of Politics', in D. Massey, J. Allen and P. Sarre (eds), *Human Geography Today*. Cambridge: Polity Press.

Melucci, A. 1991. *Nomader i Nuet: Sociala Rörelser och Individuella Behov i Dagens Samhälle* [Nomads of the Present: Social Movements and Individual Needs in Contemporary Society]. Göteborg: Daidalos.

Mohanty, C.T. 1991. 'Cartographies of Struggle: Third World Women and the Politics of Feminism', in C.T. Mohanty, A. Russo and L. Torres (eds), *Third World Women and the Politics of Feminism*. Bloomington and Indianapolis: Indiana University Press, pp. 1–51.

————. 2003. *Feminism Utan Gränser: Avkoloniserad Teori, Praktiserad Solidaritet* [Feminism Without Borders: Decolonizing Theory, Practicing Solidarity]. Stockholm: Tankekraft.

Mojab, S. 2001. 'Introduction: The Solitude of the Stateless: Kurdish Women at the Margins of Feminist Knowledge', in S. Mojab (ed.), *Women of a NonState Nation: The Kurds*. California: Mazda, pp. 1–25.

Nagel, J. 1998. 'Masculinity and Nationalism: Gender and Sexuality in the Making of Nations', *Ethnic and Racial Studies* 21(2): 242–69.

Sassen, S. 1999. 'Culture Beyond Gender', in M. Howard and M.C. Nussbaum (eds), *Is Multiculturalism Bad for Women? Susan Moller Okin with Respondents*. Princeton, NJ: Princeton University Press.

Schierup, C.U. 1991. 'The Ethnic Tower of Babel: Political Marginality and Beyond', in A. Ålund and C. U. Schierup, *Paradoxes of Multiculturalism: Essays on Swedish Society*. Avebury: Aldershot.

Schierup, C.U. and A. Ålund. 2011. 'The End of Swedish Exeptionalism? Citizenship, Neoliberalism and the Politics of Exclusion', *Race and Class* 53(1): 46–65.

Soininen, M. 1999. 'The "Swedish Model" As an Institutional Framework for Immigrant Membership Rights', *Journal of Ethnic and Migration Studies* 25(4): 685–702.

Statens Offentliga Utredningar. 2004–2006. *Utredningen om Makt, Integration och Strukturell Diskriminering* [Inquiry on Power, Integration, and Structural Discrimination]. Retrieved 4 November 2013 from http://www.temaasyl.se/Templates/Page.aspx?id=660

Tayfun, M. 1998. *Kurdisk Författarskap och Kurdisk Bokutgivning: Bakgrund, Villkor, Betydelse* [Kurdish Writing and Kurdish Publication: Background, Condition, Significance]. Spånga: Apec förlag.

Thörn, H. 1997. *Modernitet, Sociologi och Sociala Rörelser* [Modernity, Sociology, and Social Movements]. Göteborg: Göteborg University.

Wahlbeck, Ö. 1999. *Kurdish Diasporas: A Comparative Study of Kurdish Refugee Communities*. London: Macmillan and Centre for Research in Ethnic Relations, University of Warwick.

Wallach Scott, J. 2007. *Slöjans Politik* [The Politics of the Veil]. Stockholm: Tankekraft.

Waylen, G. 1996. 'Analysing Women in the Politics of the Third World', in H. Afshar (ed.), *Women and Politics in the Third World*. London: Routledge, pp. 7–25.

Yuval-Davis, N. 1997. *Gender and Nation*. London: Sage.

Yuval-Davis, N., F. Anthias and J. Campling (eds). 1989. *Woman – Nation – State*. London: MacMillan.

PART II

HOME POLITICS, HOST POLICIES AND RESISTANCE

6

LEARNING PROCESSES AND POLITICAL LITERACY AMONG WOMEN IN THE NORWEGIAN KURDISH DIASPORA

Kariane Westrheim

Introduction

Historic turbulence in Kurdistan, caused by external and internal conflicts, war and deportations, has resulted in the dispersion of Kurds from their original homeland to diaspora communities all over the world. Large Kurdish diaspora communities have formed in European countries like Germany and France. In the Nordic countries, Sweden has the largest Kurd population and a multitude of Kurdish organizations and communities, while Norway has a relatively small Kurdish diaspora population numbering approximately 5,000 Kurds, the majority of whom come from the autonomous Kurdish Region in North Iraq. It is difficult to determine the exact number of Kurds in Norway because migrants there are registered according to their national citizenship. Kurds from Turkey, for instance, count as Turks statistically.

This chapter focuses on Kurdish women from North Kurdistan (Turkey)[1] in the Norwegian diaspora. Many women from traditional Kurdish families have typically had limited possibilities of engaging in activities outside the home. However, the political situation in recent decades has brought Kurdish women from North Kurdistan to the forefront of the political and armed struggle. Since the Kurdistan Workers' Party (PKK) entered the stage in the 1980s, it has actively recruited younger-generation diasporic Kurds to join its ranks (Curtis 2005). Many of them, however, have been educated in Norway and other diaspora countries. With their diverse educational or professional backgrounds, recruits from the diaspora differed from those who hailed from the Kurdish countryside. Some diaspora recruits had a university diploma, vocational schooling or academic, professional or technological skills that could be of use to the struggle. The knowledge and skills the recruits brought with them became valuable social transmittances, according to Espen Gran (2008).

In the Norwegian diaspora, these and other experiences have been crucial to female politicization. In many ways, Kurdish women function as a 'bridge' between countries of origin and the diaspora where experiences, knowledge, skills and thoughts are exchanged. This chapter argues that joint efforts between Kurdish women in diaspora and in the homeland have changed the role of women within Kurdish society. A key factor in this development is that women's emancipation and political engagement have enhanced learning processes and political literacy, prompting the question 'How do knowledge and learning in diaspora enhance political awareness and political literacy among Kurdish women?' Here I discuss this question in light of excerpts from interviews conducted in previous qualitative studies on Kurdish issues (Westrheim 2005, 2009, 2010).

This chapter is organized as follows. First, I will describe the term 'diaspora'. As this chapter deals with the Norwegian context, it seems necessary to show that Norway is not solely a host country for people who seek refuge or better life conditions. In the past, thousands of Norwegians left in order to seek a better life in America. Then I will briefly overview some characteristics of the Kurdish diaspora in Europe. The third part will focus on Kurdish women in diaspora and discuss how learning experiences in diaspora can strengthen women's awareness and political literacy.

The concept of diaspora is not an easy construct. It is often applied in general and categorizing ways that fail to absorb the histories, experiences and nuances of women's diaspora life. Shahrzad Mojab (2000: 89) finds it difficult to apply the concept of diaspora when it comes to women. A large part of diaspora literature, she claims, has been a masculine construction made up of texts, often with a nationalist overtone, that lack content enabling description of the experience of women. Furthermore, Minoo Alinia (2004) argues that most research studies on diaspora have neglected the gender dimension or lack nuance, often presenting women as a single category despite differences in background, experiences, personal preferences and political affiliation.

Recent diaspora literature is often seen in relation to transnationalism. Gran's (2008) work on transnational activities discusses the term *social remittances*: ideas, behaviours, identities, gender patterns or social capital flowing from diaspora communities to the country of origin. These transfers occur when migrants make return visits and communicate through letters, emails, videos or phone calls. Social remittances also refer to professional or educational skills acquired in Europe and utilized in the country of origin (Gran 2008: 121–22). For women in diaspora, social remittances are also crucially important to political participation. In this chapter I regard social remittances as a form of social, cultural and political capital that Kurdish women take with them from Norway. When they go on return visits or communicate in other ways, they pass on transformed social, cultural and political experiences and knowledge. In various ways, political developments in Kurdish politics appear to have depended on such exchanges.

Some diaspora groups maintain strong national ties to their homeland (Anderson 1998). They are involved in politics in both their homeland and the host country and might even support a political or armed movement fighting for liberation or fundamental change through so-called politics-oriented remittances (Tharmalingam 2011: 170). Kurds constitute one such group. A significant number of Kurds in Turkey and diaspora actively support the PKK and its political wings (Westrheim 2005, 2009).

At present, the large body of literature focused on diaspora is seriously lacking in research and scholarly literature on Kurdish gendered diaspora in Norway. As Norwegian scholarly contributions are scarce, this chapter will also make use of studies on diaspora experiences outside Norway. One scholarly work I would like to mention in this context is Marianne Rugkåsa's article 'The Traditional, the Modern and the Political: Politics and Gender Ideology among Kurdish Immigrants in Oslo' (2004). In a review of this work, Birgit Blaettel-Mink underlines the need for a stronger understanding of the importance of gender in studies of Kurdish daily life in Kurdistan and diaspora (2006: 39) and argues that Rugkåsa's (2004) article provides a valuable focus on female politicization in the Norwegian diaspora. She asks how Kurds in Oslo relate to the liberation struggle in their homeland, which in this context refers to the struggle of PKK. Her question is perhaps even more relevant today, a decade later. Rugkåsa identified characteristic tendencies of three main groups in her material: (1) Kurdish traditionalists, who attach crucial importance to Islam and the clans while distancing themselves from Kurdish culture and the ongoing liberation struggle; (2) Kurdish modernists, who try to fit in in the host country while also supporting the PKK ideologically or financially; and (3) political Kurds, who see themselves as modern in that they distance themselves from Islam, though they simultaneously espouse traditional Kurdish values. Women in these political families are expected to be politically active even as they reproduce the families. Some claim that 'to have a politically active woman signals that the husband is a revolutionary and lives according to the PKK ideology' (Rugkåsa 2004: 229, cited in Blaettel-Mink 2006: 40). This may be true to some extent, but it also depicts Kurdish women in diaspora as dependent on men. The belief that a Kurdish woman is solely an object serving her husband's political self-image is a diversion. Kurdish women in Norway and elsewhere might very well be 'traditional' mothers and wives while also being politically active. Despite the frequent appearance of dependence on their husbands, Kurdish women – in both diaspora and home countries – have propelled the Kurdish struggle by taking to the streets, participating in demonstrations and campaigns, carrying banners and facilitating and supporting collective action in the background and in their homes. These initiatives have been critical to the growth of the political and popular Kurdish movement (Westrheim 2009, 2013).

Kurdistan may be divided for the time being, but in recent years Kurdish women have established parties and organizations to unite across party lines and across borders. One example is the annual Kurdish National Conference of Women ('Conference for Kurdish women discusses creating global association' 2012), in which a delegation from Norway used to participate. But even though many women are active members of political parties, gender issues have often been set aside for the benefit of other political issues. In the long run, women's politicization could bring about a reinvention of Kurdish politics and traditions, superseding present imaginary borders due largely to new opportunities gained in diaspora in Norway and elsewhere.

Diaspora and the Norwegian Exodus

The term 'diaspora' is often used to describe the dispersion of Jews after their Babylonian exile. An often cited work is William Safran's 'Diasporas in Modern Societies: Myths of Homeland and Return' (1991). Safran claims that one of the most crucial characteristics of diaspora is homeland orientation: the close link between people in diaspora and their homeland, whether it is real or imagined. The very meaning of diaspora has been stretched, making the term more interesting and dynamic. Today it is not unusual to accompany the term 'diaspora' with a modifier describing the characteristics, particular condition or situation of the ethnic group or people it refers to, such as 'catastrophic' or 'victim' diaspora in the Palestinian case (Cohen 1997). As Gabriel Sheffer (2003) claims, communities of labour migrants can also be regarded as diasporas as long as they maintain emotional and social ties with their homeland (Sheffer cited in Brubaker 2005: 2). The broader concept of diaspora signifies the movement of indigenous peoples, or a population of common ethnicity, to a place other than their homeland or home region. In this perspective, emigrant groups have been called diasporas even after becoming largely assimilated (Brubaker 2005: 3).

In recent years Norway has become an attractive diaspora country, but one should not forget that Norway has a history of emigration as well. The migration of 800,000 people from Norway to the United States between 1825 and 1925 can broadly be seen in light of the diaspora concept. Their departure was motivated by a mix of push and pull factors related to economic conditions in the respective countries. Quakers leaving for religious reasons (push factors) made up the bulk of the first wave, while later groups left for economic and social reasons (pull factors). The migrants represented all social layers of society, though poor smallholders, mainly young single men and families, predominated. The authorities often paid their way, regarding the outlay as more economical than supporting these farmers back home.

According to the Norwegian historian Ingrid Semmingsen (1988), female emigrants left Norway in significant numbers to seek adventure, earn their own money or escape a future of poverty that offered no options but marriage and hard work. In the period of mass emigration (1865–1915), nearly 40 per cent of 700,000 emigrants were women. At the very beginning, only a few women made independent decisions regarding emigration. They were the exceptions. Later, especially during the next wave of emigration in the 1880s, the number of urban emigrants increased, and it became common for a husband to leave first and try to establish himself, later sending money or a ticket so wife and children could follow him. Those left behind often endured hardship while waiting, and the poor-law authorities frequently had to assist them with food or lodging or even a ticket to America. Most emigrants planned to return to Norway after a couple of years. The majority however, never returned. Women were more likely than men to settle permanently (Bergland 2011, p. 5). They settled in the Midwest, where to this day communities cling to their Norwegian background and heritage, with women, it seems, as its transmitters. Their contribution in diaspora has been significant in all areas of American society. As in the case of Kurdish women in Norway, they functioned as a bridge between the two countries. Some of the patterns found in Norwegian migrant communities in the United States mostly resemble those of other migrant groups, even when the original reasons for departure differ.

The Kurdish Diaspora in and outside Norway

A precise count of Kurds in Europe, the United States, Canada and Australia is difficult because, as Alinia (2004) observes, Kurds are registered as Iranian, Iraqi, Turkish or Syrian citizens (see van Bruinessen 1999; Wahlbeck 1999). Roughly estimated to number one million in these Western countries, Kurds constitute one of the world's largest diasporas (Özcan 2006; Alinia 2004). The Kurdish diaspora in Europe formed only recently. Whereas previous migration consisted mainly of deportations or migration from Kurdish to non-Kurdish regions and neighbouring states, from the 1960s onwards students and labour migrants dominated the migration pattern (Alinia 2004: 30f.). Following the Islamic Revolution in Iran in 1979, the military coup in Turkey in 1980 and the Iraqi regime's protracted, murderous extermination campaign against the Kurds known as Operation Anfal, successive waves of Kurdish political refugees arrived in Western Europe and, to a lesser extent, North America. Launched in 1992, the Anfal campaign of forced evacuation and destruction of Kurdish villages increased the Kurdish exodus to Europe ('The Kurdish Diaspora' 2013). The process of defining a Kurdish identity and sense of nationality must take these political conditions and historical events into consideration (Westrheim 2005: 108).

Nearly 85 per cent of the Kurdish diaspora in the West comes from Turkey. Discussing migration from North Kurdistan (Turkey) to Europe, Vera Eccarius-Kelly (2002) argues that the 1980 coup d'état proved a crucial event for Kurdish radicalization in Europe. Gunnar Karlsen argues that from a historical viewpoint, present-day Turkey's legacy of violence and torture dates back to this military event (Karlsen 2007: 3). One reason for the coup was the increasingly popular support of the PKK, which the authorities regarded as a threat (van Bruinessen 1988). The PKK was hit particularly hard by military repressions (White 2000: 33) that imprisoned thousands of its members (McDowell 2000: 420). Several hundred thousand Kurds fled to Germany, France, the Netherlands, Belgium and Scandinavian countries to escape persecution (Eccarius-Kelly 2002: 92).

After the military takeover in Turkey, violence and armed clashes between military units and the PKK escalated in the Kurdish regions in the southeast. Asylum applications from Turkish citizens, to Germany in particular, skyrocketed at this time.[2] Refugees' claims of cultural and political discrimination in Turkey were, to a certain degree, accepted, and political refugees who received asylum transferred their political resistance networks to Europe. 'This changed the Diasporas from predominantly a-political guest worker communities established during the 1960s and 70s, to political networks and more homeland-oriented political activism' (Eccarius-Kelly 2002: 93).

Features of the Kurdish diaspora communities in Norway and elsewhere seem, to some extent, to accord with the three elements that Benedict Anderson (1998) claims are constitutive of diaspora: (1) dispersion, which in the case of the Kurds has primarily been forced (for various reasons); (2) orientation towards a real or imagined homeland, which becomes the authoritative source of value, identity and loyalty; and (3) boundary maintenance, which means maintaining borders vis-à-vis the host country as a means to strengthen the Kurdish community and promote solidarity among its members, but also refers to looser social relationships that cut across state boundaries to link members of the diaspora in different states into a single, transnational community (see Brubaker 2005). Studying the Tamil diaspora in Norway, Øyvind Fuglerud (1999: 3) found that keeping up connections to the country of origin through families and friends and staying informed about the situation in the home country were more important than maintaining relationships with Norwegians (Fuglerud 1999: 3; Wahlbeck 2002: 224; Tharmalingam 2011). This also seems to be the case in the Kurdish diaspora in Norway (Westrheim 2005). In a previous study on the PKK and the Kurdish movement (Westrheim 2009), one female informant told me she had fled Turkey after her release from prison. Although she would have preferred to continue her struggle in her home environment, she said, she found that her stay in Norway broadened her political perspectives. She maintained frequent contact with former political allies in Turkey, such as the women's organization she was affiliated with that kept her informed about political developments in her homeland. Meanwhile, her diaspora position gave her fresh perspectives on the struggle. As her main goal was to advance her people's struggle and improve the situation for women, the Norwegian political system proved a tremendous inspiration to her political work and personal development in diaspora.[3]

As Östen Wahlbeck (2002: 228) argues, political allegiances in the society of origin have special significance. The strong political orientation towards a Kurdish homeland is different from the relations other migrants have towards their countries of origin. As Andy Curtis has argued (2005), diaspora communities can influence the views and actions of Kurds in the homeland. On the other hand, without the diaspora, the Kurds living in Turkey and elsewhere might not have developed into a topic of political interest in Europe (Eccarius-Kelly 2002, cited in Westrheim 2009: 33).

Kurdish communities in Europe display a multitude of different political orientations, religious beliefs, linguistic groups, social classes and educational backgrounds, and consequently represent a broad range of gendered experiences. Wahlbeck (1999, 2002: 225) refers a comparative study of Kurdish communities in Britain and Finland. Whereas he found Kurds in these parts of Europe to be very heterogeneous, transnational social relations were a common feature among them. When refugees in Britain were asked if they felt that they belonged to an 'ethnic minority' in the UK, many of them had trouble understanding the question. This indicates that their ethnicity was primarily defined within the context of social relations with their countries of origin. This orientation towards Kurdistan makes it difficult to regard Kurdish refugees as an ethnic minority within the framework of the countries of exile (Wahlbeck 1999).

Although many Kurds in the Norwegian diaspora, including women, are well integrated, Curtis (2005) argues that second-generation migrants tend to be more nationally oriented and identify more with their historical background. Difficult integration processes and feelings of alienation are two reasons for this. Many Kurds in diaspora live in societies that do not want them; thus they reject the host nation and look towards a homeland for acceptance. Curtis contends that second-generation youth also are more likely to want to return to the homeland in the belief that the establishment of a Kurdish state will solve the problems their parents faced. It may indeed be easier to idealize the homeland at a distance, and for many, the notion of Kurdistan has become a unifying political ideal (Curtis 2005; see also Westrheim 2005, 2009).

Because of the Kurdish people' diffusion there is no given place all Kurds can refer to when asked where their homeland is (Alinia 2004). Even so, many have learned to imagine Kurdistan as their common land. Diaspora members maintain close ties to what they perceive as home and their homeland, and to relatives living in other countries. Almost every Kurd in Kurdistan has at least one relative abroad, and it is not unusual for families to have members scattered all over the world. The idea of a Kurdish homeland blends political discourses with individual wishes, conceptions, longings and experiences (Alinia 2004: 219). Kurdish diaspora can be regarded as a space where the individual emerges more strongly and identities are deconstructed and reconstructed (Alinia 2004; Hassanpour 1994, 1998; van Bruinessen 1999). Kurdishness emerges through the image of a real place, and at the same time derives from mental images nourished among others, and from diaspora experiences (Westrheim 2005, 2009). In the past few decades, Kurdish media and communication via TV channels have supplemented this development (Alinia 2004; Hassanpour 1998). Anderson's (1991) 'imagined community' aptly explains this notion of a state without a geographical territory. Many Kurds in Norway have never been to Kurdistan, so the younger generation's idea of 'home' seems based in their imagination, combined with other people's narratives of the homeland. A female Kurdish student in Norway made the following point in a research interview in 2005: 'Sometimes people ask me: Where is your country? Then I will answer Kurdistan. Then they say: Show me on the map, it is not there' (cited in Westrheim 2005: 108–12). The student had a concrete image of Kurdistan in her head. Her family had arrived in Norway when she was a child, and she had come to identify with both her diaspora community and what she regarded as her homeland. She found her answer adequate, but those who questioned her understood that she could not name a country as they defined it and continued to challenge her by asking her to point to it on the map. Her answer, 'Kurdistan', holds many of her conceptions and dreams, coupled with her parents' narratives and experiences of the place. Kurdistan becomes a utopia she has only visited through her parent's stories. In Edward Casey's words, she is not *at* the place but still *of* the place – independent of physical presence (Casey 1996: 19).

This rather strong physical and imaginary sense of belonging to Kurdistan is transformed into an urge to take part in political developments there. This is probably why Kurds often express a wish to work for the 'Kurdish cause', even when they live in Europe (Wahlbeck 1999). Women are no exception in this regard. Mainstream Kurdish nationalism may hinder their political work on gender rights, but women continue their political work with great success. Diaspora provides women with opportunities to work on women's issues and to establish women's associations to raise awareness of gender-related issues and develop political literacy. The response of one of my former Kurdish respondents indicates that this may also impart a sense of responsibility: 'Women have to work to improve their situation; no one can do the work for us. It is important to use the opportunities we have living in other countries. Women can improve their lives, educate themselves and do many things that were impossible at home. Kurdish women in diaspora have an obligation toward women at home. What we learn here can be of great value to them' (F35).

Many Kurdish women living in Norway are aware that diaspora creates a space with opportunities for education and self-development.

Kurdish Women of the Diaspora:
Political Participation and Learning

Literature shows that Kurdish women in both the diaspora and the homeland make efforts to change the role of women within Kurdish society, which these women continue to relate to the country of origin in one way or another. The distance between the home country and countries of diaspora does not seem to hinder their activities. Referring to Iraqi Kurdistan, Shahrzad Mojab and Rachel Gorman (2007: 75) argue that 'almost all the groups in Iraqi Kurdistan have access to the diaspora and engage in activism there'. The process by which immigrants forge and sustain social relations to their origin is generally termed *transnationalism,* a widely applied concept. I will not explore the concept further in this context, but I find it somewhat useful as a backdrop to understanding how women relate to other women in their home country. Wahlbeck (2002) refers to Linda Basch, Nina Glick Schiller and Cristina Szanton Blanc (1994) when defining transnationalism. In their studies among migrants from the Caribbean and the Philippines living in the United States, Basch et al. describe how the migrants' social, economic, political and cultural networks involve both society of origin and society of settlement: 'We define "transnationalism" as the processes by which immigrants forge and sustain multi-stranded social relations that link together their societies of origin and settlement. We call these processes transnationalism to emphasize that many immigrants today build social fields that cross geographic, cultural, and political borders' (Basch et al. 1994: 7 cited in Wahlbeck 2002: 223). Alynna Lyon and Emek Uçarer (2001) describe Kurdish political activism, as it is manifested in Germany, as a 'transnational ethnic conflict', while Martin van Bruinessen (1999) refers to Anderson's term 'long-distance nationalism' (e.g., Anderson 1994: 376–77) to explain the ways in which the Kurdish diaspora connects to the Kurdish movement in the Middle East (Anderson cited in Wahlbeck 2002: 228).

The question is whether the term transnationalism or long-distance nationalism is at all apt to describe the processes that engendered the Kurdish diaspora in Europe. A useful way of understanding diaspora in relation to feminist organizing, according to Floya Anthias (1998), is to think of it as a historical rather than cultural phenomenon: 'A historical understanding of diaspora would focus on the events of and precursors to war or oppression (before a dispersal, if there has been one), or oppression (in the diaspora itself). These are the historical events through which a community comes to understand itself as a political entity' (Anthias cited in Mojab and Gorman 2007: 79). As Mojab and Gorman stress, Kurdish feminists in the homeland and in diaspora share common histories of political struggle in relation to national oppression (2007: 80). Kurdish women have a long history of political activism and resistance in the states that divided them and in the diaspora countries where they are dispersed.

Some Kurdish youth are actively engaged in politics in diaspora as well as in the home country, but others are not. One young woman explained: 'As I came to Norway when I was 7 years old I didn't quite engage in my homeland's politics. As a Norwegian citizen I find it more important to be informed and active in the country where I live.' Nonetheless, examples abound of young Kurds raised in the Norwegian diaspora who continue their parents' struggles, albeit in new ways. Kurdish diaspora youth use Norwegian political parties and organizations to promote political issues in the home country. As members of organizations or parties, they learn to analyse and discuss various political challenges nationally and internationally while using their own or their parents' previous experiences and political knowledge. In the following I will discuss one example of this.

Bano, Gizem and Jamil

The terrorist attack on Utøya in Norway on 22 July 2011 took sixty-nine lives and shocked the entire world. Among the dead were three female Kurdish students, Bano Rashid (18), Gizem Dogan (17) and Jamil Rafal Mohamad Yasin (20), born and raised in politically active families that had fled their countries of origin to escape retaliation for oppositional political activities. In diaspora, Bano, Gizem and Jamil became affiliated with the Norwegian Labour Party's youth organization, Worker's Youth League (AUF) Family experiences and memories of the past, as well as national and international political issues became strong motivating factors in the engagement of the three young politicians. They came to regard peaceful political means as the only way to fight oppression, injustice, racism and gender inequality, and maintained that democratic processes should be promoted through openness and debate. The knowledge they developed meaningfully benefited their Kurdish environment and influenced and strengthened Norwegian society as well. Through their various efforts, members of the young diaspora generation act as ambassadors in a transnational process. Bano, Gizem and Jamil are shining examples of a young Kurdish diaspora generation of women. Raised in political environments, they maintained a link to their homeland by highlighting political issues in a Norwegian context.

They saw the importance of knowing their family background well and combining it with future political aspirations and visions.

The history of Kurdish women has documented generations of strife and renewal. Many Kurdish women in Norway and Europe have experience of areas of war, violence and conflict. Some of them are not in a position to narrate these experiences, other than to close family members. In diaspora, they often find themselves alone and without a female network. Yet many Kurdish women have used the opportunities provided in diaspora to develop as politically aware human beings. They mobilize their previous experiences, Mojab (2000) claims, as resources in their struggle to create alternative spaces and homes in diaspora. Many, having escaped from war-torn, patriarchal, colonial environments, joined the armed liberation movements in mountain camps where they educated themselves and developed practical skills that proved invaluable for organizing women in the diaspora.

This is also the case in Norway. After a meeting of a cultural association in Norway, a former female freedom fighter shared her thoughts with me: 'It came to the point of no return; I had to join the armed forces in the mountains. After having followed an education course here, I went to the mountains. I worked with press statements and media presentations, but primarily I worked on gender issues. Finally I had a feeling of doing something useful for my people' (F21).

On the other hand, the reorganization of the struggle in diaspora also creates opportunities for mobilization, recruitment and political lobbying to strengthen the struggle (van Bruinessen 2000), not least in terms of different educational activities and recruitment in Kurdish communities. In Kurdistan, as in diaspora, significant numbers of women participated in the education courses initiated by the PKK and Kurdistan Free Women's Party (Partiya Azadiya Jin a Kurdistan, PAJK)[4] as teachers or as students. Those who leave the mountains often continue to work and teach in diaspora. Educational and political activities, often designed for women in particular, have not only taught many illiterate women to read and write but also brought them political literacy as they learned to question their gender position within the family, society and diaspora (Westrheim 2009).

By participating politically in the struggle, the many Kurdish women engaged in political, social, cultural and educational work in the diaspora gain learning experiences and knowledge that subsequently benefit far more women than them. Their learning experiences form a basis for transformation, growth and change in themselves, their communities and politics. In this transformative process, women actively get involved and take control of their lives and futures (Westrheim

2009, 2010). Their motivation to work on gender issues might derive from an urge for liberation from oppression and violence perpetrated by husbands, male relatives or representatives of the military or the state.

We know from history that oppression fosters counter-initiative, and that people who are subjected to oppression over time often channel such initiative into organized rights work. Kurdish women past and present have fought the same battles as men and are still at the forefront of the struggle, suffering its consequences. Mojab and Gorman (2007) underline that many women in Middle Eastern war zones 'have extensive political backgrounds acquired through years of political and armed struggle in the region and in right based organizing' (2007: 59). Diaspora provides these women with opportunities to make their voices heard in their communities as well as in the larger society. A former research participant told me about getting the chance to work for other women after she came to Norway: 'I have met Kurdish women who had nothing in the past, who suffered domination by their fathers, husbands and sons. They never went to school; they could not even read or write their name. At the beginning it was difficult for them even to get permission to come to the cultural club, but little by little some of them opened up, they learn and feel empowered' (F30).

In this way, Kurdish women in Norway can act as conscious agents of transformative politics both in the home country and in diaspora. Sonja Lokar (2007) argues that women can change the very pattern of development and the understanding and practice of democracy, an ability crucial to their future participation in society and in politics. Women side with men in the actual political struggle, but history shows that they tend to be invisible, silenced or pushed aside in formal politics. This form of silencing women's voices and rendering women's political activities invisible originated in the home country and continues in diaspora. Referring to the case of Turkey, Handan Caglayan (2008) finds that the public sphere still preserves the masculine characteristics and patriarchal ideology that prevent women's visibility.

The desire to influence Kurdish politics to the same extent as their male politicians, or to participate in politics in Norway, is not something women should have to ask for; rather, they must claim or struggle for it. Even though political conflicts can complicate women's lives and set back their struggles for gender equality, Simona Sharoni (2001) claims that in a different context (e.g., the diaspora) a political conflict can become a springboard for gender equality, providing new opportunities and a source of learning and transformation for many women. It is often claimed that women's traditional domestic role in the family is an obstacle to public political action, that the world of the home and the world of the polity are sealed off (Sharoni 2001). However, many Kurdish women see domestic and political life as inseparable, whether in their home country or in diaspora. In this regard, Norwegian diaspora provides a space of opportunity for women's emancipation, political literacy and political participation in future politics.

The Kurdish Struggle as Learning Site

Within the PKK movement, women organize independently of their male comrades, a practice that eventually expanded their opportunities to organize both civically and politically (Westrheim 2009, 2010). Over time, PAJK gradually took over the coordination of ideology and its members' education, focusing on gender issues as part of the overall education programme (Flach 2007: 53). PAJK became a 'movement within the movement', maintaining that freedom for the Kurdish people and emancipation of women in Kurdistan depended on women's liberation. PAJK had been a key factor in the growth of the Kurdish freedom movement within Kurdish society and diaspora communities, and in the development of the struggle as a learning site for women.

In many parts of the world, women have occasionally turned to militant means to gain their legitimate rights and make their voices heard, be it in Europe or Africa, Palestine or Kurdistan. Many women's movements that once resorted to militant means in their struggle for rights are now mainstream movements that are taken for granted as part of the political landscape. It is easy to forget the militant past of women's movements that later succeeded in gaining political influence and status. This is important to bear in mind regarding Kurdish women still in the midst of their struggle.

The development of Kurdish women's political awareness in Kurdistan and diaspora has highlighted questions of equality, participation and choice, but so far, none of these goals are fully achieved for Kurdish women, regardless of where they live. As mentioned above, the PKK emphasized women's rights within Kurdish communities and recruited women from all classes, backgrounds and educational levels. In the last three decades, political participation has increased among Kurdish women in general, largely because of the PKK and pro-Kurdish parties like the Peace and Democracy Party and its predecessor, as well as political, cultural and social branches in diaspora. Mojab claims that 'recruitment of women ... draws them out of the domestic sphere and into the public sphere of life. In this process, women join the rank and file of political organizations, establish women's groups, publish journals, and contribute to society's consciousness about unequal gender relations' (2000: 93). As Laura B. Perry (2005) emphasizes, women in oppressed societies have a special interest in fighting for their rights. One way is to participate in collective political events, thus softening the border between the private and the public sphere.

In a previous interview study, one of the interviewees – a woman in her mid-thirties – answered this when asked how women can use opportunities in diaspora to develop political identity: 'Women can use their previous experiences and their current position in diaspora to develop a stronger political awareness among others by participating actively in different political organizations – Norwegian and Kurdish. This will open a world of new opportunities' (F37).

Indeed, numerous examples show that diaspora provides many Kurdish women with opportunities to develop as women and become politically aware. This same respondent related how her mother came to be politically aware. It all started in a small town in Norway:

> My mother came to Norway many years ago with her husband and children. She used to participate in a local women's association where women of different nationalities and ethnicities came together. She often said that she learned what her rights were but more important though was that she learned to cooperate with women of various backgrounds: illiterate, highly educated, young and elderly, single and married women. They had different political, social and cultural preferences but shared some common experiences as women in diaspora.' (F37)

Starting with small-scale political participation, Kurdish women have become leaders, mayors and deputies in their country of origin and in diaspora. This does not mean, however, that they have an easy political life. They still struggle against gender-based suppression by male colleagues in politics.

Despite women's important contributions to political development in Kurdistan as well as in diaspora, many problems remain unsolved. However, the tradition and struggle of women willing to sacrifice their positions and lives for a democratic society with equal opportunities for all will probably continue. The communities of women in diaspora play a significant role in this struggle. As humans, Paulo Freire (1982) argues, we are not only *in* the world, but also *with* the world and have the capacity to adapt to reality, to make choices and transform reality (Freire 1982: 3f). Kurdish women in diaspora are *with* the world as liberation fighters, participants in many forms of collective action and agents for change – often parallel to the women's resistance in the home country.

Many Kurdish women have managed to transform prior experiences into learning. Referring to an interview study on developing political awareness and learning in diaspora, Mojab (2006) describes how the respondents began to explain the history that led to increased awareness. Their histories unveiled up to twenty years of history of the political struggle, organizing and resistance to the state that led to flight, and revealed that they were still struggling politically in diaspora, although in a different way (2006: 168–89). Many Kurdish women are still far from getting a formal education. When access to formal learning sites is blocked, knowledge is sought elsewhere. With reference to Giroux (2007), Mojab (2006) argues that education and knowledge, whether gained inside or outside formal institutions, must include issues of gender, power, history and self-identity, and the possibility of collective agency and struggle.

Learning happens everywhere, and informal learning is taking place when women come together for discussion. One female respondent expressed this as follows: 'When I came to Norway in 1995 there was a group of women who met three times a week over a meal and talked. We learned to read and write, and we sang. The most important though was that we learned about each other. We listened to each other's stories and longings and discussed how we could improve our own and other women's lives' (F37). Historically speaking, women's groups, organizations or movements have always been empowering learning sites for women of diverse backgrounds by providing equal opportunities for all, from illiterates to academics. The Kurdish women's movement, as it is organized in North Kurdistan and diaspora, is no exception. The aim of this kind of education, according to Ira Shor, is to educate critical and conscious citizens, a goal that can only be achieved if people become aware of their subordinated position (2000: 25). By the same token, the fact that many Kurdish women in diaspora have political experience does not necessarily mean they possess political literacy, which is the ability to *understand* and *react* adequately in political situations and acquire new knowledge and new skills (Westrheim 2009, 2013). Political literacy also means becoming aware of one's democratic rights, and gradually becoming better equipped to participate in democratic life (Crick 1998: 3). Furthermore, political literacy implies the ability to read political situations and be aware of one's own position in the world (Lister 1994: 63). For all women, and particularly to women in areas with political and male dominated suppression, it is crucial to understand oneself as situated in a certain historical and political time and place, and at the same time to gain knowledge of the structures and patterns of the past, that is, history, culture, politics and socio-economic conditions and the power relations that shape them. Because individuals cannot easily obtain this knowledge and understanding, women's organizations in Norway and elsewhere have prioritized connections with women's organizations in home countries – and vice versa.

A respondent in a previous study grew up listening to family members' political discussions at home. She already had political experience when she came to Norway, but she had never reflected on how this knowledge and literacy could influence her own and other women's emancipation and political situation. She stressed the importance of diaspora with regards to developing political awareness:

> I came to Norway as an adult but grew up in a very 'political' family in Kurdistan. Actually, I was far more politically aware than any of my schoolmates. Politics was part of my daily life. Diaspora made me more attentive to the politics in Kurdistan and even more towards gender issues, rights and new ways of thinking and acting as a woman. Diaspora opened many doors to me and I will use these opportunities for the good of my people and women in particular. It is important that women in Norway and at home join forces. (F38)

Flach (2007) sees education as vital to the Kurdish struggle and the emancipation of Kurdish women, given the difficulty of addressing these issues without knowledge about why there is a struggle (Flach 2007: 86). Thus, transformative education is key to developing stronger political consciousness among women. Mojab (2006) mentions the example of a Kurdish freedom fighter in Sweden, an illiterate woman who had lived under governmental suppression. In diaspora, she gathered and mobilized women for the national cause; taught herself reading and writing in order to read the political literature; and learned to manage a large community of youth, support them, give them hope in life and inspire them to work for a better life in the future. Under conditions of war, this Kurdish woman was *learning for life*. This is informal learning, although we are not used to thinking of learning this way (Mojab 2006: 168; Mojab and Dobson 2008). The struggle for the Kurdish cause and a just and democratic society is also a struggle for learning and educational opportunities – and learning sites can be found everywhere.

Since the early 1990s, Kurdish women have refused to accept being alienated and silenced and taken to the streets to collectively claim their rights, a phenomenon growing in parallel with political development in Turkey. In this transformation process, women in North Kurdistan and in diaspora have learned how to organize and how to raise their issues in public (Westrheim 2013).

Kurdish women in Norwegian diaspora use diasporic opportunities to create spaces for self-development and learning. Even when facing obstacles, suspicion and challenges, many women try to pass on what they have learned to women in their home country. This is not an easy task. One respondent said she had to be careful when doing so: 'It is difficult to tell my female relatives and friends in the country I come from about my experiences in Norway. They find my thoughts about women and women's emancipation very strange as it comes from a foreign culture. I must be very careful in the way I present my ideas' (F36). But she remained convinced that diaspora has been critical to her learning and knowledge. She also learned that women in her home country can contribute meaningfully to women's movements in the West:

> Even if I come from a very liberal family, it was a shock to discover the way women think and act in Norway and how gender issues are handled politically. I also realized that Western women have a stereotype perception of women from the Middle East. Living in two countries taught me to understand both women living in the west and women from the more traditional east. As I have learnt a lot from living in Norway, women here can learn a lot from the struggle of women in my country. (F36)

When women become critically aware of their situation and of the powers that oppress them, Nadera Shalhoub-Kevorkian (2008) claims, regardless of the site or what shape the oppression takes, their resistance to occupying forces in the face of imposed patriarchal practices creates contradictory tensions. Nonetheless, women in diaspora use their learning experiences and the knowledge gained by participating in different voluntary and organized activities in diaspora to promote women's rights and enhance the political, social and cultural situation of women in both home and host country.

Conclusion

The historical political unrest in North Kurdistan (Turkey) and its conflicts, war and displacements have resulted in the dispersion of some one million Kurds of different social, educational and political backgrounds to diaspora communities all over the world. Large Kurdish diaspora communities have formed in European countries, Norway included, as well as the United States, Canada and Australia. Despite the difficulty of estimating exact numbers, it is fair to assume that women constitute a major part of Kurdish diaspora. The Kurdish diaspora in Norway numbers an estimated 6,000 people, primarily from Iraq but also from other parts of Kurdistan, like the southeastern regions of Turkey.

The Kurds have, as Mojab affirms, been targets of genocide, ethnic cleansing, linguicide and ethnocide (external war) in Turkey, Iran, Iraq and Syria. But at the same time, male members of the Kurdish nation wage an internal war against women. These two wars interlink in complex ways (Mojab 2000: 89). Kurdish women from traditional families often have limited possibilities to engage in activities outside the home. In North Kurdistan (Turkey), however, many women have been on the front lines of the PKK's political movement and armed struggle since its foundation in the late 1970s. For many women this became a site of experiences that have proved key to the general politicization of Kurdish women in North Kurdistan and the Kurdish European and Norwegian diaspora. Women's emancipation and political engagement have encouraged them to seek knowledge and definitely fostered learning.

In the introduction I asked the question 'How do knowledge and learning in diaspora enhance political awareness and political literacy among Kurdish women?' When access to education is prohibited, knowledge and learning are sought elsewhere: in the mountains, in prisons or in collective action in the streets (Westrheim 2008, 2009, 2010, 2013). Excerpts from the respondents' interviews reveal that Kurdish women in diaspora claim to have learned a lot while living abroad, from becoming aware of women's rights to establishing women's organizations where they arrange social and cultural events. Women's associations in diaspora also organize language courses. For many decades the Turkish authorities have alienated and suppressed the Kurdish language, which is still banned as a tool for learning within the formal educational system. Many women came illiterate to Norway or other host countries but claim to have learned to read and write thanks to the initiative taken by, among others, Kurdish women's organizations, not least organizations affiliated with the PKK and PAJK. In addition, women seem to have raised their critical awareness about issues concerning the general situation for Kurds to the extent that it has fostered a political awakening. Through this kind of transformative educative learning experience in diaspora, Kurdish women have gradually developed political literacy, becoming able to read political situations and gain awareness of their situatedness in the world. With this comes an urge to transfer some of these experiences to other women in the homeland.

Diaspora functions as a bridge between countries of origin and host countries. This chapter has argued that knowledge gained by Kurdish women of the diaspora has been valuable to their own development, and that many women pass the benefits of diasporic experiences on to female relatives and friends in the homeland in a joint effort to change the role of women within Kurdish society. This is not an easy task. One of the respondents mentioned the need for caution when talking about this in traditional, male-dominated environments, whether in diaspora or in her homeland. But despite the challenges Kurdish women face in their country of origin and in diaspora, many have acquired education and become active participants in the diaspora communities and the wider society – like Bano, Gizem and Jamil, now remembered as important political and cultural contributors to both Norwegian society and their Kurdish communities.

Notes

1. The Kurdish regions in the southeast of Turkey are termed North Kurdistan.
2. About 350,000 Turkish citizens applied for asylum in Germany between 1980 and 1990 (Eccarius-Kelly 2002: 93).
3. This example comes from an interview with a 29-year-old woman (F29). Data were collected between 2006 and 2008 in Turkey, England, Belgium and Norway. Data cited in this format have not been published previously.

References

Alinia, M. 2004. 'Spaces of Diasporas: Kurdish Identities, Experiences of Otherness and Politics of Belonging', Ph.D. dissertation. Göteborg: Göteborg University, Department of Sociology.

Anderson, B. 1991. *Imagined Communities*. London and New York: Verso.

———. 1998. *The Spectre of Comparisons: Nationalism, Southeast Asia, and the World*. London: Verso.

Bergland, B.A. (2011). Introduction, in B.A. Bergland & L.A. Lahlum, *Norwegian, American Women. Migration, Communities, and Identities*. St. Paul, MN: Minnesota Historical Society Press, pp. 3–18.

Blaettel-Mink, B. 2006. 'Gendered Kurdish Lives', *Feminist Europe. Review of Books* 6(1): 38–41.

Brubaker, P. 2005. 'The 'Diaspora' Diaspora', *Ethnic and Racial Studies* 28(1): 1–19.

Caglayan, H. 2008. 'Voices from the Periphery of the Periphery: Kurdish Women's Political Participation in Turkey', *IAFFE 17th Annual Conference on Feminist Economics, 19–21 June 2008, Torino, Italy*. Retrieved 25 July 2010 from https://editorialexpress.com/cgi-bin/conference/download.cgi?db_name =IAFFE2008&paper_id=276

Casey, E. 1996. *The Fate of Place: Philosophical History*. Berkeley and Los Angeles: University of California Press.

Cohen, A. 1997. *Global Diasporas: An Introduction*. Seattle: University of Washington Press.

Crick, B. 1998. *Education for Citizenship and the Teaching of Democracy in Schools: Final Report of the Advisory Group on Citizenship (the Crick Report)*. London: QCA/98/245.

Curtis, A. 2005. *Nationalism in the Diaspora. A Study of the Kurdish Movement: Nationalism, Ethnicity and Conflict.* Utrecht: University of Utrecht. Retrieved 22 October 2013 from https://cs.uwaterloo.ca/~a2curtis/courses/

Eccarius-Kelly, V. 2002. 'Political Movements and Leverage Points: Kurdish Activism in the European Diaspora', *Journal of Muslim Minority Affairs* 22(1): 91–118.

Flach, A. 2007. *Frauen in der Kurdischen Guerilla. Motivation, Identität und Geschlechtersverhältnis.* Cologne: Papyrossa Verlag.

Freire, P. (1982). Education as the practice of freedom. In *Education for critical consciousness* (pp. 1–84). New York: The Continuum Publishing Company.

Fuglerud, Ø. 1999. *Life on the Outside: The Tamil Diaspora and Long-Distance Nationalism.* London: Pluto Press.

Gran, E. 2008. 'Imagining the Transnational Lives of Iraqi Kurds', Ph.D. dissertation. Oslo: University of Oslo.

Hassanpour, A. 1994. 'The Kurdish Experience', *Middle East Report* 24(4): 2–7, 23.

———. 1998. 'Satellite Footprints as National Borders: Med-TV and the Extraterritoriality of State Sovereignty', *Journal of Muslim Minority Affairs* 18(1): 53–72.

Karlsen, G. M. 2007. *Turkey: Need for Firm Leadership on Human Rights.* The Norwegian Helsinki Committee, Report 25. Retrieved 1 January 2007 from http://humanrightshouse.org/Articles/5748.html

Lister, I. 1994. 'Conscientization and Political Literacy: A British Encounter with Paulo Freire', in P.L. McLaren and C. Lankshear (eds), *Politics of Liberation: Paths from Freire.* London and New York: Routledge, pp. 62–73.

Lokar, S. 2007. 'Democracy in Eastern Europe: Women's way?' *Development* 50: 110–16. doi:10.1057/palgrave.development.1100341.

Lyon, A.J. and E. Uçarer. 2001. 'Mobilizing Ethnic Conflict: Kurdish Separatism in Germany and the PKK', *Ethnic and Racial Studies* 24(6): 925–48.

McDowell, D. 2000. *A Modern History of the Kurds,* 2nd ed. New York: Taurus.

Mojab, S. 2000. 'Vengeance and Violence: Kurdish Women Recount the War', *Canadian Women's Studies* 19(4): 89–94.

———. 2006. 'War and Diaspora as Lifelong Learning Contexts for Immigrant Women', in C. Leathwood and B. Francis (eds), *Gender and Lifelong Learning: Critical Feminist Engagements.* London: Routledge, pp. 164–75.

Mojab, S. and S. Dobson. 2008. 'Women, War and Learning', *International Journal of Lifelong Education* 27(2): 119–27. doi: 10.1080/02601370801936283.

Mojab, S. and R. Gorman. 2007. 'Dispersed Nationalism: War, Diaspora and Kurdish Women's Organizing', *Transnational Theory, National Politics, and Gender in the Contemporary Middle East / North Africa,* special issue, *Journal of Middle East Women's Studies* 3(1): 58–85.

Özcan, A.K. 2006. *Turkey's Kurds: A Theoretical Analysis of the PKK and Abdullah Öcalan.* London and New York: Routledge.

Perry, L.B. 2005. 'Education for Democracy: Some Basic Definitions, Concepts and Clarifications', in J. Zajda (ed.), *International Handbook on Globalisation, Education and Policy Research.* The Netherlands: Springer, pp. 685–92.

Rugkåsa, M. 2004. 'Die Traditionellen, die Modernen und die Politischen: Politische Ausrichtung und Geschlecteideologie unter kurdischen Migranten in Oslo', in S. Hajo, C. Bork, E. Savelsberg and S. Dogan (eds), *Kurdologie Band 6: Gender in Kurdistan und der Diaspora*. Münster: Unrast-Verlag.

Safran, W. 1991. 'Diasporas in Modern Societies: Myths of Homeland and Return', *Diaspora* 1(1): 83–99.

Semmingsen, I. 1988. 'Kvinner i norsk utvandringshistorie', in *Migranten* [The Migrant]. Oslo: Nasjonalbiblioteket, pp. 7–23.

Shalhoub-Kevorkian, N. 2008. 'The Gendered Nature of Education under Siege: A Palestinian Feminist Perspective', *International Journal of Lifelong Education* 27(2): 179–200.

Sharoni, S. 2001. 'Rethinking Women's Struggles in Israel-Palestine and in the North of Ireland', in C. Moser and F. Clark (eds), *Victims, Perpetrators or Actors: Gender, Armed Conflict and Political Violence*. London: Zed, pp. 85–98.

Shor, I. 2000. 'Education Is Politics: Paulo Freire's Critical Pedagogy', in P. Leonard and P. McLaren (eds), *Paulo Freire: A Critical Encounter*. London and New York: Routledge, Taylor & Francis Group, pp. 25–36.

Tharmalingam, S. 2011. 'Remittance Practices and Transnational Social Spaces of Tamils and Somalis in Norway', *Nordic Journal of Migration Research* 1(3): 166–75. doi: 10.2478/v10202-011-0017-x

The Kurdish Institute in Paris. 2013. 'The Kurdish Diaspora'. Retrieved 5 November, 2013 from http://www.institutkurde.org/en/kurdorama/

The 2nd National Congress of Kurdish Women. 2012. 'Conference for Kurdish women discusses creating global association'. Retrieved 22 April 2013 from http://www.ekurd.net/mismas/articles/misc2012/5/state6240.htm

van Bruinessen, M. 1988. 'Between Guerrilla War and Political Murder: The Worker's Party of Kurdistan', *Middle East Report* 153: 40–46, 50. Retrieved 19 November 2012 from http://www.let.uu.nl/~martin.vanbruinessen/personal/ publications/2851(198807%2F08)153%3C40%3ABGWAPM%3E2.0.CO%3B2-3

————. 1999. 'The Kurds in Movement: Migrations, Mobilisations, Communications and the Globalisation of the Kurdish Question', Working Paper No. 14, Islamic Area Studies Project, Tokyo, Japan. Retrieved 21 April 2008 from http://www.let.uu.nl/~martin.vanbruinessen/personal/publications/index .html

————. 2000. 'Transnational Aspects of the Kurdish Question', working paper, Robert Schuman Centre for Advanced Studies, European University Institute, Florence.

Wahlbeck, OÈ. 1999. *Kurdish Diasporas: A Comparative Study of Kurdish Refugee Communities*. London: Macmillan

————. 2002. 'The Concept of Diaspora as an Analytical Tool in the Study of Refugee Communities', *Journal of Ethnic and Migration Studies* 28(2): 221–38.

Westrheim, K. 2005. 'Cultural Identity and Oppression Experienced through the Kurdish Liberation Struggle', in H. Akman and O. Stoknes (eds), *The Cultural Heritage of the Kurds*. University of Bergen: BRIC. Center for Development Studies, pp. 105–28.

————. 2008. 'Prison as Site for Political Education: Educational Experiences from Prison Narrated by Members and Sympathisers of the PKK', *Journal for Critical Education Policy Studies* 6(1). Retrieved 12 December 2009 from http://www.jceps.com/?pageID=article&articleID=120

———. 2009. *'Education in a Political Context: A Study of Knowledge Processes and Learning Sites in the PKK'*, Ph.D thesis. Bergen: University of Bergen, Norway.

———. 2010. 'Choosing the Mountains: The PKK as Alternative Knowledge and Identity Project', *Politics, Culture and Socialization* 2(2), pp. 99–122.

———. 2013. 'Taking to the streets! Kurdish Collective Action in Turkey', in C. Gunes & W. Zeydanlioglu (eds), *The Kurdish Question in Turkey: New Perspectives on Conflict, Representation and Reconciliation*. London, New York; Routledge, pp. 137–61.

White, P. 2000. *Primitive Rebels or Revolutionary Modernizers? The Kurdish National Movement in Turkey*. London and New York: Zed Books.

꧂ 7

TERRITORIAL STIGMATIZATION, INEQUALITY OF SCHOOLING AND IDENTITY FORMATION AMONG YOUNG IMMIGRANTS

Bolette Moldenhawer

Introduction

Since the publication of the OECD's authoritative report on the disadvantages students from immigrant backgrounds suffer in comparison to their ethnic-majority peers in terms of performance and advancement in Europe's highly varied school systems (OECD 2006), ethnic differences in education have become a prime target of research and policymaking within national frameworks and at the continental level. At the same time, policymakers and parents alike are concerned about both the increasing importance of educational qualifications and the problems associated with multicultural urban and educational contexts (Butler and van Zanten 2007). The facts of ethnic differentiation within and by schools are widely acknowledged, but their explanations show great variations. Based on major findings from the EDUMIGROM research project,[1] this chapter will apply an analytical approach that aims to reveal how the complex interplay among the prevailing key factors of social background, ethnicity, gender and residential segregation produces and reproduces disadvantages for immigrant youth in compulsory education. The focus, in particular, is on gender's impact on the ways school systems, students' practices and social relations relate to the symbolic and social order of local residential areas and become superimposed on the stigmata of ethnicity. Inspired by Wacquant (2007, 2008a, 2008b), this symbolic work around schooling will be conceptualized in relation to mechanisms of territorial stigmatization in the age of advanced marginality. Moreover, by dealing with the concept of transnational community, the analysis will take into account changing patterns of identity formation among young immigrants and ways they affect female students in the context of territorial segregation and stigmatization.

The chapter consists of four parts. The first part looks at students' school achievements and outlines two sets of factors that contribute to the function of ethnicity in assessing immigrant students' performance: (1) differences in familial conditions, and (2) differences according to the socio-ethnic profile of the schools. The next section delineates Wacquant's theoretical contribution to the modality of territorial stigmatization and the additional concept of transnational community. An empirical analysis of the multiple hierarchies of social backgrounds, gender, residential areas, schooling and ethnic discrimination in selected Danish and French cases follows. In the final section, I conclude by proposing a discussion of Wacquant's work that rethinks the implications for research into identity formation among young immigrants and the mechanisms of territorial and ethno-racial stigmatization that operate via the functioning of school institutions.

Inequality of Schooling and the Role of Ethnicity

The findings in this section are based on a survey of young people aged 14–17 in their final year of compulsory education. The aim of the survey was to gain quantitatively comparable information about young people's thoughts and experiences concerning the role of ethnicity in schooling and in their everyday lives (Szalai, Messing and Neményi 2010).[2] The point of departure was the study of relative social disadvantages affecting people from minority backgrounds that are manifested in ethnically informed differences. In other words: How does the role of ethnicity add to the role students' gender and family conditions play in shaping their achievements, by emphasizing implied cultural differences?

The first set of factors contributing to the role of ethnic differences in school achievement[3] is the students' familial conditions. The overarching conclusion is that parental educational attainment, as an indicator of cultural capital, is the most important constituent of acknowledged performance. As our data show, 'students from highly-educated families have close to five times greater chance of attaining an "excellent" qualification than fellow students from a very poorly educated parental background' (Szalai 2011: 9). The family's socio-economic position and the related factor of income regularity also induce differences similar to those concerning cultural educational background, although their impact is milder than the latter's. Moreover, the data show that ethnicity plays a distinct role in the students' level of achievement, since ethnic minority students' assessed performance has disparate prospects of catching up with that of majority peers of similar social backgrounds. More specifically, the data show that '[w]hile the difference between the proportions of "excellently" qualified students of majority and "visibly" minority backgrounds is 6 per cent in the case of those coming from poorly educated families, it jumps to 26 per cent among students of highly qualified parents' (Szalai, Messing and Neményi 2010: 40). This widening of the ethnic gap points clearly to an important conclusion, namely, that the higher the respondents were positioned in the social hierarchy, the more intense the ethnic distinctions in evaluations became. Meanwhile, in a closer look at how gender intersects with social backgrounds in relation to students' performance, the data confirm what is already known about the significance of gender in education, namely that the impact of gender is milder than that of the students' social background (Archer 2003: 7–26). Furthermore, girls are performing better than boys independently of social background, or to put it differently, girls apparently adjust better to the official requirements of schooling than boys do (Szalai, Messing and Neményi 2010: 37).

The survey study reveals a second set of factors contributing to the role of ethnic differences in school performances in the socio-ethnic profile of the schools. Regarding clusters of schools according to the ratio of ethnic minority students from better-off and poor backgrounds, respectively, school-level average grade scores comprised a steep hierarchy, with a gap of at least 35 per cent between 'top' schools attended by children of the local elite and other schools dominated by disadvantaged ethnic minority students. Half of the 'top' schools are so-called elite schools that offer special courses and are known for their high level of performance. Well-educated ethnic majority families provide 72 per cent of their students, and they accept talented ethnic minority students and/or poor children in rare exceptions, if at all. It is debatable whether these differences reflect only the role of students' ethnic, educational and socio-economic background, described above. However, a closer analysis of the results shows 'that institutional distinctions by social and ethnic background play a significant role in their own right: they accentuate individual differences by organizing them into powerful institutional arrangements' (Messing and Neményi 2010: 45).

This finding is justified, considering the different opportunities students of both genders from the same backgrounds have to attain 'excellent' or end up with 'low' qualifications. Having attended a 'top' school, at least 48 per cent of ethnic majority students from highly educated backgrounds wound up with 'excellent' qualifications, while the corresponding ratio was as low as 18 per cent among those members of that group who, despite their family's high standing, attended low-ranked schools dominated by disadvantaged ethnic minority students. Moreover, the data reveal distinctions in institutional differentiations in average performance work in identical directions for all groups of students: depending on the school's position in the hierarchy of the educational market, students from similar ethnic and social backgrounds are evaluated differently, suggesting that the value of the same cultural capital was different in schools with different positions in the education market hierarchy. The role of this differentiating level of performance has further implications in that it conceals existing differences in ethnic and social structures and converts their compound impact into educational ranking. This lays the foundation for qualitative comparisons that seem fair by taking only a single marker of identification into account, namely, the ranking of the school institution in the educational market. At any rate, this way of positioning of schools in a widely recognized, market based institutional hierarchy is legitimized by the way 'the invisible institutional addition to assessments on the individual level boosts ethnic-social differences in performance, and thus informs and legitimizes further selections, while assisting in socializing all the involved actors to look at the distinctions as "natural" and "inevitable" givens carried by the impersonal structure of schooling' (Szalai 2011: 13).

To sum up the above findings on the socio-ethnic aspects of differences in students' performance for both genders: European school institutions act as agents of social production and reproduction, although differently. At the same time, the survey study indicates that the amalgamation of these two fundamental social categories of the students' position plays out in a rather complicated way. On the individual level, the significance of ethnic differences contributes more fully to the importance of socioeconomic differences. As described above, when similar social backgrounds are compared, schools are predisposed to evaluate students of ethnic majority background at higher grade levels than ethnic minority students. As for the institutional level, the findings point to the function of institutional segmentation as one of the most powerful ways of institutionalizing, legitimizing and smoothly reproducing ethnic distinctions. In the local environments where the schools are located, the acute differences in these schools' socio-ethnic structures are further enhanced by the differences in assessed individual performance, thus deepening the ethnic divides in school achievement.

It is hard to read this interplay between the individual and institutional dimensions of the socio-ethnic ordering of schools as anything other than a further educational segmentation of ethnic minority students, who end up in local schools with bad reputations that make it difficult to envisage an acceptable educational future. And because the socio-ethnic ordering of schools is also affected by mechanisms of residential segregation marked by unemployment and low educational level, it can lead to further negative consequences, such as a concentration of social problems and marginalization. The institutional dysfunction of schools that are not powerful enough to counteract the impacts of a wider scale of socio-spatial and ethnic processes that increase segmentation and segregation can label their attendees with an 'undesired differentness', and hence 'a stigma attached to territory which becomes superimposed onto and redoubles the stigmata of race and poverty' (Wacquant 2010: 217). Ethnic minority people trapped in schools and districts widely perceived as 'problem areas' might respond by deploying a strategy of either symbolic self-protection, in which the residential segregation can act as a protective shield from the ethnic majority society, or by reinforcing the experienced differences, disadvantaged position and division line between themselves and their ethnic majority peers.

Both questions – how school segregation is tied to varying forms of residential segregation, and how it affects the stigma attached to the image of 'problem people' in general and girls in particular – will be analysed more fully in the empirical section on the Danish and French cases. The next section will delineate the conceptualization of territorial stigmatization, ethnicization and transnational community as a background to the empirical analysis.

Territorial Stigmatization, Ethnicization and Transnational Communities

In the early days of the new century, territorial stigmatization is a novel dimension of inequality and urban marginality in both the United States and Europe. This new social reality, Wacquant argues, is generated by the scarcity and instability of work as well as the changing role of the state that is further confused by what he describes as the ethnicized idiom of immigration, discrimination and 'diversity'. Rather than denoting various forms of ethnic group formation (Hamaz and Vasta 2009: 10), ethnicization receives attention as a mechanism pushing issues of 'immigration' and 'ethnic minority discrimination' forward as prominent social problems, and thus serves to obscure the more important social problem of insecure work and the consequent formation of marginal urban populations (Wacquant 2008a: 116). Fundamentally, territorial stigmatization is a socio-spatial order determined by the dualizing hierarchy of class and place, thus breaks with the errors concerning place which are inscribed in substantialist thought that ignores the study of relations between social structures and physical structures. Wacquant developed his overall theory of advanced urban marginality as 'a theoretically guided empirical comparison of the (hyper)ghetto of Chicago and the (post-industrial) working-class periphery of Paris' (Wacquant 2008b: 166). Even though *banlieues* are seen as enclaves of pluri-ethnic zones with a high concentration of immigrants and their descendants, it is crucial to note that ghettos and *banlieues* are the legacies of different urban trajectories and arise from different forms of social classification: in French working-class *banlieues*, social classification primarily proceeds on the basis of class position, moderated by ethnic categories and categorizations and mitigated by public policy and institutions, whereas in black American ghettos, social classification occurs more readily on the basis of a historically ethno-racial membership.

The concept of stigma is taken from Erving Goffman and Pierre Bourdieu, respectively, to highlight how the public disgrace afflicting these 'problem areas' devalues their residents' sense of self and corrodes their social ties (Wacquant 2008a: 116). Wacquant argues that territorial stigma is akin to the third type of stigma in Goffman's analysis – that of 'race, nation and religion' – because they can both be transmitted through lineage and easily affect all members of an ethnic group, kinship or family (Wacquant 2007: 67). Moreover, he builds on Bourdieu's relational sociology, which calls attention to the search for homologue relations between social, spatial and mental structures and consequently investigates how social space, at once inscribed in spatial structures and in mental structures partly produced by the incorporation of these structures, is the site where power is stressed, no doubt in its subtlest form, as symbolic violence that goes unperceived as violence (Bourdieu et al. 1999: 126).

Based on an empirical analysis of local belonging in a working-class, ethnically mixed residential area in Denmark, Jensen and Christensen argue that the way Wacquant employs territorial stigma is closer to the concept of symbolic violence taken from Bourdieu than to the concept of stigma taken from Goffman (Jensen and Christensen 2012: 77–78). In their view, further empirical analysis may challenge the way social and geographical structures are held to be incorporated as mental structures influencing conceptions of self among residents in deprived areas. In the next section I undertake this challenge by showing how the stigmatized school with a high concentration of ethnic minority students certainly stands out as a zone of exception – that is, it is understood as a sanctuary from negative representations of 'immigrants' in public and political discourses. Additionally, I explore the role of symbolic power, characterized as power that makes itself known as legitimizing categorizations and classifications in relationships with group structures, and the way in which these function as distinctions based on ethnicity, gender, place and class. I draw on Sylvie Tissot (2007) and Melissa Nobles (2010) in order to discuss how ethnic stigma, together with territorial stigma, alter one more obstacle in the path to schooling.

In order to analyse the patterns of identity formation, I draw on a conceptualization of 'migrants' who, as identified by Sayad (2004), are simultaneously agents of emigration and immigration. Identity formation among immigrants is hence understood as constant processes of coming to terms with one's history of emigration and immigration. This approach counters immigrant-state-centred research on integration and migration along the power structures that socially locate immigrants as belonging or not belonging by taking the 'here' – the 'national' or the 'local' setting – as a granted analytical device without attending to the way the 'local' or the 'national' is transnationalized (Wimmer and Glick Schiller 2002, cited in Hamaz and Vasta 2009: 9). Moreover, racialization as a form of power relation embedded in the history of emigration and immigration has been the object of study in this approach. Gilroy (2009) for example explains how racial relations are embedded in the history of European nation-building, especially by looking at the way in which the Britain's languages of 'race' and nation have been articulated together. Efforts to combine them are noticeable in the discursive and structural framework where the 'host' society negotiates and reifies belonging. Race and racism are as such related to a powerful dimension of social differentiation that works to shape social, economic and cultural relations and designate unequal positions.

Gilroy does however also deliver a critique of the uncritical celebration of the reification of cultural differences. He argues against the 'cultural diversity regime' that affirms blackness as an open signifier and seeks to celebrate complex representations of black particularity internally divided by class, gender, sexuality and age (2009: 565). Wacquant, on the other, introduces his concept of ethnicization to demonstrate how the cultural diversity regime and the assertion of complex identities has failed to take into account the discourses and structures that maintain inequality and social problems confronting many ethno-racial communities. The powerful territorial stigma attached to residence in areas that are mixed in terms of both ethnic and social classification, along with the presence of school institutions that will be the focus below, enables us to identify the main factors accounting for the muted social potency of gender and ethnic classification in the selected French and Danish urban peripheries.

The Danish and French Empirical Cases

The Danish and French cases are selections from a total of nine country studies by EDUMIGROM. Although I was in charge of the Danish country study (Thomsen, Moldenhawer and Kallehave 2010; Moldenhawer, Kallehave and Hansen 2010; Moldenhawer and Padovan-Özdemir 2011), here I will build on the findings in the country study reports made by the French research team (Felouzis et al. 2010; Schiff 2010a, 2010b, 2011). A comparative approach can be a powerful tool to 'make the familiar strange and the strange familiar' in order to highlight what we take for granted in our own 'national context' (Broadfoot 1999; Osborn et al. 2003: 24). The purpose of choosing the French case, in addition to the well-known Danish case, is to further unravel the interplay between school segregation and the varying forms of residential segregation, and how it affects the stigma attached to the image of 'problem people' in general, and the role of gender in particular. I argue that France and Denmark are fruitful national cases for comparison because they differ substantially. First of all, Denmark's educational system has historically been differentiated, specialized and decentralized, whereas the French system has been unified, systematized and centralized (Archer 1979; Schiff et al. 2008a). The cases furthermore differ concerning relations between the public and the private, the individual and the collective, marketization (Moody and Thévenot 2000; Pedersen 2011; Raveaud and van Zanten 2007), the colonial past and immigration history (Schiff et al. 2008b; Noiriel 1996) and the categorization of 'the immigrant' linked to different models of citizenship (Jønsson and Petersen 2010; van Zanten 1997). The comparative approach aims to discern key invariants and variants in the social, spatial and mental structures of territorial and ethnic stigmatization and schooling.

Residential Areas and the Schools

The scale of residential separation varied between the Danish and the French schools in the study.[4] One Danish school is in a neighbourhood dominantly or exclusively inhabited by immigrant groups, and the other is on the edge of a segregated ethnic minority community. By contrast, the schools in France are located in the a general catchment area that provides education for students – depending on their course of study – who come both from local neighbourhoods and from further away. The French schools are located in a disadvantaged, working-class Parisian suburb of the Seine-Saint-Denis district where the proportion of immigrants is higher than the national average. In line with the features of the chosen residential area, the schools' student population is ethnically very diverse (especially immigrants[5] of Maghrebian origin and from Turkey or the African continent), but socially rather homogeneous and overwhelmingly lower-class, with two thirds of the students having parents with low or very low levels of educational certification. One of the schools – a mixed vocational and technological upper secondary school receiving a predominantly male population of close to 700 students – is positioned lower in the educational market hierarchy than other vocational schools in the area because the socio-economic background of the student body available for enrolment is even less favourable than at the other schools. Moreover, the school is required to enrol students whose very poor academic performance rules out their acceptance elsewhere (Schiff 2010a: 25). The other school is a large technological and vocational school of over one thousand students (of both genders) surrounded by several disadvantaged public housing complexes well known for their high rates of unemployment and crime. The school has striven to improve itself as a vocational high school by offering real employment opportunities and options for continuing to higher education, and moreover by opening one general class and several technical streams. However, this has not sufficed to counteract the poor reputation associated with the immediate neighbourhood and the school's former status as a vocational school (ibid.: 27). Consequently, the school environment has suffered a 'moral panic' similar to that delineated by Wacquant in his study of the *banlieues* (Wacquant 2008b: 138) because of its association with the French version of the 'ghetto' and all its social problems, poverty, unemployment, single-parent households and immigration, and its further association with the poor reputation of the immediate neighbourhood. Yet another dimension of the school environment is the presence of bureaucratic institutions that have long been known for their initiatives on behalf of immigrants and their descendants.

The two schools selected in Copenhagen, Denmark, are located in the same catchment area of the city but in two rather distinct neighbourhoods of differing socioeconomic and ethnic composition. Both are public schools.[6] One is in an area dominated by the middle class and lower middle class, private housing and working-class rental apartments. In the couple of year, the total number of students (of both genders) rose from 500 to 750 due to the closing of a neighbouring school dominated by students of immigrant backgrounds. Consequently, the share of students with an immigrant background rose from 15 per cent to about 40 per cent. The other school is in a social housing area that is geographically isolated from the rest of the community. Its student body of almost 475 (of both genders) almost exclusively comprises students with immigrant background and from lower social-class backgrounds. The differences dividing the neighbourhoods are further reflected in the very different levels of public and political attention paid to them. While the former neighbourhood seems to receive very limited public and political attention, the latter is often referred to as a 'ghetto'.[7] Built during the period from the 1950s to the 1970s, this neighbourhood was conceived as a model town offering 'a decent life' for all social groups. Rental apartments in the two- and three-storey buildings organized around a public school and other welfare institutions. However, this development of an archetypical Danish model area with a clear character of unity and neighbourhood never became the healthy, differentiated social landscape it was meant to be (Gaardmand 1993: 50–51). In the 1970s, the first immigrants to move into the neighbourhood were mainly Turkish guest workers, followed by family settlement in the 1980s. Today more than 60 per cent of the residents are immigrants and their descendants, while 50 per cent of the adults are part of the workforce, leaving the other 50 per cent of adults with income from different types of social security schemes, such as early retirement, unemployment benefits or cash benefits for uninsured persons (Thomsen, Moldenhawer and Kallehave 2010). Being increasingly economically marginalized and politically doomed as an area for outsiders, the neighbourhood has received massive attention and supplementary funding from the municipality, public housing corporations and NGOs to support 'integration' (Moldenhawer and Øland 2011).

Residential Segregation and Inequality of Schooling

The historical organization of the French school system was based on the ideas of universalism and republicanism. The state had an obligation to free its citizens from the influence of religion and promote a strong national identity and social solidarity. This fundamental understanding of education as an institution to promote equal citizens of the Republic explains why the notion of differentiated teaching according to perceived needs is so difficult to implement there: the system is strongly influenced by the formal national commitment to a unified system of provision. The school system in Denmark differs considerably from the French system. Even though the compulsory education curriculum has become even more centralized in the last decade, the school system has a strong tradition of communitarianism grounded in a tradition of local democracy and social partnership (Osborn et al. 2003: 38). Consequently, the system strives to impart differentiated education to each individual so that everyone has the best chance of developing according to his or her abilities within the Danish school system. Meanwhile, in both Denmark and France there is strong emphasis on the idea of egalitarianism – providing the same education for all, regardless of differences in family background. In fact, however, both educational inequality and school segregation exist in more or less subtle ways in both systems.

The case studies reveal a pattern of different connections between school segregation and forms of residential segregation. In France, it is rather exceptional to leave a given school district, whereas parents in Denmark exercise a high degree of freedom to seek out the school they consider most appropriate for their child. However, some have argued that despite the lack of an official policy of choice, French parents, in particular middle-class parents, do choose schools beyond the catchment area, either by sending their children to private schools or by moving close to the school they consider best for their children (Raveaud and van Zanten 2007: 111). This shows how difficult it is for even the most egalitarian parents to reconcile equality for all with their children's success in heterogeneous classrooms. The parents' dilemma is, on the one hand, the equal opportunity all children deserve for academic achievement, and on the other, the problems they face when teachers have to pay too much special attention to 'problem students'. The considerable strength of this perception in France is due to the combination of a long tradition in academic qualifications and the system's tradition of limited pedagogical differentiation (ibid.: 121).

In the French schools in the study, the enrolment of students entails similar processes of social and ethnic segregation. Even though it is mandatory that students attend their designated local school and that schools admit all students residing within the catchment area (although this rule is more loosely applied in upper-secondary schools), members of upwardly aspiring, mainly lower middle-class parents wishing to improve their children's prospects resort to border-crossing. Indeed, the existence of vocational and non-vocational upper secondary schools, and of a wide variety of different study programmes with unequal levels of desirability, leads to the departure of better-off students. This produces further inequalities between schools, thereby exacerbating the effects of the institutional segregation of schooling (Schiff 2011: 11).

In the neighbourhoods of the Seine-Saint-Denis district where the schools are located, non-European residents are quite seldom in the majority. Citing Preteceille (2009), Schiff writes that '[t]wo thirds of non-European minority households live in neighbourhoods in which they represent less than 30 per cent of the local resident population', arguing: 'It is probable therefore that the high concentration of these groups in certain schools is due as much to differential educational choices and strategies of majority and minority families than it is to the effect of increased residential segregation' (2011: 5–6). Studies of students' experience of streaming at the end of lower secondary school confirm that students with North and Sub-Saharan African immigrant backgrounds, particularly those who have been enrolled in vocational programmes, often begin their upper-secondary school career with a sense of having been negatively selected and unjustly constrained in their educational options (Schiff 2010a: 31). Student interviews make clear that low-performing immigrant students are much more likely to fail because they have developed a 'school culture of opposition' fed by feelings of both stigmatization and disillusion at having been placed in programmes for which they did not apply, or that do not correspond to their true aspirations. Especially immigrant girls in a vocational class in the food services industry described their disappointment at having been 'placed' in what they perceived as a dead-end programme. Many of them had professional ambitions that appeared unrealistic, and they did not seem to have come to terms with their limited educational prospects (Schiff 2010b: 11). Conversely, immigrant boys who had likewise been enrolled in a vocational programme other than the one they wanted appeared less dissatisfied with their lot than the girls, probably because of their much better professional prospects and chances of continuing their studies. Thus immigrant students in general, and immigrant girls in particular, are more inclined to blame their failure on the school system and teachers than are ethnic majority students, who are more grateful to the vocational school for keeping them, despite their educational problems and personal failings (Schiff 2010b: 34).

In Denmark there was some tension between the traditional image of consensus and homogeneity, and the tendency within the two schools to move towards a more consumer-oriented philosophy of education, encouraging an individual school identity. In addition, now that the relaxation of regulation of school catchment areas allows parents to choose schools outside their area, 'reputation' has increased significance as a 'marker of identity'. In each of the two schools, pedagogical interventions have been developed to qualify the school identity. Generally, these interventions have taken compensatory approaches in which 'immigrant' schools (i.e., schools with a substantial number of immigrant students; 25 per cent appears to be the 'magic' number) receive financial compensation via allocation of extra resources. In recent years, many of these schools have embarked on major image makeover projects to attract and retain ethnic majority students. The one school where immigrant students make up 40 per cent of the student body is making a significant effort to reverse the process of being an 'immigrant' school. The school's strategy for maintaining a good reputation is to increase the proportion of ethnic majority students from middle-class backgrounds, and at the same time reduce the proportion of immigrant students from 40 to 30 per cent. The school is described as 'an inclusive school', that is, oriented towards developing a common Danish school culture, with particular emphasis on citizenship education and tolerance building. After compulsory school hours, it offers mother-tongue education in Albanian and a homework café for students at all grade levels. The other school has to cope with a stronger structure of ethnic and social segregation. While none of the enrolled students come from outside the catchment area, several children of ethnic Danish background attend schools outside the area. The school promotes itself as 'whole-day school' (in Danish: *heldagsskole*) that combines schooling and extracurricular activities into one compulsory eight- to fifteen-hour school day. This extended schooling model moreover keeps the 'exposed' immigrant students off the streets and out of their supposedly deprived homes by engaging them in healthy activities at school. This model and its method must thus be understood as congruent with the school's location in a highly multi-ethnic, economically disadvantaged urban neighbourhood.

Clearly, the Danish case schools have indeed become more competitive in the school market in the catchment area. Again, one school is located in a more privileged residential area, whereas the other, least desirable, school is in a low-income, densely populated immigrant residential area. This jockeying for position within the school market has an obvious impact on students, who, depending on which school they are admitted to, face a continuous devaluation of their educational opportunities. This leads me to assume that the development of pedagogical interventions more deeply intervenes with the pattern of school segregation in the Danish system than in the French system of centralization, which traditionally remain impermeable to pressure from civil society, including calls to adapt pedagogical interventions to the particular social and cultural needs of the students. Furthermore, the relatively high proportion of immigrant students in schools in the Danish case is a consequence of ongoing 'white flight', due generally to parents' free choice of schools, and specifically to the institutional reorganization of schools, that is, the closure of an 'immigrant' school and the merging of two schools. In the French case, meanwhile, 'immigrant' schools result primarily from the educational mechanisms of 'exclusion from within', namely, the system of educational differentiation, streaming and selection of students. In this sense, contextual factors and differences born of structural inequalities between schools, classes and educational tracks play a central role in shaping the immigrant students' perceptions of themselves and their educational and professional opportunities.

Residential Segregation and Ethno-racial Stigmatization

The residential case study areas are marked by considerable cleavages between 'us' and 'the others'. Although group-specific attributes (e.g., migration history, religion, ethnicity, culture) may differ among the neighbourhoods studied, the rationale behind the contrasting categories is largely based on the notion of a line of division between the (often white) majority population on one side, and the diverse immigrant population on the other. In Denmark, the term immigrant came into use as an administrative category in the 1970s, replacing the previously used term foreigner (Alsmark, Kallehave and Moldenhawer 2007; Jønsson and Petersen 2010). However, before long 'immigrant' was associated with generalized stereotypical conceptions of Others and different types of social problems (Horst and Gitz-Johansen 2010). This line of division between 'Danes' and 'immigrants' – basically, non-Danes – is present in both the political and public discourse, often in the form of generalized stereotypical images. Categorization as an immigrant often correlates with difficulties in basically all societal arenas, for example, the labour market (unemployment and ethnic discrimination), housing (housing segregation and a high concentration of immigrants in socially disadvantaged neighbourhoods) and education (lower grades and a lower likelihood of transition to higher education). A further implication of this division is that children of immigrants are also considered immigrants, that is, second-generation immigrants, even if they were born in Denmark and have lived their entire lives there. Since the 1980s the term bilingualism has also been used, especially within the educational sector, to illustrate the distinction between 'Danes' and 'non-Danes' (Thomsen, Moldenhawer and Kallehave 2010: 3).

In France the distinction between 'us' and 'the others' is clearly meaningful. However, because the Republican principle of equality opposes any form of differentiation based on ethnicity (Brinbaum and Cebolla-

Boado 2007: 446), references to cultural, racial or social categories are subsumed by references to residential categories, especially the major distinction drawn between the *jeunes des cités* ('ghetto' youth) and others (Schiff 2010a: 78). In fact, urban identities synthesize all the various dimensions of immigrant youth's social, ethnic and even academic identities, while also permitting a degree of mingling between various ethnic groups (Schiff 2010a: 77). Despite some incidence of immigrant students making distinctions in their social relations based on ethno-racial categories such as 'black', 'Muslim' or 'Arab', ethno-racial tensions are never manifest in a 'pure' form independent of other dimensions of social relations involving distinctions based on such factors as residence, academic performance, style and immigration.

Nobles (2010) questions whether ethno-racial identities actually play a role in recent developments in France's *banlieues,* as Wacquant argues. Pointing to how Wacquant overlooks the role of public and political opinion, certainly during the 2005 riots, she argues that ethno-racial identities are undeniably growing in political and social significance in France. Tissot's (2007) discussion of Wacquant's comparison between the United States and France is on a par with Nobles's critique. She examines his argument on the respective roles of race and class in the French *banlieues,* going one step further by arguing that his concept of ethnicization blurs the objective structures of ethnic-racial inequalities. For Wacquant, ethnicization is the erroneous importation of foreign categories, namely, race, discrimination and immigration, as described above. Instead, Tissot argues, 'Its crucial feature in France has been the refusal to address the obstacles race creates for the racialized people.' (ibid.: 368). The serious difficulties that immigrants and residents in the suburbs continue to face in relation to education and the labour market were never described in terms of racism and discrimination, but in terms of the problems they supposedly presented for the French Republican model of integration, or in other words, the principle of non-differentiation of citizens on the basis of their ethnic origin. Schiff (2011) explored further, finding that even when specific policies are developed in response to the unequal distribution of immigrant and non-immigrant students in the vocational schools positioned lowest in the educational market hierarchy and regarded as immigrant ghettos, their careful formulation does not refer explicitly to the significance of racial or ethnic categories, but rather to the significance of their 'disadvantaged' social position (ibid.: 2). Varying experiences of ethno-racial discrimination, both argue, should be regarded as part of the stigma attached to the image of the 'ghetto' youth that combines all the processes of differentiation and exclusion that impede their prospects for social inclusion.

In the Danish case, 'ethnicity' as a signifier of cultural difference is more outspoken. Ethnic categories associated with the 'immigrant' category become a burden and a label of failure and disintegration. From the perspective of immigrant students' non-assimilative experiences of schooling, it is clear that they are attempting to escape the general stigmatization of the 'criminal trouble-making immigrant'. Generally, this stigmatization relies on the grounds of the deprivation regime (Horst and Gitz-Johansen 2010: 147). However, when ethnic categories are seen in relation to residential categories, making the immigrant neighbourhood into a major distinction between 'us' (inside the ghetto) and 'the others' (outside the ghetto), the school stands out as a zone of exception (Moldenhawer and Padovan-Özdemir 2011: 10). Although some immigrant students describe interethnic interaction outside school, primarily in connection with sports activities, they form a residential community that draws on distinctions based on 'us' (inside the residential area) and 'the others' (outside the residential area). In this specific local environment, the ethnically diverse school may function as a sanctuary from negative representations of immigrants in public and political discourses, especially when it comes to social interaction and the social well-being of the students (Moldenhawer, Kallehave and Hansen 2010: 57).

Since most of the immigrant students in the French school cases come from disadvantaged urban neighbourhoods outside the school district, social and residential differences do not entirely overlap with ethnic categories in the schools. In this situation, the schools' environments appear relatively well protected from the harsh realities of urban life, and furthermore seem an important stabilizing element in the students' lives, even though many legitimately feel that they have been relegated to the bottom of the academic hierarchy. During interviews, students often mentioned problems relating to drug dealing, gang violence, police brutality and control, very uncomfortable housing conditions, delinquency and muggings, which made life within the confines of the school appear relatively peaceful (Schiff 2010a: 56). An important finding, however, is that the students seemed to feel less affected by negative comparisons between neighbourhoods, schools, classes, race and class within the *banlieues* than by the stigma they experience 'from the outside', where social, ethno-racial and residential distinctions are more significant. To conclude, 'In the Parisian suburbs segregation paradoxically protects young people from confrontation with the "other" which may remind them of their disadvantaged status' (ibid.: 56–57).

Identity Formation, Schooling and the Role of Gender

Identity formation takes place in the field of unequal power relations that exist within and across local, national and transnational boundaries. In the Danish case, we have identified three strategies of identity formation among immigrant students (Moldenhawer, Kallehave and Hansen 2010; Moldenhawer 2011). The strategy of *ethnic pride* takes the form of the student's nurturing of close relationships with his or her parents, extended family and the wider ethnic community in Denmark and abroad. The second strategy, termed *reflexive ethnicity,* is characterized by adherence to a cultural diversity that perceives mixed ethnic identity affiliations as an advantage. This identity formation strategy also demonstrates a positive attitude towards the values of the school system. Third, we have identified a strategy of *downplaying ethnicity,* manifested as a distancing from ethnic identification in favour of promoting mixed ethnic/immigrant identities that are converted into subcultural, residential anchored identities (i.e., 'hip-hop' attitudes). This strategy seems to result from a general feeling of not being accepted as belonging to the 'host' society, and of being in opposition to the society outside the residential area.

By looking more closely at the role of gender as regards correlations between strategies of identity formation and schooling, we identified three configurations of immigrant students' perceptions of themselves and their educational and professional opportunities. The first configuration concerns immigrant girls who are committed to schoolwork and represent either a reflexive ethnicity or an ethnic pride identity formation strategy. The fact that these girls do well in school is popularly explained as an outcome of a quite disciplined, traditional upbringing by immigrant (read Muslim) parents who strive to keep their daughters away from 'Danish' leisure activities. However, the girls interviewed strongly emphasized their strategic use of various ways of negotiating expectations and categorizations of ethnic identifications that combine adherence to the emigrant- and immigrant-situated contexts of claims and attributes with educational goals.

The second configuration shows evidence of a male gendered relation between schooling and a strategy of downplaying ethnicity. These immigrant boys do well in school but feel rather burdened by the unsettling categorization 'criminal troublemaking immigrant.' To escape this negative categorization, they downplay their individual ethnic backgrounds, replacing them with a mixed minority identity that turns the problematized 'immigrant' category upside down. They reinvent, so to speak, the immigrant category through a positive subcultural youth strategy of empowerment among interethnic immigrant peers. Yet they still feel a need to outperform the majority students in school to escape the aforementioned exclusionary categorization as a troublesome (male) immigrant. As such, this points to immigrant students' continuous issue of identification and categorization of 'the immigrant' or 'the ethnic othering' in regard to their positioning in and outside school.

The third configuration includes both immigrant boys and girls who display an instrumental approach to schooling by investing more effort in sustaining their social relations within the ethnic community, thereby showing an ethnic pride identity formation strategy. These students' school performance is often poor due to their families' scarce educational capital. However, the boys seem able to parlay the advantage of close relations to the family and larger transnational ethnic community into prospects of employment in family business, though they may be failing at school. Girls, however, do not seem to have this opportunity and therefore are more at the mercy of the school system.

The French case study has analysed identity formation as the manner in which young immigrants define themselves and 'the others', and the composite and changing nature of their multi-faceted identities (Schiff 2010a: 74–85). In this case, however, the gendered role of difference is not significant for the way identity formation relates to the symbolic and social order of residential segregation and ethnic stigmatization. Both male and female immigrant students, when asked in interviews whether they felt proud of their ethnic origins, apparently considered ethnicity such an obvious part of their identity and everyday lives that they did not take time to ponder the question, which they saw as somewhat incongruous. Generally, female and male immigrant students alike are to some extent familiar with their country of emigration, but they assert their ethnicity in symbolic rather than traditional cultural terms. When distinguishing among themselves, as described above, they refer more readily to their neighbourhood, but in a way that can both reinforce and transcend ethnic boundaries. And when young immigrants of either gender come into contact with urban youth of European origin outside the neighbourhood, their interaction encourages association between local peer groups and strengthens the ethnic, racial and religious dimensions of their collective identities. On the other hand, when young immigrants connect with people from their own emigrant background, both their local urban identities and their French identity tend to become much more salient, thus weakening the feeling of ethnic belonging that they assert so strongly when distinguishing themselves from the members of the 'host' society. The pattern is indeed that the local neighbourhood identity is highly ambivalent, encompassing both a sense of belonging among other immigrants who have disassociated themselves from their parents' sense of community, and/or a feeling of a distance from the dominant French identity (ibid.: 77).

Following the different ways of linking school segregation to forms of residential segregation, the finding in both cases reveals a strong territorial stigmatization of the 'ethnic' category (for both genders), in which the residential area becomes the main distinction of belonging for immigrant students – hence their dismal prospects for educational success and future 'integration'. At the same time, the content of this distinction is not entirely dysfunctional: it implies complex strategies for forming identities that simultaneously belong to a certain neighbourhood and long for something else outside the 'ghetto'. Thus, the notion of the school as a zone of exception intensifies with regard to a school situated in a so-called ghetto area.

Conclusion and Discussion

The purpose of this chapter has been to study ethnic differences in education and in the problems associated with multicultural urban and educational contexts. Major findings from the EDUMIGROM survey study document that immigrant students are still severely disadvantaged in the educational market. At the individual level, it is quite significant that ethnic differences are contributing extensively to the impact of socio-economic differences. At the institutional level, the findings point to the function of school segregation as one of the most powerful ways of institutionalizing, legitimizing and evenly reproducing ethnic distinctions. In view of this general conclusion, the French and Danish cases were selected for an in-depth analysis of socio-racial-ethnic and gender differences in both education and the problems associated with disadvantaged and multicultural urban and educational contexts.

To conclude, beyond differences and similarities between the country-specific cases, social and ethnic structures, once they are inscribed in mental structures, are reproduced via schooling in immigrant and ethnically mixed areas, even though the schools themselves stand out as 'safe havens'. This is depicted in the selected environments, which are clearly considered to be areas of possible threats – areas distorted from 'places' into 'spaces' (Wacquant 2007: 70) that become social forces of marginalization. The social basis for being part of and participating fully in society appears to be lacking, due to the history of immigration and the historical structure of social forces concentrated there. In this setting, the school paradoxically offers innovative attempts at various forms of 'inclusive' interventions along gradients of inequality.

Because they are trapped in schools and districts that are widely perceived as 'problem areas', immigrant students (both genders) cannot ignore the symbolic force of the territorial stigma. Yet despite the stigma attached to the residential area, the study found that young immigrants respond similarly to the stigma regardless of country-specific differences. We have seen how they have applied strategies of symbolic self-protection, in which the residential and school context stands out as a zone of exception; or have reinforced the experienced differences, disadvantaged positions and division lines between themselves and their ethnic majority peers. This conclusion echoes some important points of Wacquant's overall argument that territorial stigmatization is a central dimension of inequality and urban marginality in both the United States and Europe. However, the persistence of the growing salience of ethno-racial divisions and tensions in the disadvantaged and multicultural urban areas studied may also indicate the main factors accounting for the social potency of ethno-racial classification in both Denmark and France. To some extent, this conclusion indeed suggests that a further discussion of ethnic stigma together with territorial stigma would merely alter one of many obstacles on the path to schooling.

The 'cultural diversity regime' and its erasure of continued structures of disadvantage and discrimination is problematic, but it is nevertheless important to acknowledge a space of positionality among immigrants that retains the recognition of diversity within interethnic, transnational communities without losing sight of the commonalities of experience – socio-economic, territorial and cultural – that also exist. By recognizing both internal differentiation, especially around class and gender, and the questions this differentiation raises, such as space seriously contemplates an intersection of culture and structure that hinders easy reification of either ethnicity or culture. The conclusion is that the concepts of race, racialization and ethnicization can be more fully developed within Wacquant's overall theory of advanced urban marginality through further theoretically guided empirical comparative studies of segregated schooling and ethnic discrimination in Europe.

Given the present extension of mandatory schooling in many European countries and the corresponding entry into the academic enterprise of social categories that previously excluded themselves, or were in practice excluded, subtle forms of 'inclusion from within' have increased (Bourdieu et al. 1999: 421–26). One of the most paradoxical effects of this process of 'democratization' has been the discovery, by the most disadvantaged and previously excluded students, of the conservative functions of the supposedly equalizing and liberating school system. By prolonging and consequently spreading out the process of elimination, segmentation and differentiation, the school system becomes a permanent home for potential outcasts, who bring to it the contradictions and conflicts associated with a type of education that is an end in itself. After an extended school career that often entails considerable sacrifice, the new, highly culturally disadvantaged student population risks ending up with a devalued degree.

Strongly demonstrated in the French school cases, exclusion seems most aggravated among 'problem students' in the sense that they have 'had their chance', and because the school system tends to define social identity more obviously. Clearly, the educational paradox of a common ethos of 'schooling for all', on the one hand, and patterns of 'exclusion from within' on the other, has created even more problems for ethnic minority students, who are trapped in a school system that is 'regarded more as an involuntary recipient of the negative effects of discrimination in areas over which it has no jurisdiction or control (housing inequalities, avoidance strategies by parents, discrimination in vocational employment schemes, etc.) than as a factor of producing ethnic and racial inequalities' (Schiff 2011: 2). This situation calls for future research into the dysfunction of school institutions that, relegated to a separate space of institutional social inferiority and immobility, are in blatant violation of the ideology of unitarist citizenship.

Notes

An earlier version of this chapter was presented at the International Seminar: Space, Place and Social Justice in Education, 13 July 2012, Manchester Metropolitan University.

1. The EDUMIGROM research project aimed to study how ethnic differences in education contribute to the diverging prospects for ethnic minority youth and their peers in multiethnic urban settings. The project lasted for three years and was finalized in February 2011. Its point of departure was the recognition that, despite great variations in economic development and welfare arrangements, recent developments seem to lead to similarly constructed disadvantages for certain groups of second-generation immigrants in Western European countries and of Roma in Central European countries. By including selected multiethnic communities and schools in the Czech Republic, Denmark, France, Germany, Hungary, Romania, Slovakia, Sweden and the United Kingdom, the project explored how educational practices in compulsory education in markedly different welfare regimes ultimately

reduce, maintain or deepen inequalities in young people's opportunities for advancement and their access to the labour market, and concurrently contribute to new forms of involuntary segregation, marginalization and second-class citizenship among people affiliated with these groups (http://www.edumigrom.eu).

2. In the second phase of the EDUMIGROM project, a survey was run among youths aged 14–17 who were in the final year of compulsory education and attending the concluding grade in the selected schools of the chosen multi-ethnic communities. The survey took the form of self-reporting, anonymous questionnaires, filled in by all students in the selected schools of the chosen multi-ethnic communities. Respondents from twenty-five ethnic minority groups represented in the investigated school communities completed 5,086 questionnaires. In the participating post-socialist Central European countries, the Roma ethnic minority was selected, whereas in the two countries with significant colonial pasts (the U.K. and France) the prominent ethnic groups of Pakistani, Caribbean, Maghrebi, and Black African origin were singled out; in countries with labour immigration (Germany, Denmark, and Sweden), mainly the large Muslim groups of Turks, Kurds, people from former Yugoslavia, Somalis or Africans were chosen (Szalai 2011: 6–8).

3. Our approach to considering achievement is based on the students' self-reported recall of their grades in a set of core subjects at the end of the preceding semester. Obviously, students may somehow have altered the written results, e.g., in thinking that their performance was better than the teacher's evaluation reflected, but we trust the wisdom of empirical research findings that overall, people do not 'lie' systematically (Szalai, Messing and Neményi 2010: 33).

4. The third phase of the EDUMIGROM project focused on the minority groups selected in each country for in-depth investigation. Applying a combination of methods (personal interviews and focus-group discussions with students, parents and teachers; classroom observations; ethnographic work in and outside the schools; and case studies on civil organizations), this qualitative phase of the study was designed to reveal the deep-seated motivations and dynamics behind ethnic minority identity formation and the shaping of interethnic relations. In each country, two urban communities were selected where the chosen ethnic minority groups were known to represent a substantial proportion of the local community. Only one community was selected in Denmark and in Sweden. The study targeted established multi-ethnic communities that could be considered to be 'typical' in terms of their occupational structure and living and housing conditions, as well as in their composition by age and household formation. Therefore, mostly working- or lower-class families were present in the communities. Thereafter, hosting schools providing compulsory education for children in the community were selected. Except for the community study in France where upper secondary schools were selected. In this section of the chapter I rely on community study findings from one urban context and two schools in Denmark and France each.

5. I use the term 'immigrants' in this section to highlight the fact that the ethnic minority students in the study are of different immigrant backgrounds.
6. Within the Danish educational system, a public school is a comprehensive school that integrates elementary, lower and upper secondary levels.
7. Since October 2010 the neighbourhood has been included in the government's outline of 'ghetto areas' in Denmark (Regeringen [The Government] 2010.

References

Alsmark, G., T. Kallehave and B. Moldenhawer. 2007. 'Migration og tilhørsforhold' [Migration and Belonging], in G. Alsmark, T. Kallehave and B. Moldenhawer (eds), *Migration och tillhörighet. Inklusions- och exklusionsprocesser i Skandinavien*. Stockholm: Makadam, pp. 7–20.

Archer, L. 2003. *Race, Masculinity and Schooling: Muslim Boys and Education*. London: Open University Press.

Archer, M. 1979. *Social Origins of Educational System*. London: Sage.

Back, L. and J. Solomos. 2009. 'Part Six: Changing Boundaries and Spaces', in L. Back and J. Solomos (eds), *Theories of Race and Racism. A Reader*, 2nd ed. London and New York: Routledge, pp. 561–64.

Bourdieu, P. et al. 1999. *The Weight of the World: Social Suffering in Contemporary Society*. Cambridge: Polity Press.

Brinbaum, Y. and H. Cebolla-Boado. 2007. 'The School Careers of Ethnic Minority Youth in France: Success or Disillusion?', *Ethnicities* 7(3): 445–74.

Broadfoot, P. 1999. 'Not So Much a Context, More a Way of Life? Comparative Education in the 1990s', in R. Alexander, P. Broadfoot and D. Philips (eds), *Learning from Comparing. New Directions in Comparative Educational Research, Vol. 1: Contexts, Classrooms and Outcomes*. Oxford: Oxford Symposium Books, pp. 21–31.

Butler, T. and A. van Zanten. 2007. 'School Choice: A European Perspective', *Journal of Education Policy* 22(1): 1–5.

Felouzis, G., et al. 2010. *Ethnic Differences in Education in France: Survey Report*. EDUMIGROM Survey Studies, Budapest: Central European University, Center for Policy Studies.

Gaardmand, A. 1993. *Dansk byplanlægning 1938–1992* [Danish City Planning 1938–1992]. Copenhagen: Arkitektens forlag.

Gilroy, P. 2009. 'The Dialectics of Diaspora Identification', in L. Back and J. Solomos (eds), *Theories of Race and Racism. A Reader*, 2nd ed. London and New York: Routledge, pp. 564–77.

Regeringen 2010. *Ghettoen tilbage til samfundet. Et opgør med parallelsamfund i Danmark*.

Hamaz, S. and E. Vasta. 2009. ''To Belong or Not Belong': Is That the Question? Negotiating Belonging in Multi-ethnic London', Working Paper No. 73, Centre on Migration, Policy and Society, University of Oxford.

Horst, C. and T. Gitz-Johansen. 2010. 'Education of Ethnic Minority Children in Denmark: Monocultural Hegemony and Counter Positions', *Intercultural Education* 21(2): 137–51.

Jensen, S. and A.D. Christensen. 2012. 'Territorial Stigmatization and Local Belonging. A study of the Danish neighbourhood Aalborg East', *City* 16(1–2): 74–92.

Jønsson, H.V. and K. Petersen. 2010. 'Danmark: Den nationale velfærdsstat møder verden' [Denmark: The National Welfare State Encounters the World], in G. Brochmann and A. Hagelund (eds), *Velferdens grenser*. Oslo: Universitetsforlaget, pp. 131–209.

Moldenhawer, B. 2011. 'Etniske fællesskaber' [Ethnic Communities], in S. Brinckmann and E. Jensen (eds), *Fællesskaber*. Copenhagen: Akademisk Forlag, pp. 105–29.

Moldenhawer, B., T. Kallehave and S.J. Hansen. 2010. *Community Study Report Denmark*. EDUMIGROM Community Studies. Budapest: Central European University, Center for Policy Studies.

Moldenhawer, B. and T. Øland. 2011. 'Disturbed by 'the Stranger': State Crafting Remade through Educational Interventions and Socio-moral Reactions', submitted to *Globalisation, Education and Society*.

Moldenhawer, B. and M. Padovan-Özdemir. 2011. *Policy Brief: Policy Recommendations on the Domestic Context of Denmark*. EDUMIGROM, Final Project Report. Budapest: Central European University, Center for Policy Studies.

Moody, M. and L. Thévenot. 2000. 'Comparing Models of Strategy, Interests, and the Public Good in French and American Environmental Disputes', in M. Lamont and L. Thévenot (eds), *Rethinking Comparative Cultural Sociology: Repertoires of Evaluation in France and the United States*. Cambridge: Cambridge University Press.

Nobles, M. 2010. ''Here a Ghetto, There a Ghetto': The Value and Peril of Comparative Study', *Urban Geography* 31(2): 158–61.

Noiriel, G. 1996. *The French Melting Pot: Immigration, Citizenship, and National Identity*. Contradictions of Modernity, Vol. 5. Minneapolis and London: University of Minnesota Press.

OECD. 2006. *Where Immigrant Students Succeed: A Comparative Review of Performance and Engagement in PISA 2003*. Paris: OECD.

Osborn, M., et al. 2003. *A World of Difference? Comparing Learners Across Europe*. Glasgow: Open University Press.

Pedersen, O.K. 2011. *Konkurrencestaten – forhandlingsøkonomiens institutionelle historie* [The State of Competition: The Institutional History of Negotiation Economy]. Copenhagen: Hans Reitzels Forlag.

Raveaud, M. and A. van Zanten. 2007. 'Choosing the Local School: Middle Class Parents' Values and Social and Ethnic Mix in London and Paris', *Journal of Education Policy* (22)1: 107–24.

Sayad, A. 2004. *The Suffering of the Immigrant*. Cambridge: Polity Press.

Schiff, C. 2010a. *Community Study Report France*. EDUMIGROM Community Studies. Budapest: Central European University, Center for Policy Studies.

———. 2010b. *French Case Study Report on Ethnic Minorities*. EDUMIGROM Background Papers. Budapest: Central European University, Center for Policy Studies.

———. 2011. *France Country Findings and Policy Recommendations*. EDUMIGROM Final Project Report. Budapest: Central European University, Center for Policy Studies.

Schiff, C., et al. 2008a. *Country Report on Education: France.* EDUMIGROM Background Papers. Budapest: Central European University, Center for Policy Studies.

———. 2008b. *Country Report on Ethnic Relations: France.* EDUMIGROM Background Papers. Budapest: Central European University, Center for Policy Studies.

Szalai, J. 2011. *Ethnic Differences in Education and Diverging Prospects for Urban Youth in an Enlarged Europe.* EDUMIGROM summary findings. Budapest: Central European University, Center for Policy Studies.

Szalai, J., V. Messing and M. Neményi. 2010. *Ethnic and Social Differences in Education in a Comparative Perspective.* EDUMIGROM Comparative Survey Report. Budapest: Central European University, Center for Policy Studies.

Thomsen, J.P., B. Moldenhawer and T. Kallehave. 2010. *Ethnic Differences in Education in Denmark: Survey Report.* Budapest: Central European University, Center for Policy Studies.

Tissot, S. 2007. 'The Role of Race and Class in Urban Marginality. Discussing Loïc Wacquant's Comparison between the USA and France', *City* 11(3): 364–69.

van Zanten, A. 1997. 'Schooling Immigrants in France in the 1990s: Success or Failure of the Republican Model of Integration?', *Anthropology & Education Quarterly* 28(3): 351-74.

Wacquant, L. 2007. 'Territorial Stigmatization in the Age of Advanced Marginality', *Thesis Eleven* 91: 113–18.

———. 2008a. 'Ghettos and Anti-Ghettos: An Anatomy of the New Urban Poverty', *Thesis Eleven* 94: 66–77.

———. 2008b. *Urban Outcasts: A Comparative Sociology of Advanced Marginality.* Cambridge: Polity Press.

———. 2010. 'Urban Desolation and Symbolic Denigration in the Hyperghetto', *Social Psychology Quarterly* 73(3): 215–19.

8

THE ABSENCE OF STRATEGY AND
THE ABSENCE OF *BILDUNG*

When Integration Policy Cannot Succeed

Tina Kallehave

In the 1990s, migration and the integration of migrants became particularly controversial political issues in Denmark, resulting in changes to the Aliens Act in 1997, the passing of the Integration Act in 1999 and media debates in which participants were often highly critical of migrants. A primary purpose of both acts was to improve the basic system for the so-called integration of citizens from migrant backgrounds. Denmark had been accepting refugees, foreign labour and immigrants wishing to join their families in the country since the end of the 1950s, but despite regular changes in legislation and political discussions on the challenges and benefits that stemmed from migration, it was not until the 1990s that the issue attracted such a high level of political attention.

The Aliens Act was intended to contribute to migrants' integration by tightening immigration rules and reducing the number of new citizens from migrant backgrounds. The Integration Act was introduced, as the name suggests, to ensure the integration of citizens with migrant backgrounds into Danish society – a process that had not been particularly successful up until then. A central tenet of the Integration Act, and therefore crucial to the political perception of integration, requires new arrivals from abroad to become self-supporting as quickly as possible, and to understand the country's basic values and norms. The Integration Act includes a number of regulations from *Lov om Aktiv Socialpolitik* (The Active Social Policy Act), some of which relate to the receipt of social benefits. Previously, refugees arriving in Denmark had been offered an eighteen-month introductory programme run by a non-governmental organization, the Danish Refugee Council. The act scrapped this, replacing it with a three-year introductory programme that covers both refugees and family reunification, and assigns responsibility for the task of integration to local authorities. The legislative work and transfer of responsibility for administration of the act to local authorities underline the political prominence of the integration question: integration had become, and still remains, a volatile political issue.

Anyhow, the continuous sociocultural and political differences between migrants and citizens of Danish background make a critical discussion of the political perception of integration relevant. Using the case of Somali migrants in Denmark, this chapter examines the political concept and aims of integration by highlighting how the means applied to secure so-called integration relate to the different sociocultural processes generating very different everyday lives – sometimes in terms of social exclusion – among Somalis. Somali women experience this social exclusion on various levels simultaneously, as women and as racial and religious others. Examples will illustrate some of the ways Somali women challenge these policies, thereby carving out more room for their inclusion in Danish society. The concepts of interpellation and life-modes make up the theoretical foundation of this critical analysis.

Somali Migrants

In Denmark, the granting of asylum to refugees from Somalia largely coincided with the closer political focus on integration. The first Somali refugees came to Denmark about twenty years ago. In 1990, 551 people with a Somali background were registered in Denmark; by 2001, the number had risen to 16,219. Although not large by international standards, this is a significant number in terms of overall immigration in Denmark.

The Somalis were quickly marked out as a group that was 'impossible to integrate'. Personnel with the local authorities responsible for integration found working with Somalis a major challenge. Stereotypes quickly emerged, such as 'Somali men sit around in cafes chewing *khat*' and 'Somali women are left at home, looking after the kids and housekeeping'. In 1997, Birte Weiss, then Minister of the Interior, said:

> I also think that the Somali group constitutes a special problem because they come from a completely different culture. There is evidence to suggest they are more difficult to integrate than any other group that has come here from cultures far removed from our own. For example, the Vietnamese and Chinese have eased naturally into Danish society. ... We have initiated a whole series of special initiatives, including one to put a halt to social fraud, which was quite clearly taking place – and still does to a certain extent – among the Somalis. We have therefore started DNA tests and simultaneous interviews to establish the veracity of family reunifications, etc. (*Ekstra Bladet*, special edition, June 1997: *Foreigners*)

It is worth noting how suspicion and mistrust of the immigrant can create a relational mode where Danes mistrust and even fear Somali immigrants. This, in turn, produces mistrust and fear among the Somali immigrants themselves. In effect, this mode secures the boundaries between 'us' and 'them' and drastically reduces the chances of Somalis entering into the labour market.

The process of turning Somalis and Somali cultural practices into a problem ran parallel with amendments to the Aliens Act and the drafting of the Integration Act, and it had an impact on both. The Integration Act and its social-policy elements facilitated the stipulation of requirements as to how Somalis ran their day-to-day lives and organized family life. The right to social benefits was linked to the duty to learn Danish and/or work. The Integration Act also paved the way for many local authorities all over the country to start special programmes. These included a programme for appointing Danish-speaking Somalis to communicate Somali cultural practices to Danish social workers, projects to qualify women to be mothers in Denmark and residents' groups to ensure that Somalis learned to behave appropriately in the residential areas where they were housed. In other words, the welfare state deployed resources at an early stage, tightening up the general legislation and introducing special initiatives to ensure the Somalis' integration.

If we look at the same group today, approximately a decade since the process of tightening up integration-related measures began in earnest, we see distinct differences between Somalis in Denmark. In terms of the Integration Act's objective of making immigrants self-supporting and capable of understanding basic norms and values, some Somalis can be categorized as integrated; others, however, are classifiable as not only non-integrated but also socially vulnerable. For some Somalis, therefore, integration programmes have segued into social programmes. The City of Copenhagen, for example, has launched a number of initiatives to help Somalis who are homeless or misuse drugs and alcohol. The background of one such project is described as follows: 'In the last five years, a growing number of Somali men have ended up homeless in Copenhagen. A growing proportion of this group now suffers from alcohol and drug abuse problems, which prevents them finding homes and jobs and stops them integrating into Danish society' (City of Copenhagen 2006: 2).

One of the tools used in this particular project is described as follows: 'By using the power of example, the "good meeting" gives [substance abusers] access to integration so that they are able to understand the social system and, more generally, Danish society.'[1] Whereas the chief objective of efforts towards integration was (and still is) to help Somalis to *liberate themselves* from the social system by becoming self-supporting, the quotation exemplifies a project whose objective is to teach drug and alcohol abusers to *be users of* the benefits provided by the social system. Some Somalis who were previously defined as refugees to be integrated are now defined as socially vulnerable as well, and in need of social care. The aims of the three-year introductory programme seem far off.

Most Somalis are neither homeless nor alcohol or drug abusers. Nevertheless, this example is relevant as a starting point from which to pose a critical question about the failure of the massive integration efforts. Why is it, or has it been, so difficult for so many Somalis – and not only those who are homeless – to find their footing in Denmark? Do Somalis not 'want' to be integrated? Or were the integration efforts insufficient or inappropriate? The answer is complex (Kallehave 2005; Kleist 2007), so this chapter is limited to an examination of the very important question of whether the integration efforts were insufficient or inappropriate.

Using the concept of interpellation[2] as a starting point, this chapter defines the basic features and challenges of integration on a theoretical level. In the light of this, it discusses how the relationship between welfare-state integration initiatives and the Somali way of life has not been, or not sufficiently been, characterized by the opposite *identity* that interpellation requires. The concept of interpellation makes it possible to discern that the individual and society are not two independent entities, but in fact always mutually place conditions on, and are necessary preconditions for, one another. In particular, this essay focuses on the processes triggered in Somalis' self-consciousness by integration initiatives targeted at the extended family, the nuclear family and the labour market. Against this background, the chapter argues why welfare-state approaches to integration have to some extent led to social exclusion. This essay is primarily based on analyses of empirical material from my fieldwork carried out among Somalis in Denmark in 1998 and 2004, and a brief period of fieldwork in Somalia in 1989. These materials are supplemented with other relevant studies on topics such as Danish integration policy.

Interpellation and Integration

Interpellation (Højrup 1995, 2003b) is a theoretical concept concerning the process by which ideology forms citizens into the self-conscious subjects necessary for the state's emergence and maintenance. In this strategic process of *Bildung*, the state cultivates its domain of sovereignty into a well-functioning society comprised of complementary *life-modes*, or self-conscious subjects. Regarding the theoretical construction of the integration problem, this chapter takes as its starting point the two core concepts of interpellation: strategy and *Bildung* (Buus 2001). As for the question of integration, it is worth devoting special attention to *Bildung* and therefore to what the integration initiatives actually do to the individual and the group, given the fact that the outcomes of welfare-state approaches to integration do not necessarily correspond with their objectives. Using the concept of interpellation, it is possible to discuss the special requirements stipulated for integration programmes to make sure they bring about the *Bildung* they strive for. To make these requirements clear, this essay will take the *Bildung* process as its starting point.

The concept of *Bildung* is inspired, in particular, by G.W.F. Hegel's reading of the term in *Phenomenology of Spirit* (Kallehave 2003; Hegel 1994). In this reading, *Bildung* is not just a question of development or the acquisition of particular knowledge. It is more a question of the development of a self-conscious subject – a question of *moral* practice (Taylor 1981) reflecting an inner relationship between the subject who executes the action, and proficient behaviours in society.

The process of *Bildung* can be described as the individual's movement from being separate from something and confronting it, to being as one with it. The structure of the process by which *Bildung* is acquired involves three dimensions: *in-itself; for-itself;* and *in-and-for-itself.* In this process, the individual (in-itself) is confronted with something alien (for-itself). By meeting with and reflecting about this alien entity, the individual is transformed and defined anew, and in the process, the alien becomes a part of the individual (in-and-for-itself). This third dimension constitutes the new starting point for an ongoing process of *Bildung*. In other words, it is a dialectic understanding of *Bildung*, which here is a process of becoming a self-conscious moral subject.

Bildung should not be taken for granted, however; it should not be assumed to be always a successful process. If *Bildung* is to happen, the relationship between the individual and the alien is subject to particular requirements. *Bildung* presumes that the encounter with the alien is precisely that – something alien and opposite to the individual. At the same time, however, the alien entity must possess something that is recognizable or identical to the individual. *Bildung* presupposes an encounter with an opposite identity, something both alien and recognizable at the same time. The recognizable aspect implies that the individual is able to glimpse something meaningful in the other; the alien aspect means that there is something new to acquire. *Bildung* is not a painless process. It develops through alienation, frustration, reflection, struggle and action. And when the encounter with something else is no longer 'something else' but has become part of the individual self, *Bildung* has taken place. This also implies that *Bildung* contains a time dimension.

It should also be pointed out, however, that the individual does not become identical to the alien 'for-itself'. On the contrary, the point is that the alien is acquired and formed through the already existing individual self and subjectivity. Thus, if several Somalis who differ significantly from each other encounter the same integration initiative, the process of *Bildung* they experience will be vastly different for each of them. This is because the relationships between each individual and the alien are different and therefore contain different *Bildung* potential. In other words, the alien is acquired differently depending on the individual's starting point, and individuals become one with the alien in different ways. *Bildung* of the subject occurs in different ways for different modes of subjects.

There is a further hurdle in the process of *Bildung*, in that not every encounter with something alien necessarily triggers a process of *Bildung* in which the individual acquires and becomes one with the alien. If a woman from Somalia encounters an integration programme in which she is unable to recognize herself, which she sees only as alien, then *Bildung* is not possible for her. Instead of becoming one with the integration initiative's requirements, and thereby establishing an internal relationship between her own self-consciousness and a practice that is useful in society, she will experience alienation, which does not facilitate a moral practice. Similarly, the Somali who encounters nothing new in a programme does not experience *Bildung* either, but instead reproduces her particular subjectivity and the practices relevant for her life-mode.

This perspective, then, recognizes that the individual Somali's preconditions are of crucial importance for the kind of *Bildung*, if any, an integration initiative will lead to. Clearly, any integration programme intended to generate *Bildung* and moral practices must be organized in a way that takes into account the Somalis' different preconditions (Kallehave 2001; 2003); that is, the subjectivity already acquired through life experiences.

The concept of strategy draws the focus to the demands that have to be placed on integration initiatives. While the concepts of interpellation and *Bildung* are founded in Hegel, the concept of strategy is inspired by

Clausewitz's theory of war (Boserup 1981; Buus 2001). The first impera-tive in the concept of strategy is that the *objective* of the strategy – and therefore the result of the process of *Bildung* – has to be clear. What is the actual objective of integration in this context? Is it to encourage more young people from immigrant backgrounds to complete an edu-cation (Moldenhawer 2005, 2007)? Is it to get the maximum possible number of adults from immigrant backgrounds into work (Hvenegård-Lassen 2007; Hertzberg 2007)? The objectives must be clear, because they dictate the direction of the organization of the strategy.

The next point is that a strategy is a *relation,* and must therefore take account of the actions it gives rise to at all times. A strategy is a not a fixed plan but a *process* that must consistently factor in any opposition it faces and has to deal with. If Somalis repeatedly do something other than what is agreed with local authority staff, or if they continually resist the demands placed on them or make them into a problem, then the means that have been deployed to ensure integration merit critical examination. Why do the demands seem alien? Why do the Somalis not identify with them? What needs to be done to introduce the requi-site recognizability? Resistance, where it exists, does not (necessarily) change the objectives per se, but it does mean that ongoing reflection about and adaptation of the strategy are necessary. The strategy is a *means* of achieving the goal by initiating the processes of *Bildung.* The strategy is not in itself the objective.

The concept of strategy focuses attention first and foremost on the organization and administration of the State's political will and social institutions. Integration initiatives must have clear goals, and if an ini-tiative is to assume the character of a strategy, the institutions adminis-trating it must continually revise it, taking into account the resistance and processes it triggers in the target group. The strategy also presumes that the people administrating it are trained to take part in strategic planning. Initiation of a strategy thus also includes the identification of institutions and even the *Bildung* of professionals who are able to iden-tify with and handle this work (Buus 2001; Højrup 2002, 2003a).

Seen as a strategic process of *Bildung,* integration does not therefore imply that the individual becomes identical with the alien aspect, but rather that the individual makes the alien his or her own in a way that is useful to society. Integration also presupposes that the alien is pre-sented in a recognizable form when the strategy puts it before the sub-ject who is targeted for *Bildung.* Hence, in this perspective, integration should not be seen as an unconditional subjection of the individual to the state's existing order (that is, society). Neither is it a process in which we can expect the state and its society to remain untouched afterwards.

It is instead a process of mutual recognition. Nevertheless, the political will of the sovereign state is in principle the decision-maker and has the opportunity to determine and organize the nature of integration programmes. The state sets the agenda in this process, but integration implies and presumes that, at the same time, society and its institutions will reform themselves as well by taking migrant subjects' resistance into account. Integration is a mutual process; the alternative is mutual alienation. In this light, it becomes reasonable to adopt a critical stance to the officially sanctioned programmes designed to integrate Somalis in Denmark, which have enjoyed only limited success and in some cases have given rise to more complex forms of exclusion.

The *Bildung* Potential of the Strategies

As illustrated above, the Ministry of the Interior at the time showed great alacrity in legitimizing the use of DNA tests and introducing stricter practices in decision-making about family reunification cases by linking the issue to that of Somali integration. Amendments to the Aliens Act legitimized these initiatives, following up with a real threat of deportation for families who had already been proven to have reunited on a false basis. This was one of the initiatives that confronted Somalis when they encountered the welfare state. But how do such incidents fit with the strategic process of *Bildung*?

Somalis presented a number of explanations for reuniting with families in contravention of Danish legislation. The phenomenon was partly explained in terms of the person's responsibility to their extended family, which outweighed their obligations to a new and unknown country. Another reason was the importance attached ensuring that as many as possible of those who had fled together achieved protection. The Somalis did not devise their family reunification practice specifically to break Danish law. Instead, the practice resulted from their self-consciousness, a subjectivity that implies wide-ranging responsibility for the extended family. In this perspective, the Somali practice becomes a moral practice that was suddenly limited and criminalized.

Incoming Somalis were met with initiatives that acknowledged and required a nuclear family. This family structure does not recognize obligations to the extended family but limits responsibility to the nuclear family's primary relations: parents, spouses and children. This law is formulated in terms of a definition of family as the 'traditional family unit' of two married heterosexual parents and their children. Even so, immigrant Somalis under twenty-four years of age cannot invite their non-citizen parents and siblings to Denmark, according to the reasoning that 'anyone under twenty-four is less able to resist family coercion to enter into marriage' (Razack 2008: 129). Under the Aliens Act, 105 Somali refugees lost their residence permits in Denmark. It threatened others with expulsion because their family reunifications were seen as illegal from the perspective of a welfare state. To avoid expulsion, some families felt forced to freeze what were usually flexible, situationally close relations. For example, women who invited their sisters under the pretext of a mother-daughter relationship had to freeze in position as mother and daughters, even after reunification with their common mother. Thus the Aliens Act impacted on both the whole Somali group and individual opportunities for action.

The Somali populations in Denmark and other countries are a very mixed bunch. In my previous work, developing and applying concepts of very different life-modes has proven relevant to analysing Somalis' very different ways of dealing with conditions in Denmark (Kallehave 2003, 2007). Using these concepts also enables understanding of why, for some Somalis, DNA tests and family reunification cases contained elements of both recognition and alienation, whereas for others these phenomena could only be seen as alien, with no recognition. This chapter will refer to only two of the many concepts of life-modes that are relevant to understanding Somalis in Denmark: the career life-mode and the political life-mode. For the career life-mode, the legislated scope of the extended family and confining of responsibility to the nuclear family are both alien because the extended family has always been present and recognizable as something fruitful, since it is meaningful to arrange life in such a way that it promotes a personal career. For the career life-mode, the extended family can be seen as an obstruction to making the right choices and setting priorities for the individual's education and career. For the political life-mode, however, relationships with the extended family are crucial because it is precisely through the extended family that the individual understands oneself and is able to act. The nuclear family, and the personal responsibility it implies, is unrecognizable to this life-mode. Being cut off from extended family means that some of one's (mostly) meaningful daily activities are no longer possible. The encounter with welfare-state approaches to integration therefore creates the basis for two completely different processes of *Bildung:* one in which the Somalis who are best understood in terms of the career life-mode optimize conditions for exercising their self-consciousness and *Bildung;* and another in which the Somalis who are best understood in terms of the political life-mode have a restricted ability to act and are therefore partially alienated.

These processes are reinforced by the Somalis' other encounters with welfare-state integration programmes. In Denmark, units that were acknowledged as nuclear families, or parts thereof, were given 'suitable' accommodation. Local authority case officers then became key figures in the administration of the Integration Act and of the welfare state's more general welfare rights. The welfare state's universalism guarantees the individual's right to welfare in the form of, for example, free access to the health system, free schooling for children, housing and social security. This welfare in principle constitutes a safety net for all citizens. However, welfare benefits are hardly neutral categories. The ways in which benefits are organized and supplied to citizens are strongly gendered and culturally rooted. For instance, benefits are organized according to a general principle that takes the individual, not the group or extended family, as the starting point. Another example highlighting such cultural implications is the way information about welfare is communicated to Somalis: it often entails interviews about the allocation of work and responsibility between spouses, in which there is clear reference to the woman's right to self-determination and the man's duty to help with children and housekeeping. In a sense, by upending traditional norms through this 'regulation' of Somali family life, Danish migration principles, whether insidiously or unintentionally, arouse conscious defence of those norms, paradoxically reinforcing the very same stereotypes and gender inequalities that are rejected in progressive Danish society. In this same context, rules about divorce and custody of children have been used as 'trump cards' against Somali men, and the stereotype of the Somali man 'sitting in a café, chewing khat' emerged and was problematized. Allocation of benefits, therefore, is not merely a financial transaction; it also consists of interactions that impose requirements, not only on the individual but also on the internal organization of the whole family and thereby the positions and self-consciousness of the individual. These requirements apply to all citizens, not just those with migrant backgrounds, but they can be especially burdensome for migrants because their self-understanding and practice are often differentiated from the requirements to a higher degree than is the case for the majority of citizens without a migrant background.

Citizens whose self-consciousness and practice already accord with the requirements do not notice them. However, for both the career and political life-mode, the requirement of equal participation in work in the home is alien because both life-modes presuppose that this work is someone else's responsibility. For the career life-mode, the right to self-determination (and therefore also the spouse's right to self-determination) is a recognizable and basic feature, so the ideal spouse, in the career life-mode, is someone who identifies with and thereby willingly not only accepts but even insists on responsibility for work in the home. For the political life-mode, responsibility for the extended family is crucial and involves much time spent networking with other men. Again, the ideal wife of this life-mode is someone who recognizes the importance of and accepts responsibility for the extended family, and who also recognizes herself in the practical care of household, husband, children and other relatives. The conditions that pertain to welfare provision therefore have far more serious consequences for the political life-mode and its supplementary life-mode, the household life-mode, because it makes no sense for any family members to see themselves as individual persons, or to see the husband in terms of tasks defined as female or the wife in terms of tasks defined as male. Therefore the conditions, again, exacerbate alienation, especially in the case of the political life-mode and the women keeping the household life-mode. Requirements directed against the internal positions of husband and wife seem to have strongly influenced the relatively high degree of divorce among Somali immigrants and the prevalence of men living alone. The cultural implications of the obligations inherent in welfare rights transform moral Somali practices into illegal practices. And over time, the process of alienation is exacerbated as Somalis resist the demands and continually decline to adopt the new requirements, which continually are made stricter in response. In the face of this alienation and the absence of a process of *Bildung*, society has failed to reflect on the integration initiatives that are in place. On the contrary, it has tightened the requirements and created more that are even less recognizable. The Somalis' *resistance* is interpreted as *reluctance* that can be overcome by force. The supplementary means of integration, therefore, do not reflect an understanding of the nature of this resistance.

Over the years, the administration of welfare rights has increasingly been associated with imposition of duties. The former 'passive maintenance' has been replaced with a policy of 'active help to self-help' that expects prompt execution of a 'trade-off'. Like the welfare rights themselves, the duties they hinge on constitute a significant element in efforts to integrate new citizens. In this light, it becomes clear that although both rights and duties degenerate processes of *Bildung*, they also generate processes of alienation and thus the opposite of what was intended. The most common 'trade-off' is the requirement to learn Danish, followed by the requirement to find a job or join a welfare-to-work programme. In this context, one might think that the career life-mode would be in its element, but this is not the case. The critical factor in this life-mode is not employment itself but the self-fulfilment made possible through certain kinds of work. Being sent to a welfare-to-work programme, rather than training and qualifying for a job that is meaningful to the individual, is therefore extremely alien to this life-mode. The career life-mode quite clearly recognizes itself in the requirement of employment, but that employment cannot be in just any job. Meanwhile, the political life-mode does not rely on work in the private capitalist market, but rather consists of policymaking: networking to gain relevant knowledge, make decisions and protect the extended family's property and reproduction. The welfare state does not recognize this practice at the level of work but sees it mostly as wasting time. Anyhow, whereas this life-mode does recognize features of the life-modes (Buus 2008) realized via provision of welfare in the Danish public sector, the demand for 'welfare to work *now*' seldom leaves room for the education and *Bildung* required to practice this life-mode. Local authority case workers have chided many Somalis for being *unrealistic* when they asked to pursue education or training instead of being sent on a welfare-to-work programme.[3]

A close reading of the case files, in which local authority staff keep up-to-date records of the work they do with individual migrants and the agreements they make with them, confirms that administrators perceive the Somalis' resistance to the various requirements, agreements and so forth primarily as an expression of disobedience or unwillingness. This interpretation results in repetition after repetition, tighter and tighter regulation, and stronger comments. Even though these repetitions result in no change or even worsen the migrants' behaviour, these outcomes do not inspire the administrators to turn their attention to the initiatives themselves or their organization, or to appeal to higher authorities for change. To date, no revisions of the means have accounted for the factor of resistance in a way that is conducive to a strategic process of *Bildung*.

Conclusion

Illuminating the situation of the Somalis in Denmark requires more than an analysis of the changing approaches to integration. Somalis' daily life involves far more complex relationships than those covered by the state's approaches to integration. Using the concept of interpellation as a means to reflect upon integration does not exclude this complexity, because the concept insists on factoring in resistance when organizing strategies to bring about the intended *Bildung*. This essay has shown that Danish approaches to integration are not strategic in Clausewitz's sense. On the contrary, they are characterized by a lack of differentiation between the objectives of the programmes and the programmes themselves as a means, and therefore also by a lack of reflection on the programmes as an element in a strategic process of *Bildung*. This also spotlights the lack of long-term strategic thinking in Danish integration politics. This background justifies a critical approach in asking why integration programmes for some Somalis have been supplemented with social programmes, for it is at this juncture that the excluding and alienating elements of the integration work manifest themselves.

As this chapter has shown, the use of the concept of interpellation is a normative element in any discussion of the integration problem, as the concept provides a definition of certain general principles whose presence in the relationship between society and the individual is required for interpellation to take place. The concept is not empirically normative, however, as it neither provides content for the relationships through which interpellation might take place nor asserts that interpellation takes place. Yet the concept is normative in that, in addition to being a concept for mutual *Bildung* between society and the individual, it is also embedded in a more complex theory of the state (Højrup 1995) that posits that citizens' daily lives presuppose the external defence of the state as well as its internal organization – the society – and not the other way around, as is often the basic supposition in sociological and anthropological theories. The concept is not empirically prescriptive, however, so it does not assert that, on an empirical level, there is necessarily any agreement between society's organization and the daily life of the population. Such agreement is often absent in the context of integration, where it is also crucial to remain aware that the *Bildung* that takes place in the immigrant population does not necessarily occur inside a specific single state but comes about as the result of interrelationships between several different states. It is precisely the theoretical definition of the interpellation concept that makes it possible to establish an analytical/strategic view of contexts and conflicts in society and thereby also, in a more limited sphere, to adopt a critical view of integration programmes and their consequences.

Notes

An earlier version of this chapter was published in *Dansk Pædagogisk Tidsskrift* (Danish Pedagogic Review), 2007, vol. 4.
  1. Københavns Kommune (City of Copenhagen) 2006: 6.

2. The concept was inspired by Louis Althusser (1983) but is broken down here with inspiration from G.W.F. Hegel (Forster 1998; Hegel 1994) and readings of Carl von Clausewitz (Boserup 1981).
3. See also Hvenegård-Lassen (2007) for a more in-depth discussion of migrants' (un)realistic options.

References

Althusser, L. 1983. *Ideologi og ideologiske Statsapparater. Grus Arbejdstekster.* Ålborg: Grus.

Boserup, A. 1981. 'Staten, Samfundet og Krigen Hos Clausewitz,' in C. von Clausewitz (ed.), *Om krig,* vol. 3. Copenhagen: Rhodos, pp. 911–30.

Buus, H. 2001. *Sundhedsplejerskeinstitutionens dannelse. En kulturteoretisk og kulturhistorisk analyse af velfærdsstatens embedværk.* Copenhagen: Museum Tusculanums Forlag.

———. 2008. *Indretning og efterretning. Rockefeller Foundations interesse i og indflydelse på den danske velfærdsstat 1920–1970.* Copenhagen: Museum Tusculanums Forlag.

Forster, M.N. 1998. *Hegel's Idea of a Phenomenology of Spirit.* Chicago: University of Chicago Press.

Hegel, G.W.F. 1994. *Åndens Fenomenologi,* trans. J. Elster. Oslo: Pax Forlag.

Hertzberg, F. 2007. 'Arbetsförmidlare mellan individ, kollektiv och marknad. Bilden av "de andra" i arbetsmarknadspolitikens gräsrotsbyråkrati', in G. Alsmark, T. Kallehave and B. Moldenhawer (eds), *Migration och tillhörighet. Inklusions- och exklusionsprocesser i Skandinavien.* Stockholm: Museum Tusculanums Forlag.

Højrup, T. 1995. *Omkring livsformsanalysens udvikling.* Copenhagen: Museum Tusculanums Forlag.

———. 2002. *Dannelsens dialektik. Etnologiske udfordringer til det glemte folk.* Copenhagen: Museum Tusculanums Forlag.

———. 2003a. *Livsformer og velfærdsstat ved en korsvej? Introduktion til et kulturteoretisk og kulturhistorisk bidrag.* Copenhagen: Museum Tusculanums Forlag.

———. 2003b. *State, Culture and Life-modes: The Foundation of Life-mode Analysis.* Surrey: Ashgate.

Hvenegård-Lassen, K. 2007. 'Viljen til valg. Kommunalt integrationsarbejde i Sverige og Danmark', in G. Alsmark, T. Kallehave and B. Moldenhawer (eds), *Migration och. Inklusions- och exklusionsprocesser i Skandinavien.* Stockholm: Makadam Förlag.

Kallehave, T. 2001. 'Somali Migrants: Family and Subjectivity', *Ethnologia Scandinavica* 31: 25–44.

———. 2003. 'Somaliske Livsformer i velfærdsstaten. Udforskning af begreber til analyse af brydninger og processer i immigrationsproblematikken', Ph.D. dissertation. Copenhagen: University og Copenhagen.

———. 2005. 'Hjem og hjemløshed blandt somaliske mænd', *Nord Nytt* 97: 75–89.

————. 2007. 'Det Meningsfulde Arbejde – Et Livsformsperspektiv På Arbejdets Betydning for Somaliske Mænd', in G. Alsmark, T. Kallehave and B. Moldenhawer (eds), *Migration och tillhörighet. Inklusions- och exklusionsprocesser i Skandinavien.* Stockholm: Makadam Förlag.

Kleist, N. 2007. 'Spaces of Recognition: An Analysis of Somali-Danish Associational Engagement and Diasporic Mobilization', Ph.D. dissertation. Copenhagen: Sociologisk Institut, University of Copenhagen.

Moldenhawer, B. 2005. 'Transnational Migrant Communities and Education Strategies among Pakistani Youngsters in Denmark,' *Journal of Ethnic and Migration Studies* 31(1): 51–78.

————. 2007. 'De indefra ekskluderede. En analyse af inklusions- og eksklusionsstrukturer og - praktikker i en gymnasieskole for alle', in G. Alsmark, T. Kallehave and B. Moldenhawer (eds), *Migration och tillhörighet. inklusions- och exklusionsprocesser i Skandinavien.* Stockholm: Makadam Förlag.

Razack, S. 2008. *Casting Out: Race and the Eviction of Muslims from Western Law and Politics.* Toronto: University of Toronto Press.

Taylor, C. 1981. 'Hur lär vi av historien? Hegel's Sittlichkeit och de representativa institutionernas kris', *KRIS* 20/21.

⊙⟩⟩ Contributors

Haci Akman is Associate Professor at the Department of Archaeology, History, Cultural Studies and Religion, Faculty of Humanities, University of Bergen, Norway. Akman's main research areas are ethnicity, migration and diaspora, cultural heritage and identity. He has conducted many research projects focused on museums and diversity. One important contribution to the field is his co-edited work *Scandinavian Museums and Cultural Diversity,* published by Berghahn Books (2008).

Minoo Alinia is Associate Professor at the Department of Sociology, Uppsala University. She holds a Ph.D in sociology and her dissertation on Kurdish diaspora was the first major work on diaspora in Sweden. She has published a number of articles and book chapters on diaspora theory, diasporic identities and mobilizations, everyday racism, and the temporal and generational aspects of diaspora. She is also the author of *Honor and Violence against Women in Iraqi Kurdistan* (Palgrave Macmillan, 2013), an intersectional critical study of violence in the name of honor. She has also published on the way gender, sexuality and issues of gender equality have been used in racializing discourses on migrants and Muslims in Sweden.

Rikke Andreassen is Associate Professor in Communication Studies at Roskilde University and holds a Ph.D. from the University of Toronto. As a researcher, teacher and consultant in the fields of media, discrimination and equality, she addresses racial/ethnic and gender issues. She has published several articles and the books *Menneskeudstilling. Fremvisninger af eksotiske mennesker i Zoologisk Have og Tivoli* (2011) and *Der er et yndigt land. Medier, minoritieter og danskhed* (2007). She was part of the EU project VEIL, which focused on European debates and legislation concerning women's head and body coverings. She is also the coordinator of the Nordforsk network 'Re-developing International Theories of Media and Migration in a Nordic Context'.

Malene Fenger-Grøndahl is a freelance journalist and writer who specializes in ethnic minorities, integration, religion and the Middle East. She has written and/or contributed to more than twenty books on these issues. She contributes regularly to a radio programme about philosophy on Danish Broadcasting Corporation's Channel 1 and works as a moderator of public debates on religion and dialogue.

Tina Kallehave is a Danish ethnologist and Ph.D. Until 2010 she was Assistant Professor at the University of Copenhagen's education section. Her research concerns migration, with a specific focus on family-, education- and labour-marked relations. A key interest has been the everyday lives of Somali refugees and their living conditions in the Danish welfare state. In combination with empirical research she has contributed to the theoretical relevance and sensibility of state- and life-mode analysis in general and its relation to migration research in particular. Since 2010 Kallehave has worked as a sculptor.

Pia Karlsson Minganti, Ph.D., is a researcher of ethnology at Stockholm University, Sweden, and guest researcher at the University of Bologna, where she has been affiliated with the FP7 project Gender, Migration and Intercultural Interactions in the Mediterranean and South East Europe (GEMIC). She is also guest researcher at the Uppsala Religion and Society Research Centre and a member of the Impact of Religion Centre of Excellence programme. Her research fields include young Muslims in Europe, transnational migration, religious pluralism and the cultural transformations of identity and gender relations. Among her recent publications are *Muslima. Islamisk väckelse och unga kvinnors förhandlingar om genus* (Carlsson, 2007); 'Challenging from Within: Youth Associations and Female Leadership in Swedish Mosques', in M. Bano and H. Kalmbach (eds), *Women, Leadership and Mosques: Changes in Contemporary Islamic Authority* (Brill, 2012).

Bolette Moldenhawer is Associate Professor at the Department of Media, Cognition and Communication, University of Copenhagen. She is co-author of *Migration och tillhörighet. Inklusions- och exclusionsprocesser i Skandinavien* (2007) and numerous articles and reports on aspects of inequality in education, transnational migration, integration and identity formation, and the challenge it involves for the Scandinavian welfare states.

Kariane Westrheim, Ph.D., is Associate Professor at the Department of Education, University of Bergen. Westrheim's publications focus on multicultural issues, democracy and education, collective action, political movements and education in areas of war and conflict. She has conducted fieldwork in The Middle East and European countries. She is currently conducting a research project on foreign prisoners in Nordic prisons, looking at the prisoners' educational backgrounds and their motivation, desire and need for education and training. In much of her work, Westrheim's theoretical framework is inspired by critical pedagogy and the Freire tradition.

🌙 Index

www.ingramcontent.com/pod-product-compliance
Lightning Source LLC
Chambersburg PA
CBHW070928030426
42336CB00014BA/2579